WHERE THE
TRUTH LIES

Julia Hobsbawm is a pioneer of 'integrity PR' and Britain's first professor of Public Relations at the London College of Communication. She founded and now runs Editorial Intelligence, the first networking organization for people in PR and journalism, which monitors and analyses the worlds of comment and opinion.

WHERE THE TRUTH LIES

Trust and Morality in PR and Journalism

Edited by Julia Hobsbawm

Atlantic Books
London

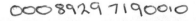

First published in Great Britain in 2006 by Atlantic Books,
an imprint of Grove Atlantic Ltd.

To the memory of Esther Kaposi, PR and Kate Carr, journalist: gone, but not forgotten.

CONTENTS

ACKNOWLEDGEMENTS

I would like to thank all the contributors for being so very generous with their time and expertise. My family coped with the chaos as I juggled the day jobs with the after-hours time it took to edit and write. My husband Alaric held the fort as he always does, and provided sage and shrewd comment. To our children, Rachael, Maxim, Roman, Anoushka and Wolfgang – I won't miss so many bedtimes again.

A number of people have helped me download thoughts, ideas and drafts a number of times, especially Toby Mundy, who is truly a great publisher. My father Eric and brother Andy both gave invaluable feedback and sound advice. To them and to my friends and colleagues who also read and commented, thank you. Particular thanks to: Sarah Benton, who was a constant sounding board and who provided additional research, Lyndsay Griffiths, Howell James, Ruth McCall, Jessica Morris, Nina Planck, Sophie Radice and Saskia Sissons. Sarah Feather at Editorial Intelligence worked closely with Karen Duffy, Clara Farmer and Sarah Norman at Atlantic; all are incredibly hardworking and enjoyable to work with.

Finally, this book is dedicated to tomorrow's PRs and journalists – in the hope that they have as much fun as those of us working in the fields do today but perhaps get more things more right, more often.

Julia Hobsbawm, London, February 2006

Introduction

Julia Hobsbawm

....

Tell all the truth if you can, and as much of it as you can if you cannot.[1]

Institute of Public Relations paper, 1970

Journalists are taught inconsistent things. We are taught to 'play it straight' or 'tell both sides' or 'refrain from comment'. But we are also taught to 'make it human' and 'engage the reader'. And that really means playing it bent – taking a viewpoint and telling one side more vividly than the other; in other words, commenting. And that 'engage the reader' form of bias changes the real world too.[2]

Andrew Marr, *My Trade*

....

'His Master's Voice'

It is hard to tell these days exactly where the truth lies in modern media. This is scarcely surprising. Rumour and urban myth, dumbed-down falsehoods and leaked spin all thrive in today's expanding, instantaneous, downloaded media world. There is no such thing as 'yesterday's news' because it is endlessly regurgitated – regardless of whether it is true or contested; placed in or out of context. And it continues to live, online, for ever.

This is fertile territory for those making and shaping information, who know as much about impact as they do about information in its raw form. Niccolò Machiavelli observed, five centuries ago, that 'among the many considerations that show what a man is, none is more important than seeing either how easily he swallows what he is told or how carefully he invents what he wants to convince others of.'3

Everyone has a truth and today's blogger-culture allows everyone to tell it; you just can't be sure whose truth is being told at any given time. The truth (or what passes for it) is filtered through the media funnel of journalism and then on to the public. Information is poured into this funnel largely by public relations, journalism's dominant source. Yet the extent of this interdependent relationship is concealed from the public. Journalism's dependence on public relations is resented among journalists, and sometimes PR uses its increasing leverage to further this antipathy. If you take all natural disasters and other genuinely spontaneous events as the benchmark for 'pure' news, the rest is less spontaneous – more orchestrated – and is likely to be linked to a hook, or a reason to cover a particular story. The exact proportion of 'the news' that is attributable to PR varies from medium to medium and fluctuates constantly, but I estimate that it can be anything between 50 and 80 per cent (and often more) of news-content on any given day.4 Not that anything like this percentage is signposted to the media consumer. News happens. And news is made to happen.

Public relations has traditionally been heard but not seen. Only the role of 'His Master's Voice', or the spokesperson, has been visible, and less so in the UK than in the USA, where the President's spokesperson started conducting on-camera White House briefings well over a decade before anyone else did the same. In the UK it was only during the Bosnian air war of the late 1990s, when NATO's spokesman, Jamie Shea, became a daily news fixture, that the actual process of public relations began to be illuminated to the public itself.

I am in favour of continuing the trend of making PR's role more public. It is difficult to see how a proper examination of the modern media can take place without dissecting the real content of media information and the context in which it is relayed, as well as the nature of the tense relationship between those most involved in its communication.

As the late journalist and social commentator Anthony Sampson noted in his *Anatomy of Britain*, the era of public relations began to dawn fully in the commercial and political world in Britain in the middle of the twentieth century. He cattily observed: 'how splendid it will be for PR wives. At last, without uncertainty, evasion or embarrassment, they will be able to reply to the neighbourhood query about their spouses' occupation: "he is in public relations". And there will be a smile of instant mutual understanding.'[5]

Sampson did not approve of the 'unseen power'[6] of public relations because the rise of PR coincided with that of the great era of investigative journalism, pioneered as much in Britain as anywhere. The idea of journalism being truly wedded to the truth, unfettered by economic interest – unlike public relations – was for a golden period in the Britain of the 1960s and 1970s something like a reality. Sir Harold Evans, probably Britain's most famous former editor and journalist – under whose editorship at the *Sunday Times* the 'Insight' investigations team discovered, among other important public interest stories, the Thalidomide drugs scandal – championed the romantic image of a journalist crusading for truth, free from outside interference. British-based journalism has an impressive tradition of brave and heroic investigators, from John Pilger, Robert Fisk, Marie Colvin, Janine di Giovanni and Ann Leslie in print, to John Simpson, Kate Adie, Jon Snow and others in broadcast journalism. It is worth remembering that many more journalists die in the line of duty than do public relations people. Journalism at its best can be a truly noble profession. Public relations may not be so theatrically heroic but it can be every bit as 'good' and morally valid as journalism. The responsibility to inform citizens and consumers of risk and reward, of truth and opportunity, or of choice and democratic process, is part of the the day-to-day work of PR.

Journalism might once have credibly argued that whatever else it did, the truth came first. But fact-finding takes time and costs money. Today's journalist, instead of standing on a doorstep clutching a spiral-bound notebook, is usually isolated from the real world in an ivory tower of glass and steel, hunched over a screen to which PR agencies can send ready-made stories. The rush to fill the ever-expanding capacity of the ever-present media leaves journalists with barely a moment to think about what the real truth is, which impacts critically on accuracy.

In newspapers, comment and opinion have become more valuable than news, its practitioners better paid and of higher profile than their counterparts in news reporting, not least because print comment remains one aspect of journalism that is poorly reproduced in a television or radio studio. But in this process 'truth' combines with opinion. Arguably it makes for more honest journalism. Journalism is at best 'a rough first draft of history'.[7] But as it distils facts and information some clarity is lost and the purity of the information becomes diluted.

From the consumer's point of view, the 'spin', the gloss, the paid-for positive message is not vastly different from the inherent institutional bias of the media itself. It is telling that the most secretive area of any media organization is its news planning conference (with exceptions such as the *Guardian*, most are closed to all but an inner circle of senior executives). A fly on the wall at those daily gatherings would hear the automatic dismissal of certain stories because they conflict with the political stance of the proprietor or editor. Similarly, that the BBC can claim that all of its presenters are impartial when some of them write impassioned newspaper columns, which are biased by definition, is evidence of the way in which journalism has become ensnared by comment and opinion.

Even the most intimate and engaging editors' memoirs seldom mention the intricate involvement of PR at almost every
stage of most stories. If, as is commonly cited by journalism's
defiant defenders, the relationship between journalism and
polititians is like a dog and a lamppost, then the relationship
between PR and journalism is like that of the prostitute
and the regular punter who relies on his 'whore', yet who is
ashamed and often resentful of his dependence on this regular,
secret tryst.

This is not to represent all PR–Journalism relations as
somehow in crisis. On the contrary, both trades are in many
senses thriving because of each other. Yet overall it is still true
to say that journalism's distrust and hatred of PR has become
internalized and institutionalized to such a degree as to be
commonplace. Writing about celebrity and sports PR in 2003,
the polemicist Bryan Appleyard declared: 'Hacks still naively
pursue something they like to call the truth. Their problem is
that it no longer exists. For truth has been destroyed by public
relations executives, or "scum" as we like to call them.'[8] I beg
to differ. Public relations may be suited to the manipulated and
hyperbolic but it is also just as much about the truth as it is
about anything else.

The 'Age of Contempt'

This, then, is the age defined by the media academic Steven
Barnett as the media 'Age of Contempt', arrived at via
'Deference' in the 1950s and 'Disdain' in the late twentieth and
early twenty-first centuries.[9] Roy Greenslade remembers, in
his history of the British press, how the tabloid baron Lord
Cudlipp found himself damning the monster he had himself
nurtured when in 1988, at the age of seventy-five, he lamented
'intrusive journalism for the prurient'.[10]

Arguably the public has good reason to decry both PR and

journalism. There is a well-documented crisis of trust in the public institutions and in information systems, explored most recently by the philosopher Dr Onora O'Neill in her famous Reith Lectures of 2002, continued by John Lloyd's book *What the Media are Doing to Our Politics* in 2004 and made a matter of national debate by the BBC, which responded to the Hutton Inquiry with an inquiry of its own, and by the subsequent announcement that it would reinstate basic journalistic ethics and values in its staff through training.[11]

As Andrew Marr noted in his candid analysis of British journalism, 'When there is less news, the newsreaders don't take the day off and the headlines don't become smaller, or less black. Journalism mimics urgency, screws up the semblance of excitement... We skate over our very thin knowledge, talking desperately, and fooling fewer than we used to.'[12] Equally, PR has become synonymous with irregularity or opportunism. The publicity surrounding Enron's shamelessly less-than-complete corporate accounts and the widespread corporate practice of public relations 'greenwashing' – to make even the most environmentally badly behaved business put a good gloss on its actions (perhaps the most scathing book about PR to date summed this up in its title, *Toxic Sludge is Good for You*)[13] – has meant that despite the highly regulated nature of financial PR in the UK, the perception is either that PR lies or that it would if it could. In the UK the best-known PR practitioner is Max Clifford, who has made broadsheet fodder out of the tabloid kiss-and-tell, so assiduous is his collection of the dirty linen of the powerful, famous and rich. This he airs, judiciously, when it suits his clients and his own personal moral motivations. This is not PR as I and fellow professionals know it. Instead, it's an example of public relations as tabloid journalism.

Even without Max Clifford's help, caricature has helped to consolidate PR's image: the spin doctor has proved even more suitable for satire than any amount of Bollinger-swigging in the BBC's classic comedy *Absolutely Fabulous* about 1980s consumer PR. In one episode of *The Thick of It*, BBC4's satire about political communications, the main spinmeister says memorably, 'I'm a man of principle. I like to know whether I'm lying to save the skin of a tosser or a moron.'[14]

Journalism may have fared better than PR in BBC drama – the 2004 thriller *State of Play*, set in a UK newsroom, brought back the idea of a journalist-as-sleuth, working his or her contact book to uncover political and corporate scandal at the highest level. But the real scandals of late have all too often featured journalists themselves, leading directly to a severe dip in journalism's reputation.

This is the era, after all, when the BBC, the world's best-known broadcaster, and the British government rowed publicly for over a year whether a report was true or not and whose line it was anyway. Government PR clashed loudly with government-sponsored journalism. Both sides argued Machiavelli's point that the other side was either cynical, naïve or both. The government's trust ratings plummeted as low as the public turnout in the subsequent general election. The BBC/New Labour row about Andrew Gilligan's *Today* report in 2002 on whether the government's intelligence reports on Iraq had been 'sexed up' epitomizes the way in which journalism and PR have become inseparable and their faults exposed.

This same row was echoed in 2005, when the Bush administration become mired in controversy and no less senior an aide than the Vice President's Chief of Staff, Lewis 'Scooter' Libby, was indicted over claims that he leaked damaging information to the *New York Times* to discredit someone who disagreed with the administration's stance on the reasons for the Iraq war. Judith Miller of the *New York Times* first went to prison to protect Libby as a source, but after her release it transpired just how biased her journalism had been; she resigned in 2005 after a riveting fiasco which saw the world's best-regarded newspaper berating her, its previously untouchable writer, for covering the war in a manner that resembled 'stenography' for the White House rather than independent-minded reporting.[15]

This is the era when the good and great say things which turn out not to be true – and then carry on as if they said something else all along. 'Read my lips: No New Taxes,' said George Bush Snr – before he raised them. His son, George W. Bush, saw his Vice President Dick Cheney tour the sofas of American daytime television in the run-up to the second Gulf war, to declare with certainty that Saddam Hussein possessed weapons of mass destruction and was linked to Al-Qaeda, when neither were true. And of course, Tony Blair insisted that Saddam Hussein could deploy weapons of mass destruction 'in forty-five minutes' and used this claim as the basis for going to war with Iraq, before being forced to admit that there was no evidence for this.

At the opposite end of the spectrum there are global celebrities like Renée Zellweger and Cindy Crawford who paid for advertising or employed publicists to confirm the strength of their relationships, days before announcing a split from their spouses. It is small wonder then that trust is at an all-time low in public life, and truth is craved like an elusive god, invoked but invisible.

Where the truth lies

Given the centrality of both PR and journalism to the question of where truth lies in the media, each day a new issue or example surfaces that could have merited inclusion here. Inevitably much will already have changed by the time this book has been published. This anthology tries to make sense of why we have ended up here, with PR and journalism both central to the architecture of public information and yet caught up in an often rancid relationship that can make things worse, not better, for their audiences.

The central questions are explored by a range of voices, some of whom will be very familiar from the firmaments of PR, journalism and public life. I am immensely grateful to each of them for presenting their thoughts so concisely and with such energy. Perhaps the central question here is the working relationship between the two practices and who has the moral upper hand. Is it that, as Simon Jenkins puts it, 'as if trapped by some original sin, both go to hell together in a handcart'?

Broadly speaking, the contributions fall into two categories: those that confront, head on, the day-to-day reality of the relationship played out between PR and journalism, and those that address the wider ethical and philosophical questions that we can ask about the professions. Some do both.

The not-so-special relationship

John Lloyd continues his debunking of many of the media's self-made myths by declaring that 'it is a crucially important part of the journalistic self-image to despise PRs' and argues that common ground can be found without compromising on the fundamental differences between us. Simon Walker of Reuters makes the bold case that the journalistic emperor is wearing substantially less honest clothing – in retail journalism at any rate – than those in PR. But the realpolitik of the interplay and interdependence is laid bare by Columbia University's Anya Schiffrin, who explains with clarity the reality of emerging economies learning about financial reporting under the guidance of financial PR agents. She also examines the pros and cons of what this means for truth: for the journalists, for the PR agents and for the public.

The brand and celebrity PR maestro Mark Borkowski tackles

the subject with his customary wit and candour. His essay, 'Is honesty the best policy?', puts forward a sound case for PR's 'good guys', without hesitating to articulate the prevalence of ruthlessness and callousness inside the industry. (It is worth noting that Borkowski actually registered as a trademark the term 'impropaganda' after PR pioneer Edwards Bernays famously coined the term as meaning PR that is not carried out with good sense, in good faith or in a moral way.)

Kim Fletcher, the former newspaper editor and now media pundit, also examines journalism's brush with PR but cheerfully admits that it is one of ubiquity: 'Open any newspaper and read the stuff: who comes up with all those holidays? Where do interviews with film stars come from? Do you think those fashion shoots happen by chance?' He contends that 'journalists retain the right to patronize PRs but rub along with them pretty well'.

Julian Henry makes the case for embracing the dog-eat-dog reality world of celebrity PR and makes no self-justifying bones about the need to 'twist the incoming data into something else, just to make sense of it'. But he opens a long-closed window on what is unsayable in much of public relations: in order to sup with the journalistic devil you have to act like one too.

Alastair Campbell was an active proponent of the position that the media is an enemy that must be fought and beaten rather than a democratic force that must be fed. Peter Oborne maintains that it is political PR agents who are corrupting the integrity of journalism, and not the other way round. He argues that Campbell's modus operandi and that of New Labour in general was rooted in a ruthless manipulation of the facts that cost the government its reputation for any kind of truth whatsoever. Colin Byrne, a former Labour spin doctor who now runs one of the UK's largest PR agencies, rebuts this point ('there are hundreds of dedicated professional Whitehall PRs who try to do their job of getting important information to us, the citizens and consumers of health, education, transport, law and order, to the very best of their abilities ... to denigrate them as distorting spin doctors is as unfair as using the case of Harold Shipman to suggest that we should never trust hard-working GPs as a group') while claiming the moral high ground above journalism. Nevertheless the truth lies, as Kate Nicholas of *PRWeek* argues, 'in the gap between perception and reality', a point which is central to the question of how truth is interpreted, and the different truths of those telling it, and on whose behalf.

Stitching stories together

During the meal he tries to be a good guest, to talk entertainingly, to fill in the silences ... he glosses over the attack, mentioning only that his car was stolen ... Stitched together in this way, the story unrolls without shadows. How he wishes it could be true!

J. M. Coetzee, Disgrace

Journalism and PR stitch stories together more than characters in prize-winning novels. They select, omit, distort and distil the facts to portray an event, client or product in a memorable or favourable way, or to convey a truth that debunks the widely held truths of the day. As new information emerges in the constant hum of the 'always on' media bubble, this information becomes refined or, just as often, blurred.

Michael Cockerell's revealing account of his unprecedented access to 10 Downing Street to film the relationship between Labour and the lobby captures the Prime Minister summing up the very problem he is accused of creating: political spin. On being asked why his government placed such importance on its relations with the media and on presentation Tony Blair declared: 'It's important to have the capacity to get on top of the news, as far as possible; because otherwise a story can be out there saying you are doing something which you are not doing at all. And these stories then take on a life of their own and start running away in the far distance.'

Two contributions in particular are vivid reminders of how journalism has become story fodder. Janine di Giovanni gives a highly personal account of becoming entrapped by an Israeli critic of her reports on the Middle East who posed as a journalist in order to accuse her of partisan reporting. Leonard Doyle describes how poacher became gamekeeper when one of his writers was accused of lying. These chapters apply a PR lens to journalistic experience and show how the tables are turned when it is the journalists who are accused of having an agenda, an accusation usually laid at the door of the PR agent. Journalists who are more familiar with factual news, war reporting and foreign affairs, find themselves at the epicentre of the modern trend of being personally disbelieved, no matter what they say.

Time is of the essence

In 1865, during the communications Stone Age, the Reuters news agency succeeded in being the first to bring the news of Abraham Lincoln's assassination to British shores by sending a rowing boat to intercept a Liverpool-bound steamer, managing to disseminate the information across Europe a full eight hours before any of their rivals. Today Reuters simultaneously transmits millions of pieces of news in a second – every second of the day.

Speed in modern communications plays a great part in the whole question of truth because the faster it goes out the faster it degrades and needs to be upgraded. As Andrew St George observes in his essay:

Crises have a pattern, like hurricanes: sometimes forewarning, always immersion and aftermath. In this, they operate not only like movies but like everyday news. Each news item appears on a news website (and that of thousands of interested investors, commentators, advisers) in order not of importance but of time: latest, thirty minutes, sixty minutes, two hours. If a piece of news is older than twenty-four hours, it falls off the site. And the site is updated, like many news sources now, every fifteen minutes. Around the world, at countless editing desks, screens, editorial meetings, the same time standard is applied. How many of these stories are true? Accurate? Researched?

Emily Bell picks up this point by arguing that the much-vaunted risks of what she calls 'this network of limitless connectivity' can in fact be forces for a far greater democratization of information in 'new' media than the proprietor-led stranglehold on opinion which has dominated 'old' media, i.e. paper- and broadcast-based information. She argues that the internet does in fact promote the truth because 'the transparency and the challengeability of your reporting becomes ever more open'. Derek Wyatt MP, who stood for eight years on Parliament's prestigious select committee on culture, media and sport, looks at trust and truth in the light of the 'the two-way street' that news has become in the digital era, where 'whatever the UK does, we can see an alternative view'.

Marshall McLuhan's seminal predictive study *Understanding Media* was first published in 1964. In the four decades that have followed many of the basic tools of journalism and public relations have remained as they were in the preceding fifty years (both practices are, it should be remembered, little more than a century old and their history is irrevocably intertwined) but the means of transmission have changed disproportionately. Today's news-dissemination is a far cry from the Reuters rowing boat. McLuhan might not have been able to imagine the internet but he could imagine the ethical significance of the new transforming era: 'Might not our current translation of our entire lives into the spiritual form of information seem to make of the entire globe, and of the human family, a single consciousness?'.[16]

The transforming era

As the American academics Robert Jackall and Janice Hirota point out, 'public relations and journalism are joined at the hip... Both occupations are storytellers engaged in fashioning moral discourse within certain frameworks.'[17]

And it is the moral framework which preoccupies several of the essayists here. Deborah Mattinson sets the scene with her study of trust in society, through an analysis of what opinion leaders think about truth. Seventy-three per cent of them think that society needs more independent media coverage – a stark figure for anyone involved in relaying information to the public via the mass media.

In her passionate look at what truth does to the dispossessed in society, Julia Neuberger looks at the values which underpin many of the stories we read. She illustrates her point by comparing coverage of Muslim youth values with stories decrying 'mad mullahs' and asks: 'How do ordinary people get a balanced view... and recognize that, whatever politicians and media may say, it is not possible to depict the world, or even our country, only in the image one would like it to have?'

The media analyst Sarah Benton writes about the heart of moral differences and values in the media and articulates the nuances between honesty, facts and lies, or what she calls the 'dishonest mistake'. Benton argues that 'we don't expect journalists to tell the truth', while the consultant and business philosopher Alice Sherwood declares that PR has a 'structural' problem with being taken seriously and provides a business dissection of communications, which argues that, despite protestations to the contrary, 'dissembling and manipulation are built in from the start'.

This is not a position which Anne Gregory, the UK's only full-time professor of public relations, agrees with. She creates something of an ethical 'how to' for practitioners and raises, as does Mark Borkowski, the critical question about whom as a PR you choose or refuse to represent, still 'the elephant in the room' for most PRs.

The BBC documentary commissioner and polemicist Nick Fraser questions, as does John Lloyd, the ethics of public service information and provision. Fraser paints a picture of the media which is at once bleak ('Media discontents are not exactly new. They form a dark thread through the predominantly utopian treatments of information in modern times') and yet resolute that the vast changes in the modern media, such as the rise of the news media in the Arab world and India, which presage a way of living with, not fighting, information chaos.

In 'Nano-Truths and the Story', the media academic Jean Seaton looks at media and information in relation to judgement as much as to truth, and puts 'news values' in the context of today's ruthlessly competitive markets: 'News both evaluates evidence and then makes a fuss to sell it to us.'

The growing cultural obsession with truth in journalism, matching an equal despair with and distrust of its suppliers in public relations, has reached what the American journalist Malcolm Gladwell defined as a 'tipping point', a cultural or commercial moment when everything is tuned to the same channel, so to speak.[18] We are now in an era that is plainly dominated by global conflict but equally plainly dominated by conflicts about information and its sibling, interpretation.

Who owns this information, and debates it, or provides, proves or disproves it to a restless, hungry and cynical public is at the centre of our political as well as cultural future and for those of us in media communications, our commercial future too. I do hope this collection helps to crystallize your thoughts and opinions.

Fact-Mongering Online

Emily Bell

When it became obvious to the whole world that the internet was neither a passing fad nor likely to remain a network used only by programmers and academics – probably sometime around 1996 – a curious thing happened.

The 'real world' of mainstream media began to gravitate around the most logical and probably the least defensible position it could: that the internet was a conduit for the perverted, the distorted and the untrustworthy. This network of limitless connectivity which might, with the most limited imagining, be the single most empowering publishing technology since Gutenberg invented the printing press, was instead vilified as a home of the con artist and the paedophile. Fuelled by an investment profile akin to that of tulips in seventeenth-century Amsterdam, flaky and over-valued, the popular image of the internet could hardly have been worse. It not only attracted pornographers and rapists, but it also apparently made smug and not necessarily very talented young people exceedingly rich; it bailed out the advertising industry and made rock stars out of computer nerds and venture capitalists – just how wrong could one technology be?

At the heart of this collective suspicion seemed to be a belief that anyone who used the internet for almost any purpose at all was almost certainly up to no good. In 2001 the Selby train crash was a marker of just how embedded this idea had become. The man who caused the accident which killed ten, Gary Hart, had fallen asleep at the wheel of his Land Rover and driven off the road, down an embankment on to a railway line causing the fatality. He received a penal sentence of five years, with the judge stressing that his failure to sleep before his journey was the equivalent of drunk driving. But the aspect of Hart's sleep deprivation most avidly dwelt on was what had caused it: 'Hours of internet chat led to Selby' read the headline in Newcastle's *Evening Chronicle*, another report in the *Scotsman* described Hart as inhabiting 'the shadowy world of the internet', as though this was in itself an illegal act. His cavalier use of the internet, it seemed, was a signifier of his character.

So this haven of the shifty and dubious was for a long time treated by many in the media as a byword for the untrustworthy. I recently found a piece written in 1997 from, of all places CNet, the online technology news site, entitled 'Truth, lies, and the internet', which highlighted an internet spoof, where a speech which was allegedly made by the author Kurt Vonnegut to the University of Chicago was in fact a column from the *Chicago Tribune*. 'The fact that a message can circulate from its point of origin or a circle of people to all corners of the worldwide network is the Net's greatest and most garish feature.'

Certainly in determining what the internet would do to the currency of news or 'truth', if one accepts that there is such a concept, this is what worried most commentators. Inauthenticity of information or testimony it was agreed would prove to be an enormous problem when the distribution bottleneck for news content was abruptly severed by the rise of the internet. But the idea that false 'facts', or deliberately malicious lies would run amok tampering with our perceptions and undermining the democratic process was the kind of thinking which belongs more to the old media than to the new media.

In the old media the malleable issue of what constitutes the truth is in the hands of proprietors and editors. If the 'truth' is that Britain should not be in favour of a European constitution then one might expect a paper's coverage to bleed with this perception – stories of Eurocrats straightening our bananas and flooding us with unwanted immigrant labour come to the fore. Subtler issues of governance in a pan-national world are suppressed. The old way would be to publish facts through a branded conduit, let's for instance say the *Daily Mail*, and then these facts might have a limited lifespan being debated between individuals or very occasionally through other media, but barring accident or libel action, this version of the truth would sit on cuttings files, in libraries and even electronically searchable archives. What this world feared was the unlicensed fact monger spreading incorrect information indiscriminately and this too passing into some vast archive of fact and counter-fact.

But what has happened is quite different. To illustrate how the internet has helped to promote truth every bit as much as, if not more than, it has threatened to distort it, I can draw on a painful and personal example. In 2003 following the invasion of Iraq, I was in charge of the *Guardian*'s website when we ran what might be politely termed an erroneous story. Without going into the hows and whys, an editor had picked up on an article from a German paper which had carried a speech given by Paul Wolfowitz the then deputy defence secretary for the US in the Far East. It was not a conference that had been widely covered and it had somehow slipped under the radar of most of the Western press. The translation suggested that Wolfowitz had said something he had not – that the invasion of Iraq was underpinned by a desire to control the oil resource. He had mentioned oil extraction and Iraq but not in the way it was reported in our story.

I had not been in the office, but within about four hours of the story being published, I was aware that all might not have been right, as emails began to trickle in with the subject field 'Wolfowitz'. This was late evening and by the early morning, when America had had a chance to read the story and kick it around, the trickle was a deluge. We had taken the story down and ran a very prominent retraction being clear about our error. If we were operating in the old world where media was distributed not electronically and instantly but within a much narrower circulation, the error would have been just as grave, but would have certainly survived longer while it reached the parts of the world – such as the Pentagon – where those who knew most about its accuracy could immediately challenge its veracity.

It was the case in the very early days of news websites that one could rely on the 'not wrong for long' motto to keep you out of trouble – make an error, take it down quickly and your relatively small audience would be none the wiser. But as the web has expanded, as search tools such as Google have proliferated and when experts can call in all stories they are interested in to their own news wires via RSS readers (Really Simple Syndication), the transparency and the challengeability of your reporting becomes ever more open.

For newspapers in particular this development is highly unsettling. Think of the national daily newspapers in the UK – eleven titles selling somewhere over 12 million copies a day all told, each with its particular angle on the news. Each community around that newspaper might 'trust' the paper's brand – for instance the *Daily Mail* has a strong community and a large readership which trusts the paper implicitly. But if stories are regularly qualified or knocked down by other sources, denied and re-edited by those perhaps who are even involved in the stories then at some point the level at which a newspaper is trusted begins to falter. Once the context into which you publish your stories alters from the 'safe' environment of your regular readership to the whole world, when your headlines appear on Google News alongside other contradictory stories, then it is far harder to defend the 'truth' of your reporting.

The *New York Times*' experience with the rogue reporter

Jayson Blair, who filed copy which was fabricated or plagia-
rized, demonstrates that in the world of high-pressure competitive news, the temptation to believe and run stories rather than
interrogate their authenticity is overwhelming even for the
most austere newspapers.

So the inevitable rise of the web has not led to quite such a
proliferation of falsehood as was originally expected; instead it
has facilitated a more open examination of facts and journalistic presentation than was previously the case. The American
technology journalist Dan Gillmor, whose book *We the Media*
predicted the erosion of the hierarchy of news provision as citizen journalists and bloggers rose in number, has a nifty
phrase which is handy for journalists to remember: 'There is
always someone closer to the story than you.' And with publishing technologies so readily available anyone can tell that
story or question other versions of the truth. Distressingly for
the mainstream media what the new-media thinker Clay
Shirky describes as the 'fame versus fortune' model is in the
ascendant now that anyone can distribute their content. In
other words there is a generation of bloggers or citizen journalists who will make their thoughts, accounts and pictures
free on the web – they may enjoy the fame that goes with the
exposure but essentially they are hobbyists, not motivated by
money and status, often with full-time jobs elsewhere.

There are several oft quoted examples of the power of the
blog versus the traditional media construct. Maybe the most
notorious case to date was that of the CBS news story aired in
the US on 8 September 2004 – where Dan Rather introduced
an item which cast doubt on President Bush's military record.
The story relied on four memos, but bloggers, including one
known as 'Buckhead', questioned the authenticity of the
memos based on what they knew of typesetting in the early seventies (the fonts and spacing on the CBS memos looked like
word-processed documents). A maelstrom of criticism and

pressure which followed ultimately saw Rather step down from his post.

The bloggers of the Republican right claimed victory. But this might prove the power of the blog or it might prove that blogs are as capable of misleading as the mainstream press in its worst mode. A highly considered article published in 2005 in the *Columbia Journalism Review* by Corey Pein pointed out that the supposed findings by the bloggers had been followed by an avalanche of mainstream coverage which converted rumour and speculation into fact and failed to make a proper examination of all aspects of the story – the speed and ferocity with which such a counter-claim moved was enough to end Rather's career and weaken CBS's reputation before the official inquiry into the affair had even concluded.

At the last count there were 27 million blogs worldwide with tens of thousands a day being added to that number. Although trying to quantify the blogosphere is all but impossible there are estimates at the time of writing that 275,000 entries are added to blogs on a daily basis and the readership of blogs across the world is somewhere around the 50 million mark. Within this modern day Babel one could argue that it is even harder to decide what might be truthful and what might be exaggerated. So won't the 'trusted' distributors of fact thrive in this environment?

Well perhaps. But as we know, in an increasingly transparent world, trust is difficult to build and easy to squander. One of the targets of politically motivated bloggers is the mainstream media's scepticism about their chosen cause. In fact what we see from bloggers is not a substitute for the mainstream press but often a replica of its best and worst attributes. High-profile bloggers tend to be white, male and middle class, they tend to divide into those who are keen to share knowledge and those who are anxious to make their view prevail. According to which category they sit in, their contributions are either enlightening and enriching or prone to selectivity and distortion – in other words pretty much a mirror to the mainstream media.

The faltering of public trust in mainstream media which is an inevitable consequence of a highly competitive and commoditized news market, has allowed organizations to use the new digital tools available to them to tell their story without mediation. In the UK's 2005 election campaign New Labour dramatically scaled back its engagement with the 'press pack', conducting choreographed photocalls and launching a series of email and blog services to keep the electorate 'informed'. But because of course it lacked any of the openness associated with the internet – no free commenting on the blogs for instance – it felt like a sorry pass at telling it like it is, it made the party feel more opaque rather than less so and it made the role of the traditional media inquisitors seem therefore more valuable.

Finding the truth can, to some, be an overrated concept. But there does seem to be in general a human instinct to uncover the truth rather than to live in blissful ignorance. Take for example the most famous example of a community-built archive – Wikipedia – an online evolving encyclopedia which anyone can add to or edit. It is not the last word in resources – again some sections are rich and balanced and others are a little lopsided, according to the enthusiasms and knowledge of those who amend the site. But on the whole it is remarkably accurate, given the overwhelming mess it could be – even small errors are diligently corrected. In online communities where recommendations are rated – the Amazon book review system is probably one of the most widely known – there will always be elements who seek to distort the system for their own gain, who lodge a good or bad review based on something other than honest opinion, but when there is a weight of opinion within these communities they can produce a more balanced picture.

The emergence of new technologies was greeted with high anxiety that they would distort and bury the truth. It is not clear that the evolution of the internet necessarily brings us any closer to knowing what the real truth is or enables us as journalists to report it, but it has created the tools whereby everyone can contribute to what the truth might be. I say everyone, but of course this is still a divided society in terms of the information haves and have-nots, there are barriers of literacy and wealth. But these are infinitely lower than the barriers to traditional publishing.

For corporations, journalists, academics, citizens and politicians, the new information hierarchies will take some time to adjust to. The sheer volume now of available source material makes it likely that errors or false reports will circulate, but the open-ended nature of the discourse means that the power to correct those reports is greater than it ever has been. My view then is essentially that of an optimist – that we are entering a new age of enlightenment for mass communication. The concerns that all change is for the worst have already been confounded, and the era of a society atomized by mass communication rather than united by it is over. And there is no reason why truth should be the casualty of this particular revolution.

A Make-Believe World

Sarah Benton

The notion of truth in journalism is startling. It is not expected in modern industrial societies. It comes from another world, of philosophy or religion, and only flourishes in sects whose members are bound by the conviction that they alone have seen the truth. The modern media is understood to be a self-sufficient world of artifice and illusion; to demand that journalists speak the truth seems as irrelevant as asking a conjuror to use no tricks. Even in the court room we doubt that the truth is told despite pledges of the whole truth and nothing but the truth being sought and spoken. The demand for forensic truth-telling lingers on from an infinitely remote time when the idea of truth was an aspect of the survival of the soul and public *confession* of the truth was the goal of a trial process. Those who are not expected to tell the truth constitute that tawdry cluster squirming in the pit of public esteem: estate agents, politicians, used-car salesmen, PR people and journalists.

But that's the contradiction. We don't expect journalists to tell the truth. Indeed, we expect them not to, just as we expect advertisers to publish nothing but deceitful froth and PR consultants to speak only what is in their client's interest, whatever that may be. Or so we say. In fact, public attitudes towards the journalistic media are deeply ambivalent. Most people do believe what they read in the papers, and even more believe what they hear on the broadcast media. Investigative journalism, a term which was coined in the 1970s, is particularly admired for its ability to discover the truth and publish it. Yet if

24

something is shown to be untrue, the same admiring people will say, 'You can't believe what you read in the papers', and not, apparently, be perturbed by the contradiction. There is a collusion here, a willingness to play make-believe, to enter into the media's world of shock, horror and scandal, and affect outrage – while also knowing it is a make-believe world so we do not actually have to do anything, or think new thoughts. So our collusive and ambivalent feelings about the truth and the media allow us to put a screen up between our real selves, who may have deep and disturbing feelings, and real facts and events which would evoke those feelings if we believed them. The problem about actual lying, which is rarer than we affect to believe, is that it throws the responsibility for public good back on to us; the revelation to us of an actual lie by a politician becomes a demand that we act to punish the liar. If we don't act, we appear to be condoning the lie or to be compliant in our own gullibility. The journalistic saw that it is the cover-up, rather than the deed being hidden, that causes the powerful person's downfall is true because it is the cover-up that involves lies.

Yet this too is a quagmire. It is now said that the media drove Peter Mandelson from office, not because he borrowed money from a friend to finance a mortgage but because he failed to declare the loan, thus implicitly lying. I don't believe it. Lies by a politician are often cited by journalists as the honourable reason for their contempt, but often the claim is merely a cover-up of the journalistic failure to be truthful about their aggression. That is, it was 'honourable' to attack Peter Mandelson for not telling the truth but it was not honourable to attack him for being someone whom they sensed was weak, or who had manipulated them with great charm in the past or whose downfall would damage the government. It is also now said, in retrospect, that the reason for hostility to Tony Blair's decision to join President's Bush's 'coalition of the willing' is that 'he lied'. Most of those who say it have no idea whether or not he lied – gave factual testimony which he knew to be untrue – for only he and a handful of people know what information was available to him at the time. It seems clear he and his cabal made dishonest use of information. This is an important distinction. Honesty is to do with worth and esteem (honour) rather than factual truth or lies as such, hence Blair's own claim that he made an honest mistake. I happen to think it was a dishonest mistake – unworthy, not in good faith – but that charge depends on my prior opinion on the utility of war and what was in the interest of the people of the Middle East in general. On this, of course, I may be wrong. As Tony Blair reiterated, it's a matter of judgement, and as he didn't say, it's a matter of political values. The claim that he lied is a comfortable shelter to protect the matter of the accusers' own judgement and values, the questions they asked at the time, or since, the analysis they brought to bear at the time, or since.

At the heart of the wretched relationship between journalists, public and media directors is whether or not people do really 'want to know'. We the public insist we do want to know. This is not true. Most of the time we don't want to know; in fact, continuing life in the maximum degree of comfort depends on not knowing, depends on blowing small bubbles of ignorance in which we can live in peace. The great quest for knowledge which was the inquiry into arms for Iraq came about almost accidentally, the consequence of a court case, not of public or journalistic questioning.

The comfort of ignorance seems to me to be an irrefutable fact about human nature, although naturally the degree of resistance to knowledge varies from person to person as it does from time to time. Children, the educated, a minority of journalists with a zeal for 'what really happened', a society in a state of generosity as the USA used to be all have a greater appetite for strange knowledge than do those who are in cults which are convinced they possess the truth, those who are preoccupied with defending the status quo, a society which has become ossified by fear and resentment as Serbia was. Then there is the matter of what it is we want to know. Most newspapers, not only the tabloids, depend on our only wanting to know what comforts us and reinforces our prejudices. Critics of a system – apartheid in South Africa, the exploitation of child labour, the 1930s purges in the Soviet Union or its 1980s senescence, the Arab Muslim Khartoum government and the Janjaweed militias – always have a greater appetite for, and knowledge of, these iniquities than have the supporters of those regimes. We, the general public, may not want to know difficult and discomfiting truths, but political activists think we ought to want to know.

And on the whole, the originating truth finder and teller has been an activist group, not journalists (which is of course not to say that all activist groups are concerned with the truth). From the 1970s onwards, more and more trade unions and campaigning groups, usually on the Left, created press departments, recognizing that they needed a medium between themselves and journalists in order for their case to receive any favourable publicity. A new group of people had to learn the art of the snappy press release, finding an angle, suggesting a peg, offering a briefing, providing a charming and articulate spokesperson. This to many seemed a Faustian pact: in exchange for some coverage in the media, the originating activist group had to accept whatever bowdlerisms appeared. Thus in the 1980s, when both CND and the Green Party were struggling their way out of obscurity, the price they paid for greater and friendlier coverage was to see their earnest speeches reduced to sound-bites, and to accept that their organizations had to be identified with physically attractive and amenable spokespersons.

This was an epiphany for the Left; its effects worked all the way through to transform the Labour Party and to clear the way for Tony Blair. A movement in the Labour Party, after leader John Smith died suddenly of a heart attack, to get Robin Cook elected as leader faltered after a few rounds when it became apparent to all that Cook's appearance and voice and manner were not 'media friendly'. No politician who appears to display disdain for or fear of the media will survive, in part because the journalists will react with hostility, in part because disdain for the media itself will be purveyed as disdain for the people watching the media – and in part because such a politician, Michael Foot for instance, will be understood to be denying the nature of the modern world, refusing to play by the rules of the new game which is media-democracy.

The obvious irony is that to enter the media world of artifice, hag-ridden by envy and Schadenfreude and malice, is to agree to the rules of a game in which real facts are illusory and what matters is sensation. The worst victims of the game are scientists, politicians and young celebrities. The science stories which get covered by the media are usually about the human body. Although most stories only enter the public domain because scientists choose to put them there, there is nonetheless almost universal condemnation by (other) scientists of the coverage. These stories, like political stories, do not usually involve actual lies (meaning falsifying facts about who, when and where); they work by blurring the source and by exaggerating the quantitative significance of the information. The effect is always to convert the egregious and peculiar into the widespread and archetypal. It is these two dishonest acts – enhancing the authority of a source and inflating the quantitative significance of data – by journalists which put many stories into the realm of urban myth. Sometimes this is very dangerous, as with the long-running scare about MMR vaccines – though here, reponsibility for the original blurring of sources and quantities lies with Dr Andrew Wakefield and the *Lancet*.

But wherever science is involved, journalists are not only particularly gullible, because they have so little scientific knowledge (including little willingness to deal with statistics); they are also most willing to rely on press releases, again partly because they lack the scientific knowledge to generate their own critical and informed pieces, but also because any press release will feed directly into the urge to produce shock and horror make-believe. Yet the PR people here are not inventing the stories – as unscientific as the rest, they depend on the science researchers who are no more free than are other human beings of the desire for fame, fortune and a sensational splash. Another example was the treatment of the press release announcing the discovery of 'Flores man' in Indonesia in October 2004; a BBC reporter, among others, announced sententiously that this would mean the whole understanding of evolution would have to be rewritten. Nonsense. As any amateur knows who has, for instance, read Stephen Gould's *Wonderful Life* (in cheap paperback and easy language), let alone browsed a few accessible magazines, evolutionary theory has long since discounted a steady and inevitable development of the modern human from slime via our primate ancestors. But who cares – it was a good, and ephemeral, story. No need to think. No need to know. Stupid to blame the originator of the press release who may have produced an accurate, if limited, piece of information. It is the journalist whose job it is to make sense of it. But dishonest too of journalists to draw a thick line between stories derived from and dependent on press releases and those developed entirely from a journalist's own researches and thinking.

Though the problem of classifying the size and significance of data is particularly acute in science-based stories – including claims about WMD – it also arises in any technical or specialist area. In 2004 there was another storm of contumely for government spin after newspapers had run front-page stories about the 'new' initiative from the Department of Health to improve hospital cleaning. This was followed shortly by reports of opposition attacks on the government for this not being a new initiative at all, but merely a repackaged announcement of an old initiative, so the Health Secretary of the day, John Reid, was lying. Surely, one must ask, the specialist health service reporters would have known this? For what distinguishes the specialists is that they have each assiduously cultivated their sources, as well as read the specialist journals. So why did the first story run at all? One answer is that the story was given by the home-page editors, not to the health service specialists but to general and/or political reporters. That is, the editors colluded with government PR to make a splash story when a moment of level-headedness would have produced a paragraph on page 9. And why do the media not make better use of this great asset, the well-informed specialist? In part because it's harder to give their stories the political spin of the day, in part because the authority of the specialist must always be less than that of the editor, in part because it may well be impossible to spin a big news story out of the daily, cumulative detail of specialist work. 'What's the angle? There's no peg to hang it on' – in other words, there is no meaning to this story outwith the established stories. A well-informed journalist demands well-informed readers in order to convey meaning. The uninformed consumer needs his or her information sexed up.

If some journalists play fast and loose with their sources, this is because they are teetering over the edge to where the medium itself becomes the authority. Something is 'true' not because the reporter has witnessed it or is reporting what has issued from a well-informed source but because the BBC or the *Daily Mail* has said it. When opinion polls were taken after the release of the Hutton Report, an ICM poll found that 31 per cent trusted the BBC 'more', compared with 10 per cent who trusted the government more – although almost half trusted neither. (An Australian journal, *Green Left Weekly*, converted this poll finding into 'A January 30 ICM poll in the British *Guardian* found that 68 per cent of respondents trust the BBC more than they trust the Blair government', though this may have been the familiar cavalier way with the statistics rather than with the truth, and an American Marxist paper converted the figure of 49 per cent trusting neither government nor the BBC into 52 per cent, lifting it neatly over the half-way mark.)

Media claims to exercise more authority and enjoy more trust than does the government suggest a pyrrhic victory. For most people working in the media are utterly without political originality; that is, they generate nothing creative. Criticism, contempt, laughs, healthy scepticism? Yes. But proposals, new ways of thinking, a capacity to represent the public across class, race, gender, age etc., an ability to reach lasting compromises? No. But by setting themselves up as more authoritative than government, they may be inviting scorn and contempt for their inability to do things which, hitherto, they have not claimed to be able to do.

Finally, if there is a problem for truth when ideology shapes meaning, but there is equally a problem when, for lack of any ideology, contempt for politicians (and the tabloid array of non-human monsters) shapes meaning, but pedantic discussion bores us supine, then what is to be done?

Is it the duty of the media to cultivate the public's willingness to know, or is it inevitable that it will ride on a preference for prejudice and comfort, duty be damned? Before this century, the almost universal assumption was that the media, like schools, had a duty to inform and educate the public. Those urging this route were not just John Birt, but also the whole of the Left and, before the 1970s, all newspaper editors and certainly the BBC in all its Reithian tradition. Entertainment was our dessert after we had struggled through the nutritious but hard to digest serious information. It was left to the tabloids to discover that lots of the public did not want to know. Or rather, what they wanted to know was a-political and trivial – the bust-size and knicker-shape of a Samantha Fox or Jordan, the wedding dress of a Lady Di or Posh, and so on. The struggle of young women with their bodies, their unwinnable conflict between the desire to be looked at and the horror at exposure, provided infinitely more copy inches than the conflict between, say, armed groups in Sierra Leone or between modernizers and traditionalists in the Chinese Communist Party.

The persistence of a cross-class preference for information about and views of the body is revealed in the internet, the wondrous invention which, in utopian theory, would have us all hungrily seeking and absorbing useful and important information about our world. In fact, or rather estimate, about 12 per cent of all websites are dedicated to pornography and 60 per cent of all web 'hits' are on pornography sites. (These figures come from surveys rather than from computer counts and are likely to underestimate.)

Does this mean humans in the age of mass commerce aka democracy are irredeemably doomed to ignorance? Can we ever know 'the truth' about political and economic life when so few of us can bear to take in the level of information which we need in order to tell truth from lies? Or rather, to get a roughly accurate picture at the time of going to press as opposed to a mess of prejudice, self-serving myth and comfort blankets?

Wanting to know as much as possible may always be a minority inclination but that is a powerful and irrepressible minority. Media publishers, editors, producers and directors – and those in PR – have a responsibility to cultivate a desire to know and responsibility to give it a morally purposeful direction – expecting the best of us rather than the worst, wanting to be part of making society more generous, courageous, vigorous.

Is Honesty the Best Policy?

Mark Borkowski

... a thing called 'Ethics' whose nature was confusing, but if you had it you were a High Class Realtor, and if you hadn't you were a shyster, a piker and a fly-by-night.

That was Sinclair Lewis, the first American to win the Nobel Prize for Literature, talking about estate agents early in the twentieth century. One biographer later claimed that Sinclair 'was the conscience of his generation and he could well serve as the conscience of our own'. I don't know who the conscience of my generation is, but I'm well aware the fashion in image management is for quick fix against long-term strategy, and that must increase the risk that we're all shysters and pikers and fly-by-nights nowadays. Certainly journalists have changed in the quarter century I've been keeping them entertained and primed with newsworthy material.

Before reality TV and the tabloid buy-up there were two idealistic young newshounds at the *Washington Post* called Carl Bernstein and Bob Woodward. They came up with the Watergate story, which grew and grew until it toppled the President of the USA, at which point the press was deemed heroic, they were promoted, the country was humiliated, and Dustin Hoffman and Robert Redford played them in the movie *All the President's Men*. A terrific film, too. But that was thirty years ago. Nowadays in the 'communications' business we're all pragmatists like Richard Nixon, and are probably as much

33

at risk of questionable behaviour in our business lives as he was. One pointer I've noticed recently is that many journalists today are in the 'game' for personal advancement *beyond journalism*. By which I mean that from the very start of their careers they're not thinking about stories and front pages and headlines and scoops and becoming Editor; they're thinking way ahead of all that 'stepping stone' stuff, to lucrative media consultancy, share options in start-ups, TV punditry. They're thinking about Getting Famous and actually being news themselves like Andrew Neil or Andrew Marr or the Lawson clan. And in pursuit of that the first casualty will be their sense of balance. Now, as we all know, lack of balance leads to instability, which in turn creates conflict, and conflict is what creates drama, and drama is the basis of all news. Balance and peace are not news: they're a vacuum and you won't get famous selling a vacuum, unless your name's James Dyson. So we're not idealists anymore, any more than most of us are religious. We're pragmatists, realists, and it's accepted and apparently *acceptable,* that we'll do whatever we have to do to get ahead.

Feel uneasy about that? Me too. 'We'll do whatever we have to do' conjures up images of desperate corporate imperialists stabbing each other in the back at the Business Class check-in, or even more desperate Tory leadership candidates trying to get taken seriously – the sort of desperate behaviour I heard about in the story of the middle-aged executive in a PR firm which held a major automotive account. Although he was excellent at his job, his position was being cunningly shadowed and stalked by a young pretender in the same department. One evening the stalker seized his chance and arranged that they should go out on what was, for both of them, a very rare evening's boozing. The younger man then helpfully saw the older back to his car, before telephoning the police as he zigzagged off. The loss of driving licence, job, respect, and subsequently wife and home which ultimately resulted seems a steep punishment for gullibility. Honour among thieves? It's a myth and always has been. In a world where Donald Trump and Alan Sugar are held up as examples of how to be a successful businessman on their respective sides of the Atlantic, it doesn't take a Harvard MBA to work out that *ruthlessness* is the Number 1 essential quality to hone if you want to get ahead.

Here in PR-land right now, is this the Age of Spin? Is this where ruthlessness and falsehood as copied from 10 Downing Street are the lifeblood of the celebrity-journalism scene, where the 'truth' is a quaint, outdated notion depending on where you're standing, and people are queuing up to sell their grandmothers? Not quite. Business is certainly tough, but personally I'm a strong believer in trying to conduct my own business with people, be they clients, employees or anyone else, in as ethical and proper a way as I can, and I don't believe I'm any sort of exception here. Yes, there's skulduggery around, and sometimes it comes a bit too close for comfort, but by and large if you treat people well they respond well, which is to everyone's benefit. There's an argument I used to give more weight to when I was much younger that the whole nature of 'business' is dishonest; that buying something from A and then selling it on at a profit to B is fundamentally cheating both A and B, who could have come to an agreement without you in the middle. It's nonsense, of course, because without the catalyst there would be no connection, and no connection means no sale.

Meanwhile, in those mythical, oak-panelled, softly carpeted corridors of power, down which I've only rarely glanced when this or that influential client has allowed me to pop my head around the door, the double-firsts-in-classics Oxford and Cambridge elite who actually run things (although they're always promoting someone from Nottingham University to prove they don't – clever) have developed their brand of pragmatism to such a level of precision that anything untoward can be dealt with quickly, efficiently and without anyone noticing. The country's fascination with conspiracy theories is easily explained by the fact that by definition most conspiracies remain undetected, so there must be *lots* of them going on all around us. This means that when the conspiracy theorist in the pub starts explaining how the Church of England had Princess Diana murdered before she married a Muslim on the orders of the Archbishop of Canterbury, I do, just for a second, consider his theory, and think of making an offer for the film rights. And when Dr David Kelly took his own life over the forty-five minutes to Armageddon press leak, it seemed extraordinarily convenient and helpful of him; so much so that MI5 seemed the most likely source of the execution squad.

Public relations has a powerful ability to direct the media's radar and set agendas in a way the advertising industry has never managed. In print, the easy-to-detect difference between the editorial areas of the page and the copy yelling from the ads remains the crucial divide between credibility and hype. However, product placement and sponsorship have blurred the lines in other areas of the media, leaving us occasionally bemused as a bowls competition turns out to be sponsored by a drugs company or a football league by a soft drink which contributes more to the world's obesity figures than any other single factor.

So what can the Good Guys do? For the PR practitioner who doesn't want to be seen as an evil, cynical, money-driven mercenary the risks are considerable but the temptations understandable in the dog-eat-dog world of business. Whatever ethical position you take, it's extremely difficult when times are hard and your loyal employees are banging their begging bowls on your door to turn down income from drug companies, arms manufacturers, GM crop researchers, cosmetic firms with a taste for guinea pig testing, gas-guzzling 4x4 makers, political parties, hell, even tobacco manufacturers, whose status in the

Western 'ethical consciousness' is now somewhat below that of Fred West or Peter Sutcliffe. They all need good PR desperately, and no one is prepared to pay more than them for a slice of your time and a turn on the media roundabout. The organized, pre-planned use of lies to create column inches and TV coverage is at its most cunning and electrifying when employed by companies or individuals with plenty to hide.

But you have to look yourself in the face, and decide deep down whether you're going to help these dodgy industries or not. Clinging to the truth in an ocean of half-truths, statistics, lies, white lies, inferences and nuances is not easy, and almost impossible to sell as a USP because everyone should be honest all the time anyway. But sticking to principle whenever you can will stand you in good stead, and in dealings with specific journalists at specific newspapers it can even save the day.

When I was young I worked at the Theatre Royal, Stratford East, a venue renowned for ground-breaking, headline-grabbing work. On one occasion we were presenting a new play by Alan Plater, the playwright famous for his TV work, including among many others *The Beiderbecke Tapes, Fortunes of War* and *Oh No! It's Selwyn Froggitt*, and my job was to drum up publicity and sell tickets. I was helped by the fact that the first interview with Plater for a couple of years was big news, and whoever conducted it would insist on exclusivity, i.e. a promise that nobody and no other paper would have the chance to talk to him until the first interview had appeared. Naturally the posh broadsheets (which were at least broadsheets then, if no posher than now) were keen to interview our star playwright, and, remembering that in those pre-email, mobile-free days people used to write real letters to each other, after word had got out, I duly received a letter from *The Times'* Arts Editor confirming that his paper would have the exclusive first interview. This clashed horribly with a telephone conversation I had just had with the *Guardian*, with whom I had agreed a verbal deal but had as yet put nothing in writing. Today there would have been an unholy row. A spoiler would have appeared culled together from old newsclippings to give the impression of a Plater interview, and bad feeling would have been rife.

Instead I rang the *Guardian* back, explained the situation and breathed a sigh of relief when the section editor said he didn't mind in the least not having exclusivity.

'What?' I asked. 'I thought it was essential. I thought being first with a story was the key to everything.'

'Not with arts reviews,' he replied with disarming honesty. 'You see, we have better writers than the *Times* so we'll do a better interview. It's as simple as that.'

I say you couldn't hope for such treatment today, but I may be wrong. Last year I was asked to handle a particularly delicate case involving a footballer's wife, the Old Bailey and a large sum of money. It was important how the press reported the story, because not only was there yet more money riding on the wife's future behaviour, but because it was a really rather sad marriage break-up, with children involved and not much honour on anyone's plate. What I decided to do was High Risk, but if it worked it would satisfy all sides. I asked the editors of the national dailies whether, if I granted them all one-to-one interviews with the F.W., they would agree to embargo the story for an extra twenty-four hours and all run it on Saturday morning. The alternative would have been a split between Friday and Saturday. They agreed, and to my delighted astonishment not a single mention of the story appeared on the Friday, despite the fact that it had made the TV news copiously on the Thursday evening. Even I had appeared on TV, standing outside the court reading a statement written five minutes before. That the ghosts of Fleet Street were still capable of keeping their word, when pressure must have been considerable to cheat ... well, I was flabbergasted, frankly, and not a little flattered.

So the modern way I recommend is to conjure up some

principles, and then do your best to stick to them. In the fullness of time potential clients will come to recognize that you're as good as your word. Some might argue that PR is no different at its core from banking or insurance, after all, and such businesses are founded on personal relationships, track records, references and a convention of absolute discretion. They can come apart at a careless remark, a broken promise or any act of duplicity. I like to think of PR as a buoyant, exciting and life-enhancing aspect of the business and entertainment worlds, but in looking for a point of difference to distinguish my 'offering' from that of my competitors it would be immensely presumptuous, not to mention pompous to stand up and announce that Borkowski PR tries to be on the edge when it comes to integrity. But hey, there's nothing in the rules which says I can't *suggest* it.

Living in Spin

Colin Byrne

I have been in PR for over twenty years, my whole working life. I have worked in politics, the private, public and not-for-profit sectors. I love what I do and have been lucky enough to work with everyone from political leaders and princes, to top companies and bright young PR consultants. Not many jobs would have brought that rewarding professional and personal experience while at the same time being sneered at and treated with such public and media scepticism. I got my new-look Chartered Institute of Public Relations (CIPR) membership card through the post recently. In the style of the late, lamented Labour Party pledge cards from the 1997 general election, it tells me that I am bound to be professional, act ethically, respect confidentiality and be transparent. It omits to mention that I am supposed to lie, distort, cover up, deceive, smarm and generally try to hoodwink the public and those brave crusaders for truth – journalists. Yet that remains the popular image of a profession that employs over thirty thousand people – an image perpetuated by many journalists.

(While we are talking of popular, PR and associated disciplines are now a top-three career choice with UK graduates. And I also want to be clear that to paint all journalists as in conflict with PRs would be a gross exaggeration. Most are just as hard-working and professional as the majority of PRs I have met, and some leading journalists that I admire, from business editors to the editor of *GQ* magazine, are happy to acknowledge that good PRs are an essential resource for good journalists.)

Living in spin

For over a decade, since the term 'spin doctor' was imported here from the USA (I reckon by Michael White, political editor of the *Guardian*) I have been amused at the irony of PRs being cast as spinmeisters by journalists who themselves have to increasingly fit their stories into the world view or editorial slant of their editor, proprietor or marketing department.

If you take a straw poll of any group of reasonably media-literate citizens and ask them to name a well-known PR person – or spin doctor – Alastair Campbell (along with the publicist Max Clifford) will usually come high up the list. Yet I found myself nodding in agreement when, in an interview given on standing down from his Downing Street role, Alastair said that the journalists always 'spun' much more than he did.

As Labour's chief press officer in the early 1990s I would routinely wake up to find my party's policies and my party leader distorted and downright lied about in the print media. Yet it was the likes of me, Peter Mandelson, Alastair Campbell and our colleagues who were derided (usually by the very same journalists) as 'spin doctors'. Indeed my old boss Peter Mandelson, dating back from his time as Labour's communications director and one of the key four architects of what became 'New Labour' (along with Tony Blair, Gordon Brown and Philip Gould), is still viewed – despite going on to be an influential national and now international politician – as the grandfather of UK spin doctors. Yet during all the press briefings and the many off-the-record conversations with lobby journalists that I witnessed or took part in with him, I honestly never heard him utter a lie or a deliberate deception. Sure, he was at pains to put a positive gloss on Labour policies and issues – that was his job as communications director in the face of overwhelming press hostility to his party and its efforts to break free of its unelectable past – but never a lie.

I must admit that occasionally I did try to cover up the facts. Politics – one of the main culprits in the widespread view that PRs distort and deceive – is one of the areas where professional PR is subjugated to the battle for influence. When I was interviewed by a panel that included Mandelson for the job of Labour's chief press officer I declared that we (Labour) were in a war with the media. A number of the panel nodded enthusiastically (Peter just smiled affectionately) because that was their experience. Just as people pledge to die for their country, I effectively declared that I would lie – or at least be economical with the truth – for my party. But in that stage of my career I was in truth more a politician than a PR. It was a war and in war, as the saying goes, truth can be the first victim. But if at that time we had had an unbiased press which reported the facts, would I have had to make that pitch? Politics is just one small fragment of the many industries and causes that PRs work hard to serve. Some – like financial PR – are so heavily regulated that 'spin' is almost impossible. They are regulated in a way that would frighten most journalists to death and drive them out of their chosen profession.

Increasingly it is common to hear a minister or business leader on the *Today* programme putting forward a policy or point of view and their efforts being referred to as 'spin'. If a firm hires good accountants or lawyers or financial advisers, they are being well managed. If they hire a PR firm – well, they must have something to hide mustn't they!

Spin – or the perception of it – has spun out of control.

Newspaper or viewspaper?

Look at the front of the *Daily Mail* or the *Independent* most days of the week. Are they reporting truth? Often the answer has to be no. They are projecting events through the prism of their editorial standpoint. A standpoint which broadly reflects that of their readership market segment. (Not always, as with the *Daily Mirror*'s take on Tony Blair and the war in Iraq under Piers Morgan's editorship.) Much of today's national media – and here I include broadcast outlets like Radio 4's *Today* programme – is in fact a mixture of news channel and 'views channel'. The *Daily Mail* now operates a policy of trying to frighten its readers to death – on health scares, crime, immigration etc. – rather than pretend to be dedicated to telling the truth.

Even the *FT*, probably the most spin-free and fact-based newspaper we have, can fall victim to the fascination with 'spin' over substance, as in a pre-2005 general election report on Labour's coming campaign where the news report was dwarfed by the accompanying picture of Alastair Campbell!

Increasingly, national public affairs journalism is the desired platform for bright opinionated people who want their views broadcast to a wider audience. It used to be politics. As my colleague, ex-*Sun* editor David Yelland, puts it : 'They are going to be better paid and less likely to be deselected.

It is interesting how many sassy, street-smart American clients and colleagues have commented to me on their shock at the cynicism of some British (largely print) journalists. Perhaps this reflects the fact that we are a cynical, glass-half-empty nation. David Yelland worked both here and as deputy editor of the *New York Post*. 'In the USA the press are protected by the Constitution.' They are part of the freedom fabric of America. 'Here, they may be called the Fourth Estate but in truth journalists see themselves as outsiders, more like the noisy kids at the back of the class throwing things' (usually at those in authority or who offend their editorial stance). Healthy scepticism is of course, er, healthy. It is part of our national character. There is a fine and robust tradition among those who comment and report on public life to take a scalpel to the pompous and pretentious. (And we have the media diaries and

Private Eye to pin-prick pompous fellow journalists.) But it can go too far. If scepticism can be healthy, cynicism is corrosive.

One government spokesman, passionate about what the government are trying to achieve in a vital area of public policy, commenting on the annual media feeding frenzy around exam results time, made the point to me that in other countries any statistics suggesting that more young people were succeeding in examinations and getting on the first rung of a good career by gaining enough qualifications to go to university would be a matter of national rejoicing. Here it is all a question of exams getting easier, dumbing down, fiddling the figures and so on. Yet if results were to get worse, those same newspapers would be screaming for ministers' and policy makers' heads to roll.

The reduced focus on facts in newspaper reporting seems to be reflected in their declining sales. Yelland again: 'People want the facts, and they are not getting them.' (Neither do they respect or believe politicians and they are consequently voting with their feet in elections.) With the broadcast media – despite the Andrew Gilligan drama – the truth is still much easier to get out there. That was the dictum that ruled the Mandelson era of Labour communications, at a time when most of the national print media were overtly hostile to that party.

I am surprised today how many business leaders in particular still fear the broadcasters. In politics the medium has been long seen as a way of going over the heads of the national print media and getting your message to citizens or consumers with less fear of editorial pollution. Also the broadcast media is regulated, by a regulator with real teeth. Is it a coincidence that the broadcast media is expanding, while newspaper circulations are shrinking? Not, as I refer to above, that the broadcast media is entirely free from this confusion of news and views. In July 2005 the leading current affairs broadcaster John Humphrys was reported to have told an audience of PR professionals that all ministers were in effect liars. Was he speaking as an influential current affairs journalist whose interviews largely colour our daily view of the political scene, or as an individual grumpy old man?

PR needs better PR

Not that the media alone need to improve their act. PR does too. As a profession we complain about not being taken seriously but are more likely to give an industry honour to Mark Bolland or a trade media platform to Charlie Whelan than to a hard-working grassroots PR. And at least journalists have proper entry-level training programmes to try to keep standards high. Despite the growth of degree level PR courses, there is still no entry qualification to gain entry to PR. In early 2005 I did a focus group of young entrants to various branches of PR on what they wanted for their profession. Here is a snapshot in a survey that was fairly free of moans about the media:

I want us to be acknowledged as experts in communications rather than miscommunications

I want us to be a bridge-building industry providing insight and understanding.

I want PR to be a serious integral management function with a recognized place in the boardroom.

I want our industry to be a leading force in encouraging organizations to behave ethically and responsibly.

I want PR to be a serious career choice for the brightest and the best.

I want PR to be seen as a decent profession based on honesty and ethical advocacy.

PR and the media

That brings me to the relationship between PR and the media, something I have observed closely for nearly twenty-five years as a PR professional.

David Yelland is one of the highest-profile defectors from the media to PR. He says: 'PR is now as important to the media as the media is to PR.' The old-school view – when I started in PR in the early 1980s – was (in the eyes of journalists at least) that the media were pivotal, independent, the ethical in pursuit of the truth and all that was fit to print. PRs were seen as slightly glamorous but lacking the power and independence of journalists and generally being in the business of flogging snake-oil for the highest possible fee.

Today – and I talk to many journalists about a move into PR as part of their career development – those views have largely changed. The media is at war with itself over declining newspaper circulation and most journalists' contact books are full of key and senior PR contacts, from politics to business, from entertainment to sports. Events like Live8 are as much about PR for a message as they are about a stage full of rock stars cheering a cause. PR is seen to be more about power and influence than glamour and flim-flam. Yes, PR continues to have poor PR. But its relationship with the media is based on something bigger than grudging respect or occasional sniping. It is rooted in a common interest – the increased importance of communications to the missions of organizations, movements and leaders. And that is a trend that can only continue.

Take the case of government communications again. For every Jo Moore or Charlie Whelan there are hundreds of dedicated professional Whitehall PRs who try to do their job of getting important information to us, the citizens and consumers of health, education, transport, law and order, to the very best of their abilities in difficult circumstances. To denigrate them as distorting spin doctors is as unfair as using the case of Harold Shipman to suggest that we should never trust hard-working GPs as a group.

If we are to understand our world, our country, our government, our own interests; if young people who are deserting the media as fast as they are deserting the democratic process are to be reconnected with the policies and people who are driving progress, or occasionally lack of it, in our society, then PRs and journalists need to work together in an endeavour which is far more important than a businessman/proprietor's views and self-interest.

The time has come to stop the name calling and the barbed mutual cynicism and to work together in the name of truth and understanding. Both PRs and journalists are in interesting jobs and influential positions. We need each other to do our jobs to the best of our abilities. Recognizing that and our mutual responsibilities to our customers, clients, voters, readers, listeners and viewers is a great platform to build on. Name calling is not.

News from Number Ten

Michael Cockerell

There is no better way of catching the attention of journalists than by making a TV film featuring them. When we had a press preview for the documentary I had made about Tony Blair and Alastair Campbell – *News from Number Ten* – no fewer than eighty hacks arrived to watch it – including almost all the top political editors. Normally you count yourself lucky if as many as five people show up for a screening.

Many of the journalists thought they were coming to a hanging party: they had arrived believing their own press cuttings. A common view, written up by those who had neither seen a frame of the film nor talked to me, was reflected by the ironical *Guardian*: 'Michael Cockerell is to make a programme revealing how the Prime Minister's self-effacing official spokesman suffers daily at the hands of brutal political hacks': I was Alastair Campbell's patsy and they were to be the scapegoats.

Naturally my view was somewhat different. But I was well aware from the start of the hazards involved in trying to make a film about the state of relations between Number 10 and the media. At its simplest, how was I going to prevent the government's spinmeister-in-chief putting the spin on us? The story of how the film was made and what we learned about New Labour's fabled publicity machine reveals how complex it can be to try to capture truth on television.

It had taken nearly six years to get Blair and Campbell to agree to my making a documentary with real behind-the-scenes access. I had first written to Campbell with the suggestion when he was appointed Press Secretary in 1994. Over the course of the next six years, as New Labour moved from opposition to government, I would repeat the request. Campbell's reply could best be summed up by the pop song 'You keep me hanging on'. Sometimes he would come up to me at a party conference or in the Commons and say: 'You'll get us one day' – a nicely ambiguous reply. At other times he would reply by letter turning down my latest request, saying, 'It's a no, not a never.'

Eventually my editor, Anne Tyerman, and I discussed with Campbell the idea of making a film about Number 10 and the media. We said we would need real access over a period of weeks to both himself and the Prime Minister and to the workings of the Downing Street press office; we would also want to film at the twice-daily briefings, whose secrecy the political editors aka Lobby journalists had always jealously protected.

But the way Campbell gave us the go-ahead was unusual. He rang me and said, 'Look on the Downing Street website.' There I discovered that Campbell had put out a notice saying that the Prime Minister and he had agreed to our making the film. It was the first time I had ever learned through cyber-space what I would be doing for the next few months.

'Given the increasing focus in the media on the issue of so-called spin, we have agreed to cooperate with the BBC on a documentary about the way we work here in Downing Street,' announced Campbell. 'I am confident that if a film explores the full range of what we do, the public will have a better understanding of the relationship between modern politics and media.' In his *The Spin Doctor's Diary*,[19] Campbell's deputy, Lance Price, used rather saltier language to explain why we had been let in to film: 'the idea of doing it is to show the Lobby journalists as a bunch of wankers interested only in trivia and personalities.'

I then spent many days shadowing Campbell in various meetings inside Number 10 and going to Lobby briefings. While seeking to be as inconspicuous as possible in far corners of rooms, without a camera, I was well aware that people would be on the *qui vive* against an outsider. The *Guardian* later published a leaked email from Blair's Special Assistant and childhood friend, Anji Hunter, advising Number 10 staff to behave: 'Michael Cockerell – plus notebook and beady eye – will be observing this meeting: so perhaps a little more cool efficiency, bonhomie towards our ministerial colleagues and decorum.'

To counter such counter-measures, my producer Alison Cahn and I constantly spent our time, off camera and before starting filming, talking to people – inside Number 10 and outside – with first-hand knowledge of how the system operated when we were not there.

And we had two further crucial weapons in our armoury once we did start filming. The most powerful was the cutting-room floor. Anything that we filmed that didn't have the ring of truth to us or we felt was put on for the cameras was consigned for horizontal filing. In his diary Price says 'AC [Alastair Campbell] deliberately started talking about a reshuffle story in the *Sun* at the Lobby today just so that Cockerell would get some film of him attacking the media for inaccuracy and trivia.' In fact that was exactly what we had thought he was doing at the time and that section never made it into the finished film. Campbell had no editorial control or rights over the film, nor did he ask for any.

The second important weapon was the length of our access. We went on filming inside Number 10 over four months and saw things that by definition you can't see if you are outside the famous black door. Also, many events we filmed were unpredictable and uncontrollable.

For instance, Alastair Campbell could not know in advance of the questions that the political journalists would ask him at the Lobby briefings. And sometimes he would emerge the worse for wear. In his diary Lance Price says, 'Monday's Lobby meeting was a disaster for us because Cockerell managed to film a ding-dong on asylum where we were clearly on the defensive. AC said he thought it was fine, but he looked a bit uncomfortable afterwards.'

There was much speculation in the Lobby about why Campbell had agreed to the documentary. Some supposed it was his vanity, others that it would be a hagiography, others that he was preparing some kind of exit strategy and he saw it as a good job application.

I felt he and Blair had agreed to the filming – despite the objections of some political advisers and officials in the Number 10 press office – because they felt the government could gain from an accurate representation of the state of play between Number 10 and the media. 'I may be making the biggest mistake of my professional career in letting you in,' Campbell told us. 'But what I want to get across is that we fulfil a basic, necessary and legitimate function. We are not the horrible, Machiavellian people as portrayed. There is a huge range of information that we have to get out in a coordinated way. But the press – hand in hand with the Conservatives – say it's all just spin.'

Campbell, Blair and Peter Mandelson had intensified the sharpness of the inevitable clashes between Number 10 and the media by the style of news management they had brought with them into government. They had followed the dictum of James Carville, President Clinton's spin-maestro: 'the politicians must always be ahead of the news cycle.' Campbell told me: 'We have to try to dominate the agenda, because good government demands it. We have to stay ahead of the media, finding new and creative ways to get our message to the public.' In practice that meant ensuring a constant supply of positive pictures and messages from the Prime Minister. Campbell's aim was to put across a coherent 'narrative' of what the government was doing and to ensure that every minister was on-message.

Or as the media put it, Blair, Campbell and Mandelson were control freaks obsessed with spin. And that was the version the public believed. Campbell made it clear that one of the reaons for letting us in was his conviction that the word 'spin' was becoming as damaging for New Labour as 'sleaze' had been for the Tories. Picking up a phrase I had once used, Campbell claimed that he and Blair were more spinned against than spinning.

Campbell's view was that much of the public disillusion with the government resulted from the way the media covered politics. In the documentary he told me that he felt that straight political reporting has become the victim of the 24-hour-a-day news media and the ever fiercer competition for viewers, readers and listeners.

The old distinctions between fact and comment had disappeared along with those between the broadsheet and the tabloid agenda, claimed Campbell: 'they are all in the same competing middle market. Newspapers have falling circulations, they don't have the promotional budgets they once had – so they have to do it editorially. The political journalists are all in the business of drawing attention to themselves. They give the sense that everything is in the fast lane – going at a hundred and fifty miles an hour: everything is a scandal, everything is a controversy. I have a drawer full of cuttings going back five years, each of which says "it's been Tony Blair's blackest week".'

The Lobby journalists would not accept Campbell's arguments. They maintained they were essential conduits to the public of what is really happening in government. They could not be expected to print just what Campbell told them – that would turn their newspapers into *Pravda*. They had to print stories that would interest their readers, who were increasingly turned off by politics.

And they rejected Campbell's view that the political journalists were the true spin doctors – imposing their own agenda and slant on what they reported. 'We are not spin doctors – we are professional decoders,' said Michael Prescott, then Political Editor of the *Sunday Times*. 'Politicians speak a strange language and it is up to us to decode it – and that leads to clashes with Campbell.'

One of the advantages of filming in Number 10 over a lengthy period, if you are unobtrusive enough, is that people do become used to you and tend to get on with the business they have to transact. Sometimes they don't even realize you are there – as with the shots of Blair rushing down the corridor to greet a VIP who'd arrived early, or when Campbell himself was caught on our camera prompting a BBC journalist to change the subject at a press conference with the Prime Minister. And there were the occasional jokey moments, as when there was a cock-up with Downing Street's high technology that failed to record the PM's webcast and, much to his annoyance, he had to do it all over again.

Probably the best spontaneous moment came when we filmed the shirt-sleeved Prime Minister coming into Campbell's room looking rather like the nervous schoolboy going into the headmaster's study. As Campbell's deputy Lance Price put it in his *The Spin Doctor's Diary*: 'TB was effectively ambushed when he walked into AC's office while they were filming.' In fact Campbell had purposely not warned the PM that we would be there. Yet I believe he thought he was acting for the best of motives – both for Blair and for our film. Campbell told me: 'If I warn him in advance you are going to be there, he will be all stiff and unnatural before the cameras.'

Blair certainly looked a little startled to see us, but soon recovered his composure when I asked him why his government placed such importance on its relations with the media and on presentation. 'It's just modern government,' he replied. 'Over the past twenty years the media has intensified – become twenty-four hours a day. So you have to try to be smarter, sharper and quicker off the mark than you used to be.

'I would prefer a situation where things happened in a far more deliberate, less frantic way than they do today – where what you wake up with in the morning is still happening at night. But nowadays, with the speed of the media it just doesn't happen like that. So it's important to have the capacity to get on top of the news, as far as possible; because otherwise a story can be out there saying you are doing something which you are not doing at all. And these stories then take on a life of their own and start running away in the far distance. So you have to be able to say: "Hang on the facts are x and y."'

Blair warmed to his theme that the media represented a barrier between him and the public: 'The greatest frustration of modern politics is that – everyone talks about sound-bites – on the main evening TV news you'll get thirty seconds, if you are very lucky – and twenty seconds, if you are not. So the number of times you can communicate with people so that they hear a structured argument is very limited. And it is partly I think because the media have become obsessed with themselves.'

But, I said, it is reported that you and Alastair Campbell spend your whole time working out how you are going to spin things so that you will win the next election. 'That's rubbish" the PM replied, 'I would be the happiest person in the world if I didn't have to give another thought as to what the presentation was. Of course when a specific controversy comes up, you have to manage the press angle and have answers for what they are going to be interested in.

'But the idea that I sit and think about presentation all day is nonsense. That is not what motivates us and it must not disturb me from doing the things that are really important for me – which are the things for this country; otherwise there is no point in doing this job. And people can believe this or not – but it is what I spend my time thinking about.'

The impact of Blair's impassioned peroration was somewhat blunted when Alastair Campbell interjected with a laugh: 'So that's why you spent the last seven minutes talking to Michael Cockerell.' I subsequently learned that it was the moment when Campbell wished he had bitten his tongue.

And the image of Campbell as the dominant partner in the relationship was one that Rory Bremner had already siezed on. By chance I was playing in a charity cricket match with Bremner on the day after the documentary went out and he told me: 'I've been studying your programme frame by frame.' In his diary Lance Price wrote after watching our documentary: 'The biggest problem is the scenes with AC and TB. AC allowed himself some little asides which play straight into the Rory Bremner image of the pair of them. AC is very articulate throughout while TB is rather hesitant and unfocused.'

After the documentary went out Campbell himself told me that he felt it had on balance justified the risk he and the PM had taken in giving us access. But from Number 10's point of view we had failed to portray the journalists as corrosively cynical enough. Nor had we dwelt sufficiently on what Campbell called 'the regular diet of trivia, froth, speculation and sheer invention that passes for so much political journalism these days'.

'I would give your documentary seven out of ten,' Campbell told me. That is about where one would like it to be: you can go back and ask for more, but you haven't made a party political broadcast.

For a political junkie like myself it had been fascinating to film for four months at the heart of the New Labour government. And I did experience some withdrawal symptoms when the filming inside Number 10 had to stop. But my abiding sense of having watched the fabled New Labour spin machine at first hand was how seat of the pants it all was. Despite all the grids, media monitoring, instant rebuttal, strategy and attack units – so much of what Campbell and his team were doing was intuitive, uncoordinated and last minute.

I was also struck by what had changed and what had stayed the same in the twenty years since Peter Hennessy, David Walker and I wrote *Sources Close to the Prime Minister*. In th7at book, we had argued that the pervasive secrecy of Whitehall was matched by a largely pliant Lobby, content to kiss the chains that bound it. And we had called for a far greater openness by both government and the media – including on-the-record Lobby briefings, televised prime ministerial press conferences and a genuine Freedom of Information Act.

Much has changed since then, under successive governments: there is far more official information available now than ever and many of the old secret taboos of Whitehall have been lifted – on such subjects as the Budget, the existence of security services and the rules governing the conduct of Cabinet ministers. MI5 has its own website and the monthly minutes of the Bank of England's monetary policy committee – which sets interest rates – are published.

And, thanks to Campbell, Lobby briefings – excluding the political exchanges – are on the Number 10 website. This was all a far cry from the Lobby's own rulebook which said: 'Never talk about Lobby briefings either before or after they have happened – especially not in the presence of those not entitled to attend them.'

Soon after our film Blair agreed to monthly televised press conferences and the government has passed a Freedom of Information Act – which despite the tight restrictions has produced some embarrassing disclosures for both government and opposition.

Yet the truth about what really goes on at the very heart of power inside a greatly strengthened Number 10 is still as tantalizingly far away as ever from the public view. Leaked documents and indiscreet memoirs provide often riveting but only partial and partisan glimpses. The bunker mentality which tends to afflict every prime minister after a long period in office has if anything intensified rather than relaxed since Alastair Campbell made his noisy exit from Downing Street. Some of the most powerful figures in the land – the Prime Minister's unelected special advisers like Jonathan Powell and Lord Birt (until his recent departure) – are unaccountable and kept away by Tony Blair from questioning by Parliamentary committees. And they refuse to speak on the record to journalists. The perennial battle as well as the mutual antipathy between Number 10 and the media is as fierce as ever.

It all seems a long way from the new dawn of 1997. Tony Blair came to power promising 'open government' and an end to the secrecy that leads to 'arrogance and defective policy making'.

Poached Gamekeeper

Leonard Doyle

My world as Foreign Editor of a national daily was turned upside down when one of my correspondents became, very controversially, the story.

A Zimbabwean stringer, Basildon Peta, had been taken into custody by Robert Mugabe's police in February 2002. In London Fleet Street questioned whether his account of his incarceration had been fabricated. It was the hurricane-strength viciousness with which colleagues in other newspapers turned on Basildon Peta – egged on by their newsdesks, whose real objective was cutting the uppity *Independent* down to size – that took me by surprise. Not many stopped to think of the consequences before taking as fact allegations against our reporter made by an organization with an anti-Basildon agenda and a clear conflict of interest. Suddenly the *Independent*'s credibility was on the line and Basildon's reputation as a prize-winning scourge of the Mugabe regime was thrashed by 'colleagues' hundreds and in some cases thousands of miles away.

The truth was just a bit too complicated for some newsdesks to think through. Once a story is offered by an enthusiastic correspondent and boiled down to an eye-catching schedule-line for the editor's conference, it can be hard to row back on it: 'correspondent admits report of Harare police cell was fabricated' was how the *Times* pitched what would become a front-page story. Nuance and detail got swept away and the resulting story would put our reporter's life in some jeopardy. In fact our correspondent, Basildon Peta, *had* been taken into custody, but a proportion of his night was spent being accompanied home by two lenient jailers to get his medication, before being returned to the police lockup. In order to protect his jailers from attack by their superiors, Basildon Peta had not disclosed this sequence of events in his original piece. This omission was costly to him, and to us, but it could have been much worse. As the media prepared to go to press on the first night, my role turned from poacher to gamekeeper and I learned some some useful lessons in the possibilities – and constraints – of damage limitation.

The onslaught would last for several days and ended with Basildon leaving his native Zimbabwe in fear for his life. He was hounded out not so much by the Mugabe regime as by the distortions printed about him on page one of *The Times* and in other UK newspapers. In the age of the internet these allegations were instantly taken as fact by his enemies in Mugabe's regime.

Trying to limit the harm to the journalist's reputation and douse the flames licking around our own credibility was an exhausting though ultimately satisfying task. But the experience of dealing with colleagues on other newspapers – little interested in the facts that might get in the way of a juicy story – was profoundly disappointing.

As Hurricane Basildon made landfall and the first winds of the controversy struck, Johannesburg-based correspondents of other newspapers began calling the editor's office. The phones were ringing off the hook as print and broadcast media called for comment. Senior executives of my newspaper had little huddles as they began to fear the worst. By the close of play, *The Times*, *Telegraph* and *Guardian* would go to press with stories that were wildly off beam, putting our correspondent's life in some danger. When the state-controlled Zimbabwean media got their teeth into the story he became a public enemy and by nightfall his story was leading the television news with accusations that his 'lies' had caused a run on the currency.

Basildon had little option but to catch a plane into exile in South Africa the next morning. He raced to the airport trying to look anonymous, while his alleged 'lies' in the British press dominated the state-controlled TV broadcasts and were front-page news in the newspapers.

Basildon's troubles began when I commissioned him to write a lengthy article about his arrest and subsequent overnight detention by Robert Mugabe's police, who were unhappy with his trenchant reporting for the *Independent*. What turned this into a category 5 media hurricane was that the accusation that he had distorted his reporting came not from Mugabe's goons, but from the combined forces of the British press, mostly via their correspondents in faraway Johannesburg.

At stake was Basildon's reputation of course, and that of his commissioning editor – myself – and in a very real way the squeaky clean reputation of the *Independent*. For about eight hours on Monday, 11 February 2002, while Hurricane Basildon blasted all in its path, and that evening's newspaper deadlines loomed, I found myself battling against uneven odds and an opposition that had scented blood and would not willingly let go.

It was to provide me with a vivid insight into some of the uglier realities of the pack instinct of the British press. No matter that most of the reporters who called me were hundreds of miles away from Harare, nothing it seemed would dissuade them from rushing into print with a story damaging to the *Independent* regardless of the risk to the reporter. This was undoubtedly because under the strange unwritten rules of the trade, that stringers, especially locally hired stringers, are somehow not as worthy of consideration as the expatriate hacks. Although Basildon had more than his share of page one exclusives in the *Independent* to his name, it seemed he was not to be considered a proper member of the British press. He was Zimbabwean and somehow the idea that he might be the victim of a vicious smear campaign emanating from inside Zimbabwe was discounted as the hack pack went for blood.

The first inkling I had of the impending storm was a totally unexpected call from my old colleague Chris McGreal, then the *Guardian*'s esteemed South Africa correspondent. Chris is one of the most respected foreign correspondents in the business and I had worked on the *Observer* with him as his foreign editor some years earlier.

With a deepening sense of gloom I listened as Chris sketched out the details of what he clearly believed was a sensational story to the effect that our Zimbabwean correspondent had fabricated his account of a terrifying night spent in Robert Mugabe's cells. I could not lightly dismiss such allegations. Chris indicated that he already had everything he needed to go to press and was simply making a final call to me to seek a comment.

But as the story would turn out, Chris's copper-bottomed source, and the same 'independent' source as used by the rest of the British media, would turn out to have a conflict of interest. But more of that later.

Reporters, commissioning editors, headline writers, sub-editors, all of us live a keystroke away from disaster. What journalist has not woken up in a cold sweat wondering whether he has got a key fact or name wrong and whether it is not too late to call back a story that unfortunately is already in the back of trucks and vans making its way to newspaper shops the length and breadth of the country.

Hurricane Basildon brought out all our worst fears at once. Was this Zimbabwean stringer whom we barely knew – nobody in the London office of the *Independent* had ever met Basildon by this stage – actually a fantasist? Worse, he might be an agent provocateur for Mugabe's propaganda machinery, who would single-handedly wreck the reputation of newspaper.

The truth, when we got to the bottom of it, was more prosaic, but by that stage much of the damage to Basildon's reputation and by extension the *Independent*'s had been done. Unfortunately it is easier to throw mud than it is to clean it up and to this day, British spooks and Foreign Office types happily spread poison at cocktail parties with comments like 'Of course, he's not very reliable, is he?'

They are joined in their whispering by diplomats from the Zimbabwean High Commission, who will tell anyone willing to listen that 'You just cannot trust his reporting.'

The truth, when I got to the bottom of it, was not quite what I expected. While it completely cleared Basildon of the charges laid against him, it raised some serious questions for me about the culture of newspapers where a final check call is often avoided as a call too many.

As I fielded one aggressive call after another from Basildon's colleagues in the field, and not knowing whether their allegations were true or false, I decided that the best way to unravel the story was to have Basildon speak for himself. I arranged for conference calls between him and the Johannesburg correspondents and listened in on most of them as Basildon patiently explained the background to the ensuing media meltdown.

The facts were straightforward. Basildon, also the head of the Zimbabwean Union of Journalists, was told to report to the police station in central Harare, which he did in the company of a lawyer provided by another organization – the Zimbabwe chapter of the Media Institute of Southern Africa (MISA), the press freedom organization (funded by Scandinavian taxpayers. Unfortunately Basildon had unwittingly provoked anger and envy at MISA because of his high-profile journalism for the *Independent*, his frequent appearances on CNN and his activist work for the Zimbabwean Union of Journalists. Indeed the reason the police wanted to question him was because he had helped organize a national gathering of journalists to oppose a draconian anti-media Bill being drafted by the Mugabe regime.

In the hothouse world of Zimbabwean opposition politics Tawanda Hondora, the lawyer who was assigned to protect him, would end up speaking freely to the media and without specific authorization about the case. MISA, which had hired the lawyer for him, then issued a 'press release' to the British press attacking Basildon's account of his time in custody. 'For the record,' the statement read, 'Peta did not sleep in police cells contrary to what is being reported.' This was the nub of the controversy as the *Independent*'s coverage of Basildon's time in custody and his incarceration in Harare central had described how he was given a few broken planks of wood 'on which to spend the night'.

By any standards this was an extraordinary act by an organization dedicated to press freedom. To issue a statement assassinating Basildon's character and attacking his journalistic integrity without even contacting him for his side of the story was staggering.

MISA also contacted Basildon's editor at the *Financial Gazette* in Zimbabwe warning that a damaging story was about to hit the headlines. Curiously, although MISA faxed the statement to the *Independent*'s competitors in Johannesburg and elsewhere, we never received it.

It was this 'communiqué' which was at the centre of the allegations and only by having Basildon tackle it head on would there be any hope of turning the tide on a story that was gathering pace as newspaper deadlines drew closer. Given the poison that now existed between MISA and Basildon, I decided to speak directly to Luckson Chipare, the head of the organization which is based in Windhoek, Namibia. I had him interrogate Basildon over the phone and establish that the

MISA 'communiqué' was a tissue of lies.

What MISA's statement did not reveal, because Basildon had kept it a secret even from the *Independent*, was that he had persuaded two of his jailers to accompany him home in the middle of the night to pick up his ulcer medication. Arriving sometime after 11 p.m. the police stayed with him at home for some four hours and brought him back to the cells before dawn. As Basildon explained things: 'The police assigned to me were told to mistreat me and they were due to keep me overnight. But after bringing me home they asked me to keep it a secret so that they would not be punished. That is why I was not explicit about where I spent part of the night. I was trying to protect two people who had been kind to me. But throughout the night, in the cells or in my home, I remained in police custody, that is what the press forgot when it rushed to print.'

Finally we knew what had actually transpired on the night in question. Then came the hard part: persuading MISA to issue a statement setting the record straight. This they finally did, but only after the first editions had gone to press in London.

The statement when it arrived from Namibia amounted to a dramatic about-turn: 'We have now established that Mr Peta was in police custody longer than what we had earlier indicated,' it read; 'he has indicated that he was in police custody for about 15 hours not the 5 hours indicated.'

From that point on it was fairly easy to persuade *The Times*' night editor to pull the most damaging story from its front page. The paper's outrageous account, by Michael Dynes in Johannesburg and Adam Sherwin in London, stated that Basildon 'has admitted that he fabricated a report about being arrested and incarcerated in a "wretched" Harare police cell'. By the second edition this highly coloured account had been yanked off the front page.

Sadly it was Mr Sherwin who, thinking he had Basildon bang to rights, fabricated his version of what he had said while explaining what had happened in Harare central police station. *The Times'* story was picked up by AFP and republished around the world – most notably in Zimbabwe. How could it be that Basildon, who spoke to virtually everyone in the British media with an interest in the story, only 'admitted fabricating' his story to Mr Sherwin of *The Times*? Was this a case of a reporter trying to sex up a story so that it lived up to the hype with which it had been pitched to the duty editor? It certainly seems so.

Over at the *Guardian* and *Telegraph* there was similar rowing back in their later editions.

While we had not quite killed the story, it was sufficiently damped down by the realization that perhaps all was not as clear at it appeared from the comfortable vantage point of Johannesburg. In fact the fairest account of Basildon's travails was in the *Telegraph*, which has a full-time Harare correspondent.

But it was the first edition of *The Times* that sealed Basildon's fate. He had got wind that the Zimbabwean police were hunting him down, armed with a copy of Mr Sherwin's page one story, which had been reprinted in the state-owned *Herald* newspaper and which they considerd 'evidence' that he had 'admitted lying' and would use as justification for throwing him in jail.

The fact that the British media, which had been considered allies of the struggle for press freedom in Zimbabwe, was seen to be leading the attacks on Basildon, a chief proponent of the battle for press freedom, left him more vulnerable. He was well known in Zimbabwe and regularly demonized in the state media. In fact Basildon was the first journalist to be arrested by Zimbabwe police in post-independent Zimbabwe when he published a story about tax evasion by government ministers in 1993, shortly after starting out as a journalist. President Mugabe's militant war veteran supporters had threatened to sort him out after the onslaught in the UK papers. And as he told me at the time, 'Anybody who had seen what they had done in white commercial farms and against the black opposition could not take their threats lightly.'

State radio even conducted talk shows in which government supporters were allowed to phone in venting their anger at Basildon for a story which the government had bizarrely claimed to have caused the stock market to crash, caused a major drop in investment and tourist inflows into Zimbabwe, and damaged the economy.

Basildon told me when I questioned him about his account of his time in the cells, 'I had nothing to gain from any fabrication. That would add nothing to my profile and only damage the cause of press freedom in my country.' He was already regularly quoted on CNN, BBC and other media worldwide. The coveted prize for journalism in southern Africa is ironically the Media Institute of Southern Africa (MISA) Press Freedom Award, given annually to a journalist who has excelled in advancing the cause of press freedom in the fourteen-member-country SADC region. It is administered from the MISA head office in Windhoek and bankrolled by Scandanivian donor countries.

To date, Basildon remains the youngest-ever journalist to have won this award having been its second recipient in 1994 at the tender age of twenty-three. He was selected by the head office of MISA in Namibia long before his detractors took over the Zimbabwe chapter of the organization. The other winners of the award have ranged from fifty to seventy years of age. Raymond Louw, the winner in 2005, a former editor of South Africa's *Rand Daily Mail*, is in his late seventies. Basildon had scooped many other Zimbabwean national awards as well as the other coveted award of 2001 Africa Journalist of the Year (Business Reporting) sponsored by the Africa Journalist Foundation.

But there were real consequences from this story which

briefly caught the imagination of the UK media. Basildon is now living with his family in exile in South Africa. While his elderly parents are extremely poor and vulnerable in Harare he cannot return to help them without the certainty of being slung in jail. Basildon now writes for the *Independent* from Johannesburg, where he is a respected commentator on Zimbabwean affairs. But his reputation undoubtedly suffered, as was proven by the whispering of FCO diplomats and the willingness of Fleet Street journalists to believe that smoke always indicates fire – even if afterwards it is shown to be a cleverly designed smokescreen.

Today the *Independent* no longer has a correspondent on t he ground in Zimbabwe. The *Guardian*'s resident Zimbabwe correspondent, who refused to participate in the smearing of Basildon, was himself slung out of the country. Both the *Guardian*'s and *The Times*' South Africa correspondents have moved on. Only the *Telegraph*'s correspondent, Peta Thornycroft, a white Zimbabwean, remains in Harare. Wittingly or unwittingly the attacks on Basildon's integrity and his flight into exile have led to the loss of a brave and articulate black journalist from his country. His reputation has been restored, but the big beneficiary of the controversy was the Mugabe regime, which did not have to lift a finger to remove one of its most troublesome critics. Instead the British press did it for him.

Sympathy for the Devil

Kim Fletcher

My first lesson in corporate public relations came from the celebrated British Airways team of the 1980s – the side that swept
all before it until hitting a run of bad form the following
decade. Our meeting came years before things went wrong, in
the days when it was possible to think of BA without the dirty
tricks campaign against Richard Branson's new Virgin airline
coming to mind. Or the moment Margaret Thatcher covered
the tail of a BA model aeroplane with a handkerchief because
the company had replaced its traditional red, white and blue
tailfins with ethnic designs.

Those embarrassing events were in the future. This was the
early 1980s. The baggage handlers were on strike and the
Sunday Times had sent me to Heathrow to find out why. I don't
recall talking to the trade union or to any pickets, though I certainly did. I do remember walking into Speedbird House to get
the management line. That's when the PR team got me.

I was a 25-year-old general reporter welcomed as if I were the
most important figure in the aviation industry. They were clearly keen to impress the *Sunday Times*. It would be difficult,
explained my new friends, to put across the complexity of the
company's position in a short interview. I must join them for
lunch in the boardroom, where we could really get to grips with
it. The men running the world's favourite airline opened a second bottle of wine and showed a gratifying interest in everything I had to say.

Did it affect what I wrote? Not as they intended, I think.

Whatever the rights and wrongs of an industrial dispute, the juxtaposition of workforce at the gate and management at the lunch table is always unattractive. I had all the priggishness of a young reporter newly arrived from the north of England. And I knew that proper reporters did not rub along with PRs.

This was a minor attempt at news management, but an eye-opener for a reporter unused to seeing PRs organize anything more than free holidays. Of course, I knew the PR industry did much more, and had done for years. But I see the last twenty-five years as a golden age for PR practitioners, in which they have gained a foothold in every area of life. Now there is nothing and no one that cannot be shined up and presented in a better light, including newspaper groups and the journalists who write for them.

Yes, even papers, as I found to my cost when I edited the *Independent on Sunday*. Mine was not a long engagement and I realized my days were numbered when I attended a management away day.

'How are you getting on with Joe, on the PR front?' asked the chief executive.

'Joe? I've not met him,' I said.

There was a ripple of embarrassed laughter around the table.

'You mean *her*. Jo – she's our PR consultant.'

We'd had a PR in for weeks and no one had told me. I was Mr Cellophane. Was that why the editor-in-chief was getting such a good write-up everywhere? I am not sure Jo could have done anything for my life expectancy, but it would have been interesting to have her try.

So it is all the more remarkable that many journalists continue either to say that they have nothing to do with PRs, or to assert their moral superiority over them when they do. Open any newspaper and read the stuff: who comes up with all those holidays? Where do interviews with film stars come from? Do you think those fashion shoots happen by chance?

Generations of journalists have taken free holidays for the travel pages, negotiated the timing of celebrity interviews and raided the fashion cupboard for frocks sent round by designers. Journalists have been happy to buy what the PR business has flogged – as long as they are allowed to cloak themselves in the integrity of 'editorial independence'.

Let us define at this point what we mean by PR. For the purposes of this discussion, it is promotion of any activity or business or person that falls short of paid-for advertising. That promotion may be for entirely positive reasons – to extol the virtues of a holiday destination, a new product, an honest politician – or for defensive reasons – to diminish concern over typhoid at the holiday destination, unreliability on the part of the new product or lies by the politician. Such promotion may require the raising of consciousness about a client's successes or the publicizing of a rival's failures. When, for example, Mark Bolland was promoting the interests of the Prince of Wales, his critics accused him of doing so at the expense of other members of the royal family. The price of making Prince Charles look a doting father was to make his younger son seem a most troubled boy.

Does PR work? You decide. A chief executive friend of mine contends that it is a sure sign of a firm heading for trouble when bosses engage PR consultants to organize laudatory profiles in Sunday business pages. The readers infer that these men and women who rise at six and spend an hour in the gym before a breakfast meeting are the gods and goddesses of businesses. My friend infers that their companies are heading in the tank and that they are about to lose their jobs.

Journalists retain the right to patronize PRs but rub along with them pretty well. Whatever they may say, the journalists are far from being the masters of the relationship. The balance of power swings from journalist to PR according to the market value of the product. A PR who wants a nice write-up for the caravan company he represents may have to work hard to find journalists to go. The PR seeking publicity for a new destination in the Indian Ocean can probably place the piece where she wants.

It is the travel world that sees the relationship at its most straightforward, with companies arranging for journalists to holiday for nothing in return for a write-up. This is the classic 'freebie'. There may be journalists who review these destinations viciously, but I haven't read them. If criticisms are made, they are written in a euphemistic manner, so that it becomes important for the reader to understand such phrases as 'basic accommodation', 'lively resort' or 'ideal for travellers on a budget'.

The other traditional areas are show business and new products. One day a PR works hard to persuade a friendly features editor to interview his new author. The next he may be able to demand front-page coverage, picture and copy approval in return for awarding an exclusive interview with a big-name star. As for products, motorcycle couriers criss-cross London every day to get the latest gadgets and gimmicks into the clutches of journalists prepared to give them a mention.

But the real developments in PR operations have been in less-visible areas. The first of these is the public services. The second – and I think more controversial – has been politics.

It is hard to find a company, council or police force operating without the benefit of PR advice. Press officers may still answer basic questions. But if there is any possible controversy, the chances are that they will be working to a script derived from a PR strategy. Working on the evening paper in Sheffield, twenty-five years ago, I would have expected to reach by phone the police officer in charge of any inquiry, heads of department of the city council and managers in local industry. Now I would be lucky to get beyond the press officer and the prepared brief, designed to anticipate my unhelpful questions.

Not surprisingly, journalists think this is a change for the worse. I was talking the other day to a provincial editor running an evening paper in a Midlands conurbation. He bemoaned the impossibility of getting straight answers from the local councils. No one was prepared to talk to his reporters directly. They conducted business on the basis of statements written by PR departments, usually in an anodyne fashion. The trend was leading to a lack of accountability, particularly in the public sector.

His irritation was understandable. Few things seem more obstructive to good reporting than the intervention of third parties who respond only after taking the time to create an elaborate brief designed to put a good shine on events. Imagine the frustration of police officers allowed to interrogate suspects only through an intermediary and after supplying notice of the line of questioning. Remember that, just like the police, journalists like to believe that they too operate to expose wrong-doing and uncover truth.

And what about the financial cost of all this gloss? We want services in return for our taxes, not an army of PRs to explain away council errors, hospital blunders and police incompetence. It's shareholders' business if private companies want to spend their money on making themselves look good. It's our business when it's the public sector.

But imagine, for a moment, that you are the council employee. You may not share the journalistic view that there is one set of facts that represents 'the truth'. You may believe that life is complicated and that there are several sides to a story. Does the reporter know what he or she is talking about? Why place your professional reputation in the hands of a young man or woman who has firm hold of the wrong end of the stick? Once you look at things from that perspective, it seems less controversial to seek help in providing explanations for conduct that could be misconstrued.

Naturally, as a journalist, I laughed at the thought of personal PR advice and took a pride in being able to explain myself to anyone. Then, once I was dealing with journalists rather than being one of them, I began to understand the paranoia of modern companies. It is remarkably difficult to persuade a journalist who thinks he has a story that his story is wrong. You soon discover that reporters are more inclined to believe an anonymous rumour than the most determined corporate rebuttal.

What advantage lay in risking personal or corporate reputation on the ability of another journalist to quote accurately? It became a relief to put those tricky questions into the hands of PR specialists, and let them take the flak for a cock-up. But even as I was passing the buck, I was depressed that media companies themselves have entered that cautious world when nothing is done without consideration of how it will look. We continue to rail at companies whose first thought in a disaster is corporate reputation, but deep down we know we have joined everyone else in asking not only 'How will this look?' but also 'How can we make it look better?'

So yes, we want the public services to spend our money on sick people and taking away the bins, but we might have some sympathy for their desire to explain themselves the best way they can.

Then we might have less sympathy for the rise of PR activity in the world of politics, where every event is now 'spun' to gain more positive coverage. The credit – or blame – for this is usually attached to Tony Blair's former aide Alastair Campbell, who used to be a political editor and knew very well how journalists worked. Under Campbell's leadership of communications strategy, the Labour government became highly efficient at putting out news to its advantage, often through background briefings of an unattributable nature.

Now, ministers have 'advisers' who are in effect PRs dedicated to promoting their interests. Many of these also come from journalism and know how their old business works. They know, for instance, that a journalist is more interested in information that is communicated on a private and personal basis.

'News is what someone, somewhere, doesn't want to see in print,' runs the old newspaper adage. 'All the rest is PR.' Sadly, too many journalists appear not to notice that many of the stories they write are derived from 'sources' and 'contacts' who very much want them to see them in print. They are under the illusion that they are breaking objective stories. In reality they are doing what the political PRs want them to, so that behind every tip, every leak, every helpful piece of advice, clarification and interpretation is an operation to boost one politician or party and do down another.

Happily, the tactic is now so well known that it is becoming counter-productive. I write this in the week that the *Today* presenter John Humphrys was rebuked by the BBC for making 'inappropriate and misguided' comments about Labour leaders during an after-dinner speech.

It was reported by other papers that a tape of the speech had been given to Tom Baldwin, a reporter on *The Times* who is friendly to Labour, by Tim Allan, a former assistant to Alastair Campbell, who now runs his own PR business. The Labour government has long been unhappy with the *Today* programme. This was seen as a means of getting back at the BBC for what the government saw as biased coverage during and after the invasion of Iraq. Public reaction to the story seemed largely to support Mr Humphrys, particularly when his speech was read in context and it became clear how it had come to reach *The Times*.

If the Labour propaganda machine starts to go wrong, it will not be the first to demonstrate that a PR operation can, ultimately, be as good only as the product it promotes. I wrote that British Airways ran a slick operation when I encountered it at the start of my Fleet Street career. As it happens, I was just about to stop working as a journalist when I came across the airline again.

A few days before the 2002 World Cup kicked off, a kind man from the airline rang and asked if I would like to fly to Japan to watch England play Argentina. We would go out for a few days, see the game and have some sightseeing in Tokyo. It was, in short, the kind of trip one might fantasize about. I was writing a media column at the time and realized that it could be a conflict of interest to take such a trip. How could I pontificate about other journalists if I were in BA's pocket? I would like to say I turned it down straightaway. In fact it was a couple of days before I rang back to say I couldn't go. I was pleased I had, for when I mentioned the offer to an American actor friend from a newspaper family, he was horrified that it had even crossed my mind to go. We may think the Americans can be pompous about ethics, but they can make the British press seem venal.

The airline itself has not had the best of fortune. Last summer it stranded thousands of passengers at Gatwick after staff walked out in support of a subcontractor catering company whose workers had gone on strike. I waited for the reassuringly pragmatic voice of the airline's Australian boss, Rod Eddington, on the *Today* programme. Astonishingly, no one from BA came on to speak, and the *Today* programme went to Michael O'Leary of Ryanair. You are losing customers, and you hand the airwaves over to your biggest rival?

How quickly reputations are damaged. BBC Radio 4 broadcast its popular comedy *I'm Sorry I Haven't a Clue* from Edinburgh the other day. The panel was invited to offer alternative definitions for words. Tim Brooke-Taylor was given 'mayfly'. He paused for a moment, before his answer brought a cheer from the audience: 'British Airways'. That airline is going to need a lot of good PR to win back its reputation.

Wolfowitz's Comb: Trouble in the Information Society

Nick Fraser

Those many millions who experienced Michael Moore's *Fahrenheit 9/11* will by now no doubt vaguely recall that the film was meant to prevent the re-election of George W. Bush. They may even acknowledge that the President was featured reading a children's book about a pet goat in the minutes immediately following the attacks. But they will surely recollect the sight of Paul Wolfowitz, Assistant Secretary of Defense, ex-professor and sometime diplomat, disciple of Leo Strauss and neocon, licking his comb before plastering his hair for a television appearance. Media comeuppances take many forms, but we may surmise that it was the comb, and not his shared authorship of a war, that caused the egghead Wolfowitz to choose the role of harbinger of peace by electing to serve as head of the World Bank.

I didn't enjoy *Fahrenheit 9/11* at all. In particular I resented Moore's pretensions. So much facetiousness ultimately exhausted any hostility I might have felt towards George Bush. But these are last year's observations in relation to a product with built-in obsolescence. More important, I was struck, again and again, by how many people (in the US, but in Britain, too, not to mention the reflexive anti-American Left in France and Germany) told me that it had proved revelatory. It was as if such people had no access to a serious newspaper, never went on the internet in search of serious news, and relied for their enlightenment on what comes between ads for haemorrhoids, or anti-ageing products, and is still called the *Nightly News*. 'We're kept in the dark,' a member of a well-heeled audience in upstate New York said to me. 'The media tell us lies.' More surprising, perhaps, was the view of a well-known correspondent of a cable network, for whom Moore's attacks, truthful or not, were a cause of shame. 'We should do these stories, and they shouldn't be left to an entertainer. But we've grown frightened of Fox News. If we criticize the powerful, we think they will take their revenge.' Still more despairing was Dan Rather, in an interview with the BBC shortly before he was forced to resign as anchor of the CBS bulletin, after documents thought to be fakes were used in a story about Bush's time in the Texas National Guard. 'It takes nothing to bring a country to war,' he said, adding that much news coverage of Iraq had resembled the paeans of praise trotted out by state-owned broadcasters in the Communist era.[20]

Indignation about the Iraq war was widespread, and justified. 'The reporting from the West looks as if it has been censored, even if this is not the case,' an Al Jazeera reporter told me last year.[21] 'How can we ask our governments to allow us to report freely when those who are our models in the West fail to do so?' More important still was the failure to address critically the Allied claim that the war was legitimate – until it was too late, and conflict had ended. As the ex-diplomat Carne Ross[22] has pointed out, the war was a catastrophe, above all of intelligence:

It is a story rich in paradox and contradictions from which it is hard to divine rational inferences or laws. The governments did not manufacture lies, but nor did they tell the truth, even when they thought they did. These half-truths bore no relation to what was actually going on in Iraq ... Things seem altogether less ordered and coherent than any logical analysis would have it. The key actors claim to have agency ... but in fact are swept away by forces they cannot grasp ...

Did the media – all but a handful of publications opposed to war for ideological reasons – report the way in which, as Ross says, 'facts ... became factoids'? No they didn't – as much as the participants, they, too, were swept away, either excited by the imminent prospect of war, or just as culpably acquiescent. Nor, with the exception of the *New York Times* and the BBC (which was of course forced to do so, because of the Hutton Report, which dealt with the deficiencies of its own journalism), did they examine why such a failure had taken place. This is a chilling prospect for those who believe that media should remain independent on our behalf, serving in the traditional role of a fourth estate.

More than the rest of humanity, media practitioners live in a space between utopia and self-loathing; but I am struck these days by the degree of hostility expressed towards journalism, whether on television or in print. It comes not just from governments (the Bush administration has been strident in its disapprobation; but then so, too, have the Blairites) but, more worrying, from the public. Most Americans no longer trust their newspapers as a source of news[23] – and one must guess that Brits ceased to do so some time ago. One acknowledged result of this is the lack of belief in politicians, which, according to numerous polls, is reaching danger levels. A more worrying effect is surely the loss of belief in information itself, and with it the pervasive decline in the notion, until recently widely held, that it is a good thing to be informed, and indeed that no citizen can call him- or herself such without some sort of sharing of public knowledge.

Disenchantment is no longer the exclusive province of the ideological Left, whose spokesmen have for many years told us about the absence of 'real' pluralism in a media economy dominated by business interests. It can be found, too, among conservatives whose websites sponsor the notion that traditional values are being destroyed by the diet of liberalism in entertainment as well as news. Even liberals, traditional defenders of openness and education, are beginning to despair of the idea of an educated public, turning away from what were called mass media in search of private networks of information. And yet this is occurring at a time when, judged purely by volume, more information is becoming daily available. Do we want to know about the weather in Adelaide, or the bibliography of an Indian savant? Google will tell us in an instant. No formal or effective censorship exists outside China, or in the remotest parts of the world. We can find out about much of what is going on via twenty-four-hour news. All this was unthinkable only a decade ago. But these innovations are, it would seem, despised when they are not taken for granted.

Media discontents are not exactly new. They form a dark thread through the predominantly utopian treatments of information in modern times. The first person to seriously deal with the question of how far the public could be educated was Walter Lippmann, later to become the most famous columnist of his generation.[24] Writing in the wake of Congress's failure to approve Woodrow Wilson's post-war vision of a peaceful, democratic world, Lippmann blamed the ignorance of the American public, attributing this to the poor quality of American newspapers. Lippmann called for a new style of civic journalism high-mindedly dedicated to the truth, in which educated writers would inform Americans about the world. He believed that this could be accomplished by the creation of what we would now call 'think tanks' – institutes for the promotion of objective, impartial truth at which journalists could graze in search of insight. Ever the liberal optimist, Lippmann believed that proprietors would be ready to print the truth, and that the public would read gratefully and attain enlightenment.

Something similar, with a British Scots slant, is to be observed in John Reith's vision for the BBC. Reith's love of monopoly was grounded in a Presbyterian vision of the singleness of truth. Notoriously, his BBC was stodgy, obsessed with the trivia of royal weddings and abhorrent when it came to anything outside the interests of the patriotic middle class. But Reith also created via the Imperial service the first world network of broadcasting. It remains striking how many radicals approved of what he was doing, enduring the horrors of working at the BBC because it seemed to them the only organization capable of telling the truth. Even George Orwell, who was censored during his time at the BBC, using the organization as a model for *Nineteen Eighty-Four*, retained a respect for its austere virtues.

Both traditions are present, albeit somewhat aged by the press of events, in contemporary media. Oddly, Lippmann's vision has worn worst. In particular, his notion that those who report on the world can somehow stand outside the fray has been widely discredited. The think tanks he prescribed exist in their dozens or hundreds, in every major capital. But in many cases their purposes have become unsubtly ideological. They exist these days not to make sense of the world, but to shape news coverage, supplying their own, highly palatable versions of reality. Either they collude with news networks or, when this is not possible, they aim to supplant them. The manufacture of argument has become a serious business, and in the United States its professionals are paid sums undreamed of by previous generations of lobbyists and apparatchiks. In consequence the idea that news can or should be impartial is fading. It is being replaced by polemicized information. Suddenly, 'attitude' has become more popular even as the public appears to be tiring of the spin of politicians. This is the real significance of Fox News and not the pervasive right-wing bias it displays daily, its own claims to accuracy notwithstanding.

But what does 'public broadcasting' mean these days? Is there such a thing as 'public media'? Much effort has been expended in definition, and it is interesting that the last, most complete statement on the subject since Reith's day came not from within the BBC, or any of its imitators, but from a commercial rival. John Birt worked in commercial television when he formulated his notorious theories in the 1970s, but his criticisms were addressed to the heart of what he saw even then as a failing system. He believed that media, and television in particular, had failed to find a way of comprehending society. Television was stuck in a shallow groove of narrative. What it showed consisted, by and large, of stereotypes constructed for the banal purpose of telling stories. Instead of distraction, television must adopt a 'mission to explain.' Birt believed that society had grown too complicated for the endless proliferation of trivia to be acceptable. A new class capable of informing the public must come into being. An assumption of his essays, never precisely formulated, is that the public not only must be informed, but will wish to be, given the opportunity.

Birt's views never found favour with journalists, who resented what seemed to them an attempt to replace reporting with high-minded pedagogy.[25] They were influential for a brief moment, and then they were jettisoned. Even in the BBC dominated by Birt, they were never implemented. Instead, public media in the age of many channels followed in the direction criticized by Birt – it became still less analytical and (if that were possible) more activated by the stimulus of celebrity. Instead of the austere satisfactions prescribed by Birt, the media gave us distraction. In time so much distraction became not a device for sustaining interest, but an end in itself.

Although it presents itself as ceaselessly new, and thus endlessly, serially renewable, television is an old medium by now, and its claims to innovate appear distinctly hollow. Many of the great discoveries of television – even the spontaneous style of reporting that comprises so-called 'rolling', or twenty-four-hour news – were made many years ago. What we know about the character or effects of television is also hardly new. The

Canadian media savant Marshall McLuhan isn't much read these days outside the Academy, and he is remembered principally for his insights into the non-rational, iconic nature of television, and the way in which, as he suggested, it was likely to replace a rational print way of perceiving with a new language of feeling. (Bizarrely, McLuhan appeared to welcome this change – and his own writings adapted catastrophically to take account of the imminent post-literate utopia he claimed to herald.) More seriously, McLuhan was also an early exponent of what media theorists now call 'convergence' – the notion that various media forms develop in tandem, so that we experience them not serially, one by one, but together and simultaneously. In the 1960s McLuhan saw print and television moving together, with the latter rapidly coming to dominate the former, thus ensuring a post-literate culture.[26]

Nowadays a similar struggle is taking place between television and the internet. The internet is said to be about to envelop television, replacing the old broadcast medium. This has led to the widely canvassed hope that print, which is supplied by the internet in near-infinite quantities, isn't doomed to be absorbed after all. I wonder whether this is a correct analysis. Those eager to write off the medium of television might examine how the internet is filling up with pictures, not all of them still. They might think how both newspapers and TV shows have come to resemble internet sites. Soon we'll be viewing not just TV shows, but movies through the internet. In this context the survival of print culture in its present form seems remote indeed.

Of course the new global market in information has brought gains, indeed some enormous ones; but the losses, too, are substantial. Few now believe that the primary purpose of radio and television is conveying information. In places like the BBC, the notion that it could be otherwise is still to be found, but the tradition is under threat. It may be worth setting out, in the form of a homage to McLuhan, the new market media orthodoxy of what a political scientist has called the World Order of Egoism:[27]

1. All media exists for a market in which we are all consumers.

2. The notion that media should supply either alternative insight or inconvenient facts is absurd.

3. There are no dissidents in the media.

4. Media is our democracy.

5. Media makes ordinary people into celebrities – and celebrities into ordinary people.

6. Analysis is bad. Emotion is good.

7. Markets dominate our times. Therefore the reality of news is merely what the market gives.

8. Irony is intermittently allowed – but in modest doses.

9. Never be serious.

10. It is futile to complain about all this.

How can truthful information survive in a world where such maxims rule? The 'manufacture of consent' to which Noam Chomsky and others have drawn our attention appears to be a fiction born of frustration.[28] In reality, the system appears too porous, and no purposeful attempt to deceive exists. It is commonplace to speak of a 'New Class' of media operatives as if these had somehow displaced old centres of power and influence, but the real story may well be a different one. Short-term, preferring simplicity to complexity, the media has proved adept at destroying reputations. The growth of so many organizations designed to shape, minimize or merely describe the effects of media has further strengthened the notion that whatever is reported comes to us packaged and should not be believed.

In the 1960s criticism of the way in which the world was run paralleled the demand for 'free media'. It was thought that broadcasting and television might be turned into a tool for social reform. But theorists of social transformation appear to have given up on broadcasting. Television and radio are too diffuse to be easily changed. Who can know any more how much information is necessary? Who can spend the time sorting out what really matters from so much truthlessness? We can all say that by now we know too much about how the media conducts their business. The notion that everything defined as news is arranged for the benefit of television is considered to be self-evident. So is the assumption that governments are bound to hate broadcasters and lie to them. For those who watch television casually, even for the declining number who read newspapers, these are only faintly important things. They matter most to those who are inside the media – appearances to the contrary not a vast constituency or even a specially influential one. And the growing contempt or indifference with which most media are regarded is the truest symptom of the growing malaise of democracy in our time.

'I watch TV news for its disconnections,' the essayist and novelist Joan Didion explains.[29] 'The elisions interest me.' In 1944, cleaning out his kitchen cupboard as the V-bombs flew over London, George Orwell came across an eight-year-old copy of the *Daily Mail*. He wasn't surprised to find so many pieces about seaside murders and peers' secret weddings and 'an idealized photograph of the man the Conservative Party were to sack like a butler a year later'.[30] Orwell noticed the topics that were not covered – anything to do with the world going to hell in places like Abyssinia or nearby Spain – and he attributed these failings, characteristically, to the greed of newspaper proprietors combined with readers' need for a 'sunshine mentality'. Freedom of expression prizes are given to those working in less fortunate parts of the world, and the assumption, fortified by the earnest, somewhat patronizing speeches and the chardonnay, is that no sparrow can fall without the attention of rolling news. Nonetheless, Orwell's observations are not so far off the mark. Who recalls the notorious 'CNN effect' – the worries expressed by politicians (and even newscasters) about the way in which the coverage of atrocities in the Balkans or Rwanda might lead to misguided humanitarian policies? Global news reporting is patchy and highly selective, one atrocity blocking out another. Even terrorism, so adroitly formulated for the benefit of rolling news, loses its impact rapidly.

But these are desperate thoughts, formulated only to be rejected. We can tell already what will be the rough shape of the coming times. There will be outrages in relation to which fresh measures of protection will be demanded by anxious publics. The rule of half-law will be further installed. Vast goings-on in the moneysphere will torment the delicate. And the destabilization of our environment will be literally apparent, not just as a scientific hypothesis. It is inconceivable that we or our children will not know the meaning of fear. For all such eventualities (and they are mild beside what the hard core doomsters are telling us) non-dysfunctional media are indispensable. We cannot survive with tainted or second-rate information.

I'm writing this during an evening after people whose disposition and motivation I can only guess at have placed bombs throughout central London, killing and maiming many. How can we assure the existence of media both truthful and capable of speaking globally, and not nationally? It should be as easy as flashing stock market signals around the world, but it isn't. Maybe someone, somewhere in the world, is busy comprehensively reformulating the purposes of public media, giving it another century's life. I hope so. In the meantime, we must learn to take our truth wherever it exists. One small and hopeful sign is the proliferation of news media in the Arab world, and now in India. One lesson of this is that no easy barriers can be constructed between the old, so-called 'Western' forms of expression, and the new ones, or indeed between private and public ones. Does it matter that Al Jazeera is funded as Voltaire was by Frederick the Great and that it can justly be called a plaything of the intermittently benign, half-constitutional monarch known as the Emir of Qatar? No, it probably doesn't matter much. Similarly there's no point in deploring the internet blurring of amateur, often unreliable blogging and what remains of professional journalism. We need to work from the assumption that no media is true all of the time, but that the postmodernists do us all wrong when they suggest that we are doomed always to live within the whale of fictions and lies. Why condemn the information chaos that surrounds us? What we have to do is construct maps each day, giving ourselves the means of navigation. And this is the same as saying that truth in the media, and anywhere else, requires constant reinvention; and that no one will do the work for us citizens. No other way of living in the world is left to us.

Writing from Israel

Janine di Giovanni

If we are talking logistics, then technically Israel should be one of the easiest countries in the world to report. The phones work, meaning you don't have to lug around a complicated satellite phone. There are fast computer lines, hot water, plentiful food, paved roads. I suppose it could happen, but you don't think about getting kidnapped and then beheaded on Al Jazeera in an orange jumpsuit like you do if you work in Iraq. You don't have to drive through the bush for hours like in Africa; or sleep outside in a tent with a rebel army. Even Gaza has a great Moroccan-style hotel now, where you can get beer and gaze out at the sea.

People talk to you, willingly and openly. Sometimes too much. One moment you find yourself at the tragic funeral of a teenaged Israeli soldier shot dead in Gaza by a crazed Palestinian gunner, the next you are sitting in an abandoned safe house somewhere not far from the Mediterranean with a teenage would-be suicide bomber for Hamas. You don't get that wall of silence you get in other countries, where people are too afraid, too traumatized, or too jaded to talk to reporters.

There are no long distances to cover in Israel, like driving from Baghdad to Basra; or Sarajevo to Srebrenica, or walking over the mountains to get inside Chechnya with snow up to your thighs. You simply fly to Tel Aviv, catch a taxi and *voilà* – you are in theatre. Sometimes, if you want to be truly lazy, you can drive to Gaza in the early morning, when the pure, hot light is just hitting the sky, and drive back at dusk so that you

can sleep in a good bed at the American Colony hotel in East
Jerusalem.

You can get to Ramallah easily if the checkpoints don't
delay you for three hours. You can drive to Bethlehem or Jenin,
even to the apple orchards of the Golan, in a few hours. 'It's a
pocket-size war,' a friend of mine said.

You rarely need an interpreter. Nearly everyone speaks
English. You don't have to make appointments in advance, or
get dozens of slips of paper signed, like in Russia. The weather is good. It's not like reporting the Bosnian war in sub-zero
degrees, being so cold your jeans stick, frozen, to chairs. Or
Chechnya, where the unbearable cold permeates everything.
Or the Ivory Coast, where you get malaria, yellow fever,
encephalitis. Or Sierra Leone, where you might get ambushed
and have your hands chopped off by rebels. Or East Timor,
where I slept each night on a doorframe in an abandoned con-
vent. Or Somalia, where you need $5,000 to hire your own pri-
vate militia to protect you. Or a million other places where the
mud, dirt, disease, bullets and mortars make reporting a near
impossible task.

No, in theory, Israel should be an easy one, as long as you are
lucky and don't get shot "accidentally" by an Israeli soldier or
get beaten up at a demonstration. Why, then, do I go into a
state of panic every time my plane arrives at Ben Gurion airport? From the first moment that I tell the passport control: 'No
stamp, please' (because an Israeli stamp in a passport makes it
difficult to get into certain other Arab countries), to the pleas-
ant visit and cup of coffee with the staff at the Ministry of
Information who have been giving me press accreditation for
nearly seventeen years? People know me. I have lots of contacts. I feel comfortable and know my way around. 'You're one
of the old timers,' one of the Ministry of Information adminis-
trators told me on my last trip there. 'You and I have grown old
together.'

It's a country I love very much, but the fact is, Israel is the most difficult place I know to work. It's a country where you must labour over every word you write, because every word can be misconstrued. The truth is never easy. Transparency, that strange buzzword of the new millennium, does not really exist. Sometimes I get through a day with several notebooks packed with information, with quotes and with interviews – but I am sure that every person I spoke to lied to me, exaggerated, or concealed the truth.

It's impossible to make anyone happy writing about Israel. Every time I write, my editor gets bagloads of complaints. Mostly they're from right-wing Jewish groups calling me anti-Semitic (a strange complaint as I was married to a Jew for nearly a decade, and until I was about ten years old, growing up in a Jewish community, thought I was a Jew), but sometimes they're from Palestinians who have, weirdly, called me pro-Israeli.

After the controversial Israeli Army 'clean-up' operation in the Jenin refugee camp in April 2002, it got harder and harder. I once Googled my name to find an obscure article I wrote about Africa: instead, hundreds and hundreds of odd links and blogs and forums came up with my name and next to it: JENIN. Even *Private Eye* wrote a funny little cartoon: 'REPORTERS FROM THE BIBLE BANNED FROM REPORTING IN ISRAEL. BY JENIN DI GIOVANNI.' And recently, I sat drinking coffee with a New York editor and he said, 'Oh, yes. You were one of those British reporters who wrote controversial things about Jenin, right?' (In fact he was wrong on two counts. One, I am not British and two, I only wrote what I saw. Is that controversial?) He did not know me for my much larger work in Bosnia; my work in Africa; or even that myself and two other reporters were the only journalists to witness the fall of Grozny in 2000. No, those things which are monumental to my career did not come to light. Instead, he remembered me for Jenin.

What happened in Jenin that so many reporters are still arguing over what happened? So that hundreds of hours of television debate between right-wingers and left-wingers prevailed? So that the outspoken wife of a one-time newspaper proprietor now in trouble with the law called us 'brownshirts'? Inquiries, reports, reams of paper were written about the aftermath. Okay, you can judge. Here are the bare facts on Jenin, no emotion added.

Between 3 April and 18 April 2002, an Israeli military operation, in response to a wave of Palestinian suicide bombings which left eighty-seven Israeli citizens dead and 570 others wounded, was launched. Jenin had long been regarded as a breeding ground for terrorists, and known as the 'city of bombers', but it was also the home of many innocent civilians.

Nevertheless, Israeli soldiers were told: 'Shoot every window, spray every house.' According to reports, doctors in hospitals were told to lower their blinds so that there would be no witnesses. During the 'operation' the camp was sealed off not only to the press, but to medical and humanitarian workers and foreigners. There were eight days of aerial bombardment from Cobra and Apache helicopters. There was regular shelling by tanks of civilian structures. There were around 1,000 well-armed and well-trained Israeli soldiers and around 200 (that's a generous figure) Palestinian fighters.

As the Israelis began pounding the place, the occupants were consistently denied food, water and medical care; nor were the dead removed. Families were used as human shields.

The aftermath: a shadowy counting of the dead, of who was a combatant and who was a Palestinian. You know what? I am not going to give the final numbers here because to me, it is irrelevant. It also plays into the hands of those bean-counters who judge war and misery by how many people died, not by how they died, or why they died. So no numbers. Look it up on the internet, if you want.

Endgame: the Palestinians deemed Jenin a massacre; Israelis deemed it an effective military operation. There were conspiracy theories afterwards, strange talk of donkeys being blown up by the Palestinians, and their blood being represented as human blood (this came from the New York editor; to be honest, I did not know what he was talking about and was too embarrassed to ask).

Now, the emotion. After the onslaught finished, I entered Jenin with four colleagues: one American Jew born in Israel; one South African-born; two Brits, walking through an olive grove under the eyes of a tank. All of us had extensive experience reporting war. One had been shot in an African war; another had lived and worked in Israel for years, and his family had fought in the Israeli war of independence. He himself served as a soldier in the war in 1973. Another was a well-respected writer who had been covering stories around the world for years. Then there was me, who had worked in war zones for fifteen years. The final reporter was the youngest but wore the badge of honour for having been expelled from Zimbabwe by Robert Mugabe. In short, none of us was naïve.

But all of us were silent as we saw the destruction, the levelling of the camp. All of us walked quietly through the debris, hearing the crying of children, seeing the man in the wheelchair trying to move over the rubble. All of us were – yes, this is the only word I can use – stunned.

And we wrote what we saw. Once I sat next to the great war correspondent Martha Gellhorn at a seminar at the Freedom Forum in London and listened to her say this: 'I think the answer is for everybody to write as well as they know how, therefore speak as well as they know how, and as truthfully as they know how. That's our job, and we must continue to do it, because any form of keeping the record is better than letting things sink into silence.'

We did not want to let Jenin sink into silence. And so we

wrote. And for a few weeks after, we got crucified. Barbara Amiel, the staunchly Zionist wife of the disgraced Conrad Black, was given vast space to air her often racist views and to attack myself and Sam Kiley, one of the reporters who was with me in Jenin. Sam shouted about suing her. I thought it best to ignore it. Bullies never win. (Witness the hot water she and her husband are now in: proof there is karma in the world.)

But perhaps the strangest experience came nearly two years later. Flash forward, the autumn of 2003. I have just returned from Israel, where I wrote a highly critical piece for *Vanity Fair* about Arafat's corrupt regime. It is not exactly flattering for him and his cronies. I am also hugely pregnant, with something the doctors call 'a high-risk pregnancy' and have had to be flown out at the advice of Israeli doctors, for emergency medical treatment. I am on complete bed rest when the telephone rings, and a Canadian reporter whom I shall call X politely asks if he can come to interview me about my work. He identifies himself as working for the CBC (Canadian Broadcasting Company). I know several reporters at the CBC very well, and think they do great work. I am friendly with him.

I also have a book, *Madness Visible*, about the Balkans, coming out in a few months' time, so the request is not so strange. I agree to see him. He says he will bring a TV crew and we arrange for him to come to my home, as I cannot move anywhere else. Before X hangs up, I ask him if he knows one of the CBC's most famous correspondents, who is a good friend of mine. He does not. In fact, he sounds like he has never heard of her. Strange, as Annamaria Tremonti is something of a celebrity in Canadian journalism. Warning bells should have gone off, but they did not.

Now, you might say: why didn't Janine di Giovanni do her homework and Google this man? Or do some check-up calls? Why on earth did a hugely pregnant woman let this stranger into her home? The fact is, I did not Google X. Now, I was being naïve. I trusted him. Journalists often help each other, and it never occurred to me that he was not a straight journalist, that he had an agenda from day one, that he was a fraud or a liar with a trick or two up his sleeve. It had simply never happened to me before.

But when X arrived, I began to get more warning bells. He had a TV crew with him, and they bustled around setting up lights and cameras, and placing me and my bulky belly on a sofa with cushions behind me. X was shifty and nervous, even as I brought out cups of tea and tried to make light chatter. He would not look in my eyes.

Then the lights were on, my lipstick applied, and he started his attack. I remembered feeling sleepy – it was my nap time – but I tried to be alert. He started in immediately, but not asking questions about my book or about the Balkans. It was about Jenin. He spoke in a high, Jerry Springer-type sensational voice. He waved a newspaper about – an article I had written. He wanted an apology, he said, for something I had written: how horrified I had been at my first sighting of Jenin. I had written that the initial horror was worse than being in Bosnia or Chechnya. I believed and still believe that. When I walked into Jenin, I was made silent by what I saw.

He wanted an apology, as it turned out so few Palestinians were actually killed. He wanted me to say the British press were anti-Semitic. He wanted me to say we got it wrong sometimes. We often do, but in that case, I did not think I did. I sat up as straight as my belly would let me and said, 'I stand by every word I wrote.' Meanwhile, I was feeling very odd: the seeds were beginning to be sown about why this weird guy was in my home.

Then X went in for the kill. The true Jerry Springer moment. He leaned forward. 'Do you see that man over there?' he said, pointing to a young man fumbling with lights. 'In fact, he is not a cameraman! He is not a journalist! He is an Israeli soldier!

And he was in Jenin! And he wants to talk to you!'

For a second, I was just confused. Then I was horrified. 'You're not a journalist?' I asked the soldier. He shook his head. 'You're a soldier?' He just stood there, looking embarrassed. Then I looked at X. 'Are you Israeli? Are you Jewish?'

He nodded violently. I was utterly confused: these people were not here in the name of journalism? But in the name of religion? I suddenly felt frightened. Maybe they were loonies sent by Mossad. Other thoughts went through my mind, but the strongest instinct was to get them all out of my home as quickly as possible, to protect myself and my baby.

In ordinary times, I would have loved to have spoken to this young soldier. He seemed embarrassed by X's theatrics, and I am sure he could have given me interesting information. I would have liked to have heard his stories. About how he might have been frightened; how he lost soldier friends whom he loved; or even how difficult it is to live in Israel, constantly worried about when a suicide bomber could strike. He was the sort of person I interviewed a lot when I was in Israel. I would have wanted to know his opinions. Young soldiers, especially, because they are fighting a difficult and emotional war.

Then it dawned on me. The whole interview was a set-up, like one of those trailer trash American talk shows where the mistress and the wife meet up for the first time on TV, and the husband is sitting there happily, then beat each other over the heads with their handbags. X never had any intention of talking to me about my book. He wanted to register my shock on television. He wanted me to rush over and hit the Israeli soldier with my handbag, or perhaps shove him out the door with my belly! He had lied to me, impersonating a journalist. I suddenly realized he was not a journalist – not the kind I work with, anyway.

The room went dead and I forgot about the camera. I just felt frightened. Who were these people? Why were they in my home? And how could I get them out? The baby began kicking violently.

'Out, all of you, now,' I said, rising awkwardly from the sofa. I asked them to turn off the camera, but not before X said excitedly to another cameraman: 'Did you get that? Did you get that?'

'You lied to me,' I said to X as he packed his gear. 'You lied to get into my home. You lied to see me.' He did not say a word. I was shaking as I let him out, shaking as I double-locked the door, shaking as I lay on my bed, shaking as I called the other journalists X said he had interviewed.

They were shaken up, too, but more resolute. He had done the same thing to them. Called, said he wanted to talk about something else, then began the Jenin routine, waving the poor soldier in front of their faces like a red flag.

'Yeah, he was a plant, probably from the Israeli Embassy,' said one.

'No, he's just a wanker who wanted to set us up,' said another.

'Forget it, what can you do?' said a third.

'I'm going to call his editor,' I said, and began dialling Canada. But although the people I contacted had heard of X – he was based in Israel, it turned out, and not in Toronto as he had told me initially – no one at the CBC had commissioned his film.

'He has nothing to do with us,' said one editor. 'He should not have used our name to get in your door. I suggest you forget it.'

Had I not have been pregnant and due to give birth, I would have pursued it. But I did not. Until the following year when X released his film *Jenin: Massacring the Truth*, and there I am white-faced, hormonal and shocked at the moment of truth: This man is not a cameraman! He's a soldier!

The interview had been butchered and manipulated. X had

edited out my words, edited out my balance and precision, edited my comments about how difficult it was for ordinary
Israelis, but left in the section where I ask the Israeli soldier
(and the rest of the crew) to leave my home. He even edited out
my pregnancy. One nasty Israeli columnist commented how I
lounged on pillows like a princess. You try having a high-risk
pregnancy; having to stay in bed for months on end, gaining
fifty pounds, and not leaning back on pillows, I wanted to
scream at her. You try having swollen ankles and weeks before
giving birth have a fake camera crew come into your home and
lie to you!

Of course, it was picked up by the Israeli press, who said I
could not bear to sit in the same room as an Israeli soldier.
They misreported that I had asked him: 'Are you Jewish?' (In
fact, I had asked if he was Israeli, trying to work out who the
hell he was and why he was sitting in my living room in
Notting Hill.) One called me malicious.

I felt violated after that, and angry. But who could I write to
and how could I complain? I had let X into my home. Before
the interview began, I had trusted him and signed his release
form. I had agreed to talk to him about my work. And Jenin
was indeed part of my work.

After the film came out, the Google hits on my name
jumped by several hundred. It was the usual stuff, but one
comment really hurt.

'My God, does this stuff still bother you? Haven't you ever
toughened up?' asked my Israeli-American friend who had
walked into Jenin with me, and who himself had been a soldier.
'Don't let it bother you, kid.'

It bothered me for a while. I would have liked to have
defended myself, I would have liked X to have made a fair film.
But there was a small thing that made me feel better. One day,
nestled among the blogs and the nasty comments about Jenin
was a Palestinian website which had picked up some of my

stories. They were complaining about how right wing and pro-Israel I was! I read it over several times, and it made me as angry as X had.

Finally I ended up laughing and laughing. The truth is, you just can't win.

The Truth and the Whole Truth?

Anne Gregory

Context

In many ways I think that ethics in public relations is more complex and difficult than ethics in journalism. The plea of the journalist is that he or she seeks out and speaks the truth in the public interest. Of course, we all know it isn't as simple as that. There are issues to do with proprietorial interference, editorial bias and pressure, personal prejudice, ambition and source integrity. Despite all this, a journalist would say that ultimately the public interest is where his or her duty lies.

Ironically, most public relations professionals would say exactly the same, but, as with journalists, it isn't as simple as that. They work for organizations and are employed to defend and promote those organizations over an extended period of time. Unlike the journalist who seeks 'the truth' about a particular story, public relations professionals are paid to tell the ongoing organizational story. Both the story and the context in which it is told are forever changing and developing. The sheer dynamism of the situation makes this difficult enough: what was perfectly true and defensible at one time may not be a month hence.

Over the past few years I have noticed a deal of self-analysis by the public relations profession. It is concerned about its image and about what is perceived as a widespread assumption that most practitioners are regarded at best as spin doctors and at worst as out and out liars.

My observation is that the big 'sleepless night' ethical decisions that practitioners have to make are few. However, the simple and inescapable fact is that ethical decision-making is not something to be kept in a box and brought out for the big occasion. For me it is a total approach to the whole business of communication; from the sort of organization you work for, to the tasks you undertake, to the way you undertake those tasks, to the outcome you are looking for.

In contributing to organizational objectives, public relations seeks to build and maintain relationships of trust that are mutually beneficial. Trust implies reliability, integrity and good faith; organizations who want to be trusted are best served by practitioners who themselves are trustworthy.

Organizations continue to exist because the public gives them a 'licence to operate'. Part of the job of public relations practitioners is to stress the requirement for public approval to their organizational masters and this should act as a regulator of organizational conduct. Indeed public relations should not only help to regulate bad conduct, but it should actively promote good conduct in the form of ethical practice and social responsibility.

Let's explore in greater detail the difference between public relations and journalism which I alluded to earlier. A story or a feature normally has fleeting impact. It is here today and forgotten in a few days. A complaint of the public relations profession against journalists is that they write in that mind-set too. Get the story, write it, then move on to the next one. The refrain is that journalists ring up often at short notice, demand information which may not be readily obtained, write the story anyway, whether it is accurate or not, and then leave the organization to take the consequences. Yes, there may be a Press Complaints Commission from which to seek redress, but by then the damage has been done and the journalist has moved on.

Public relations work on the other hand is for the long term. It takes years of painstaking and thoughtful work to build relationships of trust and a good reputation between an organization and its stakeholders. All that can be destroyed overnight by a journalist with an agenda. I am not an apologist for McDonald's, but it does strike me that anyone who eats vast quantities of the same food for a month will end up with problems and that Morgan Spurlock had a particular agenda when making his documentary *Super Size Me*.

Of course, organizations and individuals are quite capable of destroying their own reputations because they don't understand the power of communication. A few words out of turn by Matt Barrett, the Chief Executive of Barclays Bank, in October 2003 (see http://newswww.bbc.net.uk/1/hi/business/3199822.stm), who said he would not recommend the company's credit card to his children, did substantial damage to the company.

Communication for organizations is extremely complex because organizational life is complex. Organizations are multi-layered, they change constantly, the environment in which they operate changes, the people change and the stakeholders to whom they are accountable change too. The way they are perceived depends on who you talk to because there are genuinely different perceptions.

Trying to reconcile all this is a difficult and complex task for the public relations professional. Representing the 'true picture' is not easy even when the desire is there. The journalist's quest is to reduce complexity to simple, sound-bite nuggets because space and time are limited. That is their reality, but it does not do justice to the sophistication of modern organizational life. In a world where organizations are increasingly defined by what people say about them, public relations is coming under renewed scrutiny, not because it is bad at what it does, but, ironically, because it is so successful. Public relations people wield real power. They are especially powerful and influential with a resource-starved and increasingly dependent media. With power and influence comes the moral obligation to act justly and with integrity. So what exactly does that mean? Who sets the benchmark and how?

In my experience there is a great deal of confusion about morals, ethics and where and how ethical decisions are made. This chapter seeks to clarify some of these issues in order to help practitioners to be more certain about what is a very complex and messy area and to help them articulate and justify their decision-making in an increasingly accountable world.

Morals, ethics and ethical traditions

The words morals and ethics are often used interchangeably and indeed they are linked. Simply put, morals are personal values, beliefs and principles that guide behaviour. Clearly moral codes are different from person to person. Some people are guided by religious faith and may take a stance on particular issues such as abortion or euthanasia, and their morals may be different from someone without that belief. Ethics is the formal study and codification of moral principles into systematic frameworks so that decisions about what is right and wrong can be made in a reasoned and structured way.

In my view, given the controversy that surrounds the public relations industry, it is important that practitioners learn about ethical frameworks for decision-making so that situations can be evaluated systematically and consistent judgements made – hence consistent behaviour is possible. This is vital in building relationships. Being able to explain why a decision has been reached, and the thought process that has been gone through, makes that decision transparent and understandable even if it isn't agreed with.

The most basic question ethical theorists ask is 'Is it possible to know right from wrong?' Cognitivists believe that there are actual and objective moral truths. Non-cognitivists say that morality is purely subjective and is linked very much to the specific cultural contexts of individuals: there are no moral absolutes, only beliefs, attitudes and opinions.

In the pluralistic world that Western public relations practitioners inhabit, this latter school of thought seems to be most prevalent. So how do we proceed? The public relations literature is helpful here. Academics such as Pearson[31] and Heath[32] argue that truths emerge from a process of dialogue, negotiation and debate where parties to the discussion eventually agree on what the best end result is. They assert that the *process* by which the debate is conducted determines whether it is ethical or not. They stress the rules of ethical dialogue which should be followed to maintain integrity and validity. This requires participants to test and probe ideas, to have equal freedom to initiate and continue the dialogue and to set the agenda. To do this they should be free from manipulation and have equal power.

To many practitioners this is too idealistic and does not take into account the realities of power-imbalance or the requirements to make decisions quickly. However, the principle is quite clear and sound in my view. Giving people a voice and valuing their perspective accords them respect and is in itself a moral act. Pragmatically it also makes for better decision-making.

There are numerous instances where organizations have used public relations to close down legitimate, opposing voices and where the public's interest has not been served as a result. For example, for years the tobacco industry denied any link between smoking and cancer and used public relations and marketing to dispute any suspicion that there was a connection. Even today, they promote smoking in developing nations through channels that are forbidden in the developed world and do not display the same prominent health warnings. Of course, these activities are perfectly legal, but are they ethical?

Most people live their lives on the basis of some objective standards of right and wrong. For example Josephson has identified ten universal principles that can form the basis of ethical decision-making and are essentially independent of culture.[33] These are: honesty, integrity, promise-keeping, fidelity, fairness, caring for others, respect for others, responsible citizenship, pursuit of excellence and accountability. Such principles form the basis of Duty ethics. Duty ethicists say that you have a duty to act in a way that supports these moral principles.

Immanuel Kant was the principal proponent of Duty ethics and his main contribution to the debate was to introduce the notion of the 'categorical imperative'. This encouraged people to ask themselves if their action was suitable for translation into a universal principle which anyone who faced a similar situation could follow – a useful thought for public relations practitioners. One of the flaws in this approach is that Duty ethicists are encouraged to 'do the right thing' irrespective of the consequences. Thus withholding the truth is frowned on because it is in principle wrong.

On the face of it this seems sound. However, there may be times in public relations when withholding the whole truth may be a good course of action. For example, suppose there was a terrorist attack on a major British city, akin to the 7 July 2005 attacks on London. Would it be ethical to withhold the whole story and to talk about 'an incident' to prevent panic and to allow time for the emergency services to get to the dead and injured and to clarify the facts and then to release the full story? It could be cogently argued that this 'deceit' is ethical because it is very clearly in the public interest and certainly in the interests of those who were injured. It goes without saying that withholding the whole truth in this case is not the same as lying to mislead permanently or to gain personal or organizational advantage to the detriment of society at large. A variation on this theme is to be so selective about the elements of a story that people draw reasonable conclusions which are in fact incorrect, even if technically no lie has been spoken. This kind of behaviour along with a relentless effort to over-emphasize the positive is the complaint about much political communication.

It is apparent, therefore, that the consequences of decisions have to be taken into account. Indeed Consequentialist ethicists would say that it is the consequences of actions that are the most important, but there are questions over ends justifying means here. It is one thing to try to promote your organization's interests, but should that be done by any means?

Finally, most people would agree that the motivation of practitioners is important too, not just the actions *per se* or the consequences of those actions. Virtue ethicists claim character is vitally important. Was the practitioner's motivation honest? Did he or she try to be fair? With the best will in the world sometimes public relations practitioners get it wrong, but if they are seen to have had the right motives, they can be forgiven.

To make sound ethical decisions it is important to draw together all three of these elements – principles, consequences and motivation. However, my observation in practice is that pubic relations practitioners do not think about things in such a systematic way or know about the helpful decision-making tools that can be used. They end up making intuitive judgements based on the immediate circumstances, past experience and their own moral baseline.

Ethical decision-making

In my view there are three aspects to ethical decision-making that will lead towards sound results and peaceful nights.

The individual

Firstly, ethical reasoning begins with the individual. Individuals have to establish their own moral code. This is particularly important for public relations practitioners. If they are meant to be the ethical guardians of organizations then they need to have thought through their own position. A value system that provides guiding principles is essential, as is a belief that organizational representatives have certain obligations and duties, and should have a respect for others. This moral code may be religious, philosophical or self-constructed, but it needs to be reasoned, articulated and known by clients and employers. It will determine the kinds of company that the practitioner works for and the boundaries of the advocacy work that they undertake.

An example might help clarify some of the dilemmas here. Many people would believe that working for pharmaceutical companies is laudable. They are legitimate business ventures trying to find cures for diseases. However, there are issues in working for such companies. They are profit-driven and the choice of which drugs they develop is determined to a greater or lesser extent by the size of the market and the profits that can be made. Drugs to cure diseases prevalent in poorer countries, often affecting whole populations, are not developed because they cannot be sold at a profit. Other drugs like the proprietary Aids drugs were priced at such a level that they were out of reach of millions of the most needy and destitute. Drugs companies usually undertake animal experiments. They have massive marketing and public relations budgets with which they fund conferences, hospitality, merchandise and training for medical personnel, some of whom are responsible for local and national drugs budgets and purchasing policies.

With all these issues there are large ethical questions.

Some people would feel they cannot work for such organizations, some feel they can because what the companies contribute to human welfare outweighs the negatives.

Having taken the decision to work for such an organization all the issues indicated above will have to be dealt with as various stakeholders challenge the organization to justify its work. Some practitioners will find themselves as the voice of protest within their organization, bringing stakeholder concerns to the decision-making table. Ultimately they will have to consider resigning (and several do) if they cannot reconcile their own moral code with how they believe the organization should behave.

To deal with this conflict, some practitioners say there is a difference between personal and organizational ethics. Organizations acting within the law are legal entities, maybe heavily regulated, and therefore entitled to be defended and promoted. So, for example, despite a practitioner having a personal aversion to animal experimentation, they defend the organization undertaking these activities because it is a legal requirement. However, what the law allows and what stakeholders will accept do not always match and one of the jobs of the public relations professional is to point out these tensions and signal when corporate values are not commensurate with maintaining the 'licence to operate'. In order to do that, a base-line founded on legality alone is not enough.

External guides

Secondly, external guides are useful in ethical decision-making; they help validate and externalize it. The law is a good starting point, but usually only a starting point. For example, corporate social responsibility (CSR) programmes usually go beyond legal requirements. The ethical argument is not 'What is the minimum we can get away with?' but 'What should we rightly contribute?' Industry and professional codes of practice are also good external sources.

Decision-making models

Thirdly, there are some ethical decision-making models that can help the practitioner go through a logical process of thought. For example, Parsons provides five ethical pillars which can be turned into questions to help identify the ethical issues.

- Veracity – tell the truth: is there harm involved?
- Non-malfeasance – do no harm: is there a missed opportunity to do something good?
- Beneficence – do good: could anyone be misled?
- Confidentiality – respect privacy: will anyone's privacy be invaded?
- Fairness – be fair and socially responsible: is it unfair to anyone?34

I would add another: does it feel right or wrong?

One of the more well-known ethical decision-making models is the Potter Box, devised by Ralph Potter of the Harvard Divinity School.35

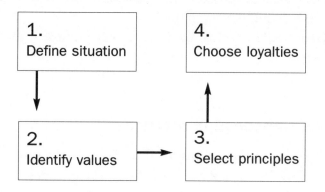

Step 1: define situation. Get all the facts. What led to the situation? Who is involved? Are there different views? What is the context?

Step 2: identify values. What personal or universal values apply, e.g. fairness, honesty? Are there company values?

Step 3: select principles. Choose your decision-making principles, e.g. company code of conduct, the law, professional body codes.

Step 4: choose loyalties. Prioritize all stakeholders who demand your loyalties.

This is a difficult process which forces practitioners to consider conflicting values and loyalties, but it brings the issues to the fore and ensures decision-making is rigorous. It may well be that two public relations practitioners faced with the same problem may come to different conclusions, but at least there is a clear and demonstrable rationale for their conclusions which will be defendable.

Sims also has a good model for public relations practitioners based on seven steps.[36]

- Recognize and clarify the dilemma.
- Get all the possible facts, list all your options.
- Test each option by asking is it legal, right, beneficial?
- Make your decision.
- Double-check the decision by asking 'How would I feel if my family found out about this?'
- How would I feel if my decision was printed in the local newspaper?
- Take action.

Ethics embedded in practice

As I said at the beginning of this chapter, ethics is a total approach to the job, not just something to be considered for the big issue. Public relations is a difficult and complex business. Practitioners need to be *technically* competent and up to date to do the job – and this in itself is an ethical responsibility. Clients and employers are not served professionally by those who are not qualified to do the job. They also need to have what I call *practice* integrity, which is ensuring the way they 'do' public relations is ethical, i.e. being honest, keeping promises and arriving at sound judgements. They must be concerned about *outcome legitimacy* – that is, ensuring the result of their work maintains and enhances relationships and builds trust for the organization and serves the public's interest. These three elements have profound ethical dimensions and are material to every project that the practitioner undertakes.

Ethical thinking is part of the very fabric of public relations planning and action, yet very few practitioners have any training in ethics and very few appear to be systematic when considering their work. This chapter has attempted to at least stimulate thinking on these issues and, at best, prompted a desire to know more and to work harder in demonstrating that public relations can be a profession with ethics at its core. Once we do that we'll have a better chance to convince journalists and the public that despite being the youngest profession in the world, we have nothing in common with the oldest.

Where the Truth Lies in Entertainment PR

Julian Henry

It is not often that the truth is considered in our shallow world of public relations. It sometimes seems to be irrelevant. We may spend many hours bickering with each other over opinion and interpretation, but the simple idea of telling the truth is rarely referred to, either in passing or as a founding principle behind our daily trade. Instead we rely on the concept of Good and Bad Information. The idea behind this is to put a value on where a story has come from and whether or not the source is valid or official in any way.

Good Information is very different from the truth. It is simply a version of events that stands up. Most importantly, a newspaper is unlikely to get sued or lose credibility with its readers for printing it. And if they are lucky their sales might actually go up. Clever newspaper editors who want to push their luck are free to embellish and talk up Good Information so that the end result resembles something quite startling to their readers. And since the interest in celebrity has spread across the national consciousness so has the pattern for taking a proactive attitude to Good and Bad Information and presenting it as fact.

It is easy to identify Bad Information with the benefit of hindsight because it can be shown to be incorrect. If you examine the content of a tabloid newspaper or an entertainment show on TV on a daily basis, you might conclude that a healthy

10 per cent of what is reported later turns out to be completely wrong. In any other business this kind of margin of error could lead to people being prosecuted. Would you get into an aeroplane if you thought that there was a one in ten chance of pilot error?

But the media, celebrities and the marketing community all have a vested interested in sustaining this busy and enthusiastic trade in Bad Information. I too am to blame, because I have been helping to grease the oily cogs of the machine for the last fifteen years of my life.

People sometimes ask if working as a publicist in the entertainment industry is a rewarding job. It's true that one of the perks is the fact that you get to develop subservient and one-sided relationships with people who are famous for one reason or another. And so when you are looking after a celebrity client at the peak of their power it can be very easy to lose sight of the truth. You might attend a glamorous party with a handful of film stars and pop talent. You find yourself having a great time. And who the heck wants to think about the truth at four in the morning when it suddenly seems that, for the first and probably only time in your life, you are actually a person of consequence and importance?

This is the upside to being a publicist. You get to hang on to the coat tails of success. Unfortunately it doesn't last. Everyone else at the party might have a Ferrari or a Mercedes. But you still have a bus pass in your pocket.

This link with reality can occasionally provide a PR executive with useful insights. We sometimes glimpse the truth. We get to hear the bad news. That the audience were lukewarm about the new CD, or that people think that the new hairstyle looks like a dog's dinner. When communicating these bald facts to our client we need to employ skill and tact. We need to paint a favourable picture, and sketch over the truth with gentle brush strokes. A consultant would call this something like situation management. Airbrushing over problems with charm and grace is one of a number of everyday lies that underpin our happy trade, and when carefully executed this can become the kind of craft that you can stand back and admire, much as one of Sir Christopher Wren's stonemasons might when work was completed on St Paul's Cathedral in 1710.

To be a decent PR person you need to have a relentlessly optimistic outlook on life and a record of obsessive behaviour. You can employ this personality trait strategically on the occasions when you might need to protect yourself from the missiles that get lobbed in your direction by jealous rivals or bitter former colleagues who have come to resent your success. You pretend that it doesn't matter. You lie to yourself.

Telling porkies can become a necessity. You might be trying to contain something fragile, volatile and potentially damaging to a large number of innocent bystanders, namely your client's king-size ego, which has the potential to explode without warning at any moment.

When living in a distorted world it becomes necessary to twist the incoming data into something else, just to make sense of it. I know this seems warped. And it will be no excuse for those who look at PR people as agents of the devil. But putting a positive gloss on things and looking at the world as an optimist is really a bare minimum requirement in the PR business.

Another familiar and easy lie in entertainment PR is the casual use of hyperbole. But it can seem legitimate to exaggerate a claim if a mentally deluded client is holding a gun to your head and threatening members of your staff.

I watched a TV show the other day and the presenter announced that 'Mariah Carey is the most successful female singer of all time.' I'd guess that this is impossible to prove. But I'm certain that Barbra Streisand, Diana Ross, Whitney Houston, Shirley Bassey, Judy Garland, Chrissie Hynde, Sheena Easton, Madonna, Debbie Harry, Annie Lennox, Stevie

Nicks, Agnetha and Frida from Abba, those three girls from Bananarama, and many, many others might beg to differ.

The repertoire of exaggeration in celebrity PR is limited through a meagre catalogue of language that is heavily influenced by advertising straplines that are normally used by big corporations as they prepare to launch something tedious like a new type of washing powder. There's an irony to this technique because it often uses a historical or geographical context when framing the claim. 'The biggest in the world', 'The first ever', 'The UK's greatest' or whatever. It seems faintly ridiculous here in the UK, where the communications business is about the most heritage-allergic and xenophobic industry in existence. Where is the 'Museum of Great Advertising from around the World'? Who has written the definitive book on what it takes to 'Be a Star Public Relations Person'? They don't exist.

But perhaps the most frequently used lie in the otherwise highly respected business of celebrity public relations is casual blackmail. This is when you phone up a journalist and tell them that you're about to leak them a great story but you'll only give it to them if they agree to your terms. It's an accepted way of doing things. And if you don't blackmail journalists on a regular basis, then quite frankly you are probably not up to the job. Aggressive and territorially minded celebrity PRs, blood-hungry political spinners, and snarling brand PR people all love the idea of packaging information and delivering it to news-hungry tabloid editors with a long list of caveats attached.

Of course, you need to exit the scene of the crime without leaving your fingerprints plastered all over the job. None of the details of the give and take involved should be visible to the naked eye, so it is often the case that a PR executive's achievement for their client is hard to estimate. Perhaps this is why the idea of a PR award seems to me to be a quaint concept and something that is actually for people in another business altogether. How can you give an award to someone who might want to deny that they had anything to do with it?

The practice of gentle blackmail of journalists starts to become a slightly dangerous way to do business as you stray beyond the cosy city limits that surround entertainment PR. In some communications sectors – healthcare and corporate – executives are paid handsomely for saying precious little while toeing an immaculately prepared line, and in others – the Civil Service and the City for example – there are strict codes controlling how information and data are fed out.

Actually the idea of blackmail being an everyday occurrence in PR seems justifiable to me, mainly because it is practised to an equal degree by the journalists, agents, lawyers, clients and other individuals with whom you find yourself doing battle. A publicist is just as likely to be bullied and intimidated with threats of broken agreements and unfulfilled promises, so we all need to arm ourselves with whatever weapons we find at our disposal.

So, yes, it is easy to go through the celebrity PR business and come up with a list of unsavoury working practices, some of which, at a push, might drive you to look at yourself and wonder if you are actually working in the right business.

It is hard to spot exactly where a PR person stands in relation to the truth. There is so much movement, so much subtle shifting of emphasis and ambiguity of intent around our work it can often be hard to establish a 100 per cent fact. Let's start by saying that the publicist in the entertainment business has become a fully functioning partner in the business of producing newspapers and TV and radio shows. We are a part of the plot because we are not just the point of access but in some cases the co-author of the story.

As an experienced PR executive you find yourself in a privileged position. While hundreds of journalists sit waiting with their tape machines front of house at the press conference, you are at the hub of the action backstage as the moment is constructed for the media. You see the tantrums. The swearing. You may be the person who writes the speech, formulates the photocall or dreams up the headline that millions of people ponder as they stare at their newspapers the next day.

In these situations you use the truth as a navigation tool to take you through whatever trials and tribulations lie ahead. If you decide to lie, you will need to carry the risk and the consequences. But is the truth enough to interest the world and get you to where you need to be? My advice would be to start by placing the truth at the top of the page. And then do what you need to do to make the rest of it happen.

For a publicist the truth is useful as a reference point when discussing your options with your client. It is also handy if you are suddenly overcome by a desire to build credibility and impress upon the world that you are a creature of quality and distinction. But it's most useful in the moments when you have to stop and try to analyse your own sense of value in a particular job. One of the best things about being an entertainment PR in London is that you can be offered a choice of moral dilemmas several times a day.

For some people I sense that the daily routine of utilizing the truth as a barometer of their actions will quickly become an unnecessary chore. It gains you little in terms of financial reward. It can mean having to make difficult decisions. But over the longer term a reputation will benefit, and the kind of relationships that will develop can only shine a positive reflection back upon your professional life.

I like the idea of being given a constantly shifting set of options and choices, each with different consequences and opportunities to determine whether or not you are able to sail with the help of what Cherie Blair supposedly described Piers Morgan as lacking – a 'moral compass'. This is what can make a publicist's job both worthwhile and exciting.

So let's be honest. Because the concept of truth is rooted in neutrality it is often horribly dull to look at. No one but a trainspotter or a stalker will be interested in a dry list of facts reported with clinical precision. You need seasoning and dressing to bring out the flavour, and it's quite reasonable to add some sizzle so the truth gets the opportunity to shine through.

When attempting to appropriate fact and take ownership of the truth you will often see publicists, journalists, authors, film makers and others with either a vested interest or a chip on their shoulder ploughing their cars spectacularly off the road and into the ditch. It can end in tears all too easily. But by carefully plucking a few granules of the truth and placing them neatly and tidily together, and then using your skill to retrieve relevant facts and forgotten nuggets of information to add to the mix, you can create an engaging proposition that is both accurate and true, as well as being something that satisfies your client and the media. It doesn't always need to be a barefaced lie.

We are often reminded of how celebrities fail us. It's easy to forget their positive qualities and their contribution in opening doors upon the truth. If you need evidence of the increasingly responsible and inspiring pop culture that seeks to connect its audience to powerful causes such as personal politics and self-enlightenment, then you should consider the work of musicians such as Bob Geldof, dramatists like Richard Curtis or comedians such as Lenny Henry. These celebrities and others exploited their talent as artists and publicists for the Make Poverty History campaign in the summer of 2005. This event was about marketing and communication just as much as about music and fair trade.

It's reassuring that a trivial medium such as pop music has so many influential celebrities like Damon Albarn, Thom York or Miss Dynamite who think beyond the boundaries of their art, despite what the Middle England media commentators might suggest to the contrary. And the desire of these youngish artists to pursue the truth in their work is what continues to stimulate the UK music industry and keep it creatively vibrant.

Their credibility and their desire to avoid cliché has given rise to an interesting sub-sect of publicists in creative fields such as music, fashion and film PR, some of whom would clearly consider themselves to be agents of truth, rather than missionaries of Satan. These PR executives have more in common with their principled and idealistic clients than they do with the working hacks of Fleet Street.

In the future it will become harder to distinguish between truth and lies. With many new types of organizations providing information and data, and our increasing need to exploit entertainment content as a means of making brands seem exciting, it is possible that we will have to pay a higher price for the truth.

And of course it's not just PR people who know how to spin a version of events to the world. The commercial ownership of newspapers, TV channels, online organizations, search engines, and telecommunication network providers will lead to their content being skewed to reflect their own version of the truth. Those of us who can be bothered may have to work harder to locate independent comment and high-quality sources of information in order to form our judgements.

It goes without saying that the process of guidance through this ever-increasing maze of new media titles, niche magazines, specialist websites and web blogs may well require expensive specialist help from a team of experts who operate on the basis of trust between individuals and a respect for honest practice. And unlikely as it may seem, there is every possibility that it might actually be a public relations agent who ends up guiding you towards the truth rather than away from it.

Inside Out Information

Julia Hobsbawm

*Campbell had to squeeze every paragraph out of an institu-
tionally cautious security service that was disinclined to gear
its work to the needs of a tabloid propaganda machine. After
considerable pressure from Downing Street, the dossier
famously proclaimed that the Iraqis 'are able' to deploy chem-
ical weapons in forty-five minutes.*

Peter Oborne and Simon Walters, *Alastair Campbell*

*Editors check articles before publication for punctuation, accu-
racy, tone and balance, conscious always of the public interest.
And if they also drive fellow journalists to great feats of hyperbole, it is on the basis that if the public is interested, it's in the
public interest.*

Peter McKay, *British Journalism Review*, December 2005

'Great feats of hyperbole' is a charge that can be laid at the door
of both public relations and journalism. Hyperbole may make
for entertaining reading and it boosts sales of newspapers and
products alike, but a public grown used to it can lack perspective when serious issues requiring their judgement, goodwill
and understanding come into play.

Hype muddies the water for those seeking the truth, and certainly for the audiences who listen, read, watch or surf through
media to gain information and make decisions based on what
they believe. Purchasing decisions. Voting decisions. Decisions
about what is true or false. People may resent it, but they have

to trust what journalists and PR people tell them and to do that they have to believe that we are sincere in what we do. The philosopher Bernard Williams points out that sincerity and truth do not always go hand in hand: you can be sincere and still lie, but to believe in sincerity is to believe in truth, through the conduit of accuracy.

When the Liberal Democrat leader Charles Kennedy was forced to resign from office by his frontbench MPs in January 2006, the *Sunday Mirror* leader column noted the following day that he 'was finished as a leader from the moment he admitted what he had tried to hide with an ever-increasing web of lies'.[37] The lie – that he was not an alcoholic when he was – went on for several years to a media that colluded with it, aided and abetted by some of the Liberal Democrat PR team and frontbench who were asked about, and denied it.

But many issues and facts are not so straightforward. Much as I would like truth-telling in PR and journalism to be clean-cut, it isn't. Things are less black and white, and more what Margaret Atwood describes as the 'spaces on the edge of the print'.[38] Contemporary issues such as nuclear power, capital punishment, selection in education, the legal limit on abortion and whether the War on Terror is justified (or even real) resist clear-cut designation, as do corporate pay, PFI and a host of other issues that are hotly debated. One person's truth is another person's lie.

Over 25 per cent of newspapers and news magazines are not news and features but comment and opinion.[39] The comment media is at the height of its powers, probably because it is by definition not attempting to convey hard fact but an interpretation of truth seen through a transparent lens of bias. It is commonplace now for UK broadsheets/Berliner papers to give as much prominence to celebrity stories or popular celebrity-led TV programmes such as *I'm a Celebrity, Get Me Out of Here* or *Big Brother* as the tabloids. There is a trend emerging to encourage audiences to be entertained by news above all else, which plays into the hands of those practitioners who don't really mind how much information is distorted to fit the bill. A familiar media crime is to report something which is so out of context as to render it plain wrong.

Journalism's job may be to seek out the truth that those in power want to hide but its job is also to sell papers and beat off broadcast or broadband competition. It is under huge competitive pressure to tell the truth selectively. Public relations is tasked with getting an issue on the agenda and trying to shape perspectives favourably in the eyes of whoever is the paymaster so it is also under pressure to tell the truth selectively. Both are under pressure to tell the truth persuasively.

In PR, tactics are reduced by critics to 'spin' and in journalism to the 'agenda'. In truth we are highly dependent on each other, like volatile and unstable elements. Depending on factors such as context, timing, and what access and information are provided and when, the information mixture differs – as does the public's understanding of it. It may sound mundane but how an article is sub-edited can be as critical to the perception of a story's veracity as the selection of information that goes in to the story in the first place. Audiences are not expected to see the very editing that can cause confusion and misrepresentation.

One 'answer' to the problem of finding where the truth lies is to have considerably more transparency about the process of defining, distinguishing, imparting and interpreting the latest version of the truth. The first decade of the new millennium is dominated by advances in information technology so that it is now possible to know everything about everyone, almost all the time, through different media. Sun Microsystems' CEO, Scott McNealy, is quoted often for his famous sound-bite: 'You have zero privacy anyway. Get over it.'[40]

The media world now spins on an axis of revelation. People's appetite for intimate knowledge about those in power or celebrity has been stimulated partly by accident and partly by design in order to create greater intimacy between people and brands, people and politics, people and each other. An inevitable by-product is that the spotlight falls on those who are behind the cameras as well as those in front.

PR and journalism should accept that the public are now savvy and cynical and expect to see the underbelly of everything – just as they do in webcams, reality TV shows, blogs and popular culture (my seven-year-old son, seeing me undressing one day, remarked that perhaps I too could become a celebrity as 'they don't wear clothes either in *Heat* magazine, do they mummy?').

The practices of PR and journalism have both historically remained hidden from scrutiny, but no longer. Journalism and PR have become 'the story'. Judith Miller and Jayson Blair of the *New York Times*, Andrew Gilligan of the BBC, Alastair Campbell of the British government are the most obvious examples of media figures in the spotlight. Although still a relative rarity, the scale of attention they command has become a symbol of the potency of the role of each practice.

The emerging trend of media transparency follows in the footsteps of culture more generally. Over thirty years ago, architecture began, via Lord Rogers's staggeringly successful 'jolie laide' Pompidou Centre in Paris, to make the guts and plumbing of a building available for all to see. Suddenly the inner workings of something had virtue. Transparency and inside-out labelling is now to media branding what the Pompidou Centre is to architecture and Louis Vuitton and Prada are to fashion.

And of course the internet enables millions of people to simultaneously surf through billions of web pages, democratizing access to that information. You can read online at any time of the day or night. You can become knowledgeable about law, politics, history, science, and any number of subjects which previously were for studying over a period of years:

'Researching health information is now one of the most popular online activities (pursued by around 93 million Americans or 80% of adult internet users). An orthopaedic surgeon complained to the *New York Times*: "I have people coming to the office who have downloaded 50 pages of stuff from the internet on minimally invasive surgery."' [41]

Rather than deny or eschew this trend, PR and journalism should acknowledge and capitalize on it, learn from it and even embrace it. And of course, being media practitioners, we should name it. I call it 'Inside Out Information' or IOI. How might this new transparency be implemented?

What measures can PR and journalists take to mitigate the effects of hype and allow the viewer, reader, web surfer or listener to properly decide where, in an ocean of information, the truth lies. The following ideas are, I think, some of the things that need to be done to improve standards in the communications industry, be it PR or journalism.

1. Always read the label

The impregnable anonymity of journalistic sources has been challenged by a hyper-competitive media that in some cases, either by accident or design, then turns on its own sources. The most visible example is Dr David Kelly, the respected government scientist who in brazen defiance of the Official Secrets Act, briefed various broadcast and print contacts. He was naïve enough to assume that he would not, or could not, be identified. The situation led to Kelly's suicide (and a near catastrophe for the Blair government). In 2005, the *Herald* came perilously close to rewarding the disloyal Scottish Conservative source (who had leaked evidence of expenses abuses by David McLetchie, former Tory Leader in the Scottish Parliament) by being prepared to publish his emails, thus revealing his identity – an outrage which was not lost on the journalistic community.

Whilst it did not eventually take place, it is an indicator, perhaps, of the changing journalistic times.

Of course anonymous briefing is often necessary and expedient. But anonymous sources are also used for dodgy purposes, and abused by PR and journalism. The leak has become a PR weapon of choice just like its counterpart, 'the exclusive'. Yet it must be best practice to be 'on the record' more often than not, to have more than one source where possible – as the BBC now urge with renewed energy post-Gilligan and post-Hutton.

The PR adviser David Michie touched on the idea of content labelling briefly in his analysis of British PR in 1998.[42] He observed that 'a fascinating picture would emerge if newspapers were required to print the names of PR consultants providing them with material in each issue, in the same way that foodstuffs manufacturers have to give details of their products' contents on the packaging'. So instead of E-numbers we would be able to know about the number of off-the-record briefings making up a story as opposed to on-the-record quotes, even if the anonymity of the source was still protected. Source material itself is relevant to piecing together the whole picture about a story, especially when it is contested (cuttings famously stay in archives and damaging inaccuracies get repeated every time archive material is sourced for new stories). If a company or individual has tried to stop publication, or has made repeated efforts to correct source material, surely it is in the public interest for the public to have access to the correspondence if they wish, so they really can judge?

I'm not suggesting that the physical architecture of a page or a programme is tampered with. Neither am I suggesting that consumers must read through screeds of footnotes like a 'running crawl' across the bottom of a TV news station such as Sky or Bloomberg. I am arguing that they should be able to opt into significantly greater amounts of historic and contextual information, similar to the way in which consumers can press a red button on their handsets for bespoke stories or repeat episodes.

They should do so via the internet. I'm not suggesting access forcing reporters to reveal their sources, but something along the lines of the academic model of citations, so that the audience for a story can really track and trace its origins, should they wish to, and understand much more fully the basis on which that story has reached them.

Content labelling is actually used more in politics than journalism, through the Register of Members' Interests. Why not create a register of journalistic interests so that we can know if a journalist writes about or interviews a friend, a former lover, or someone with whom they were at university? A juror would be dismissed if they knew a defendant; the least journalists or PR agents can do is disclose whether their personal connection creates any kind of conflict of interest.

A good, if mild, example of content labelling was a hostile story in the *Sunday Times* about the TV psychiatrist Dr Raj Persaud, by the BBC journalist John Sweeney, in which he concedes: 'To be fair, I should point out that Persaud has a real go at me in his article.'[43]

Content labelling is the best kind of self-regulation and should be employed as often as possible. It is embraced by the food industry. So why not by the information industry?

2. Conference call

And what if the media truly embraced the Inside Out approach, revealing how it chooses the news and comment to feature on any day, in any given hour? It would be remarkable for newsrooms to provide the kind of open access that allowed ordinary people to watch the extraordinary process of deciding the news agenda. This has been done fleetingly by the Guardian Media Group, and somewhat clumsily by the *LA Times*, but perhaps the BBC should embrace it as a public service obligation, and offer on the web a continuous *Big Brother*-style broadcast of the newsgathering teams making their choice of stories.

The online encyclopedia Wikipedia is a democratic, continuously evolving resource that vividly demonstrates this approach to information and decisions about truth.44 Who is to say that one senior commissioning editor or programme chief is the oracle on a subject's importance or the way it is explained?

The BBC could be the first to implement this Inside Out approach, partly because it chimes with their intense self-examination following the Neil Report of 2004, which cited the 'editorial lessons' about basic reporting technique that needed to be restated at best and, at worst, relearned.

Transparency about news and story selection could also tackle the Achilles heel of PR: poor pitching. If many clients or agency bosses listened in when their staff rang up journalists or compiled pitch material they might be surprised and unamused. The golden rules of PR should be that you can articulate your message clearly, with the facts at your disposal, and that you have a reason to be pitching to a particular journalist or forward-planning desk at a particular time (journalists often hate PR for what seems like the most minor of offences, calling at the wrong time, but it is a cardinal sin to call them unnecessarily on deadline).

The best PR agencies should also allow webcams to cover media relations activity, in order to encourage better behaviour (rather in the way that televising Parliament makes politicians just a tad more self-conscious, at least some of the time). They should certainly endeavour – as the good ones do of course – to ensure that every member of the team knows all the issues and arguments inside out, thereby avoiding the hyped or trite in favour of well-organized presentation of facts, figures and the context in which to appreciate fully the story at hand.

3. End educational separatism

It is irrefutable that the practices of PR and journalism are inexorably linked. Yet education about their theory and practice remains largely separated to the point of segregation. While I don't think that providing academic-based courses in either discipline can work without being done in tandem with direct experience, neither can learning about one practice work properly without learning fully about the other.

In 2006 there are 800 different qualifications in public relations and journalism in the UK across the qualification spectrum (Journalism Studies still outnumbers courses in PR by some margin). But only around 1% of them are PR and journalism taught together.[45] This means that the central and indisputable connections remain largely denied, that tomorrow's journalists receive an education that still perpetuates the myth that public relations is essentially there to dissemble rather than to inform. PR students are educated to believe that as practitioners they will never enjoy a level playing field with journalism and are perhaps inferior.

In America it took Edward Bernays, the PR pioneer who wrote numerous books on the theory and practice of public relations over a lifetime, to get a definition of public relations recognized by the media that meant more than just 'press agentry'. His seminal book *Crystallizing Public Opinion* was published in 1923 but it wasn't until 1939 that *Fortune* ran an article entitled 'The public be not damned', which defined PR as 'the name business gives to its recognition of itself as a political entity'.[46] Yet despite the recognition nearly seventy years ago that commercial organizations are also political organizations, with messages to communicate and preferences to shape, most journalism students today would still be hard-pressed to define public relations as anything other than 'spin'.

It should be taught that journalism and PR have inherent

and vital differences but also that the overlap is both regular and necessary. Some aspects of that overlap should be considered in case studies, and in defining a new theory of 'best practice' that addresses PR communication and journalistic communication. Students need to know that in modern information businesses 'the truth' is a complex affair and that accuracy matters.

The consensus has always been that journalism should expose the powerful who deceive and distort, while public relations is paid to expose and deceive, depending on the paymaster. This argument tends to neatly favour the idea that journalism sits atop a moral pyramid, with PR languishing beneath it, for ever consigned to the position of ethical subordinate.

The time has come to examine just how apposite this assertion is in an age of information. Is journalism right to regard itself as ethically superior to the practice to which it is permanently shackled? Examples of institutional bias and outright manipulation of the 'facts' are just as prevalent inside journalism as they are in PR.

4. Widen the watchdogs

The Inside Out Information approach is one of self-regulation. I'm not advocating that changes to higher education, or the suggested implementation of content labelling or opening up story selection become mandatory, only suggesting that it is worth noting that there is no single trade body or legally defined group that currently has at its heart the twin practices and ethical considerations of journalism and public relations. Both have their trade bodies – the National Union of Journalists and the new Chartered Institute of Public Relations. The Press Complaints Commission is not only a contentious organization (almost every element of its Code can be overridden if the editor deems the breach is in the public interest) but it also deals only with the press, not any aspect of its interplay with PR. This seems to be seriously outdated and flawed.

There are a number of active groups and initiatives dealing with media intrusion, transparency and responsibility, amongst them the Media Wise Trust (formerly Press Wise), the aims of which are 'to promote for the benefit of the public compliance with ethical standards of conduct and with the law by journalists, broadcasters and all others engaged in or responsible for the media, in the United Kingdom and elsewhere'. But defining PR as 'all others' hardly does justice to a profession that now dominates the media, attracts as many graduate applicants as journalism and broadcasting, and that has representatives in every corner of every business, public body, organization and organized group in the land.

Is there a reason not to create a Media Commission, dealing with the practical and interconnected issues between PR and journalism, which establishes a self-regulated inspectorate or panel to look into best practice on both sides? It could be made up of industry experts and lay people, politicians and academics. They could compile online league tables of the individual practitioners and/or their newspapers/programmes/PR agencies or departments which consistently receive excellent or poor reviews. It would work to an agreed code about information gathering and dissemination that is adhered to by both journalists and PRs.

I'm sure there will be people who say that there is every reason not to create a Media Commission, who will accuse me of nannying or of implying that journalism and PR are cut from the same cloth. All I can say in response is that I have worked in PR in Britain for nearly two decades as the voice of my masters, albeit voices I have chosen to represent and had the luxury of rejecting when I disagreed or disapproved of them. Most often I have engaged in media relations – the most visible and criticized bit of public relations. I have watched with fascination, amusement, incredulity and dismay as my profession – the business of promoting someone's interest to 'establish and maintain mutual understanding and goodwill between an organisation an its publics'[47] – has failed time and again to establish proper credibility, and as journalism has become, like the Emperor with no clothes, that most gullible of all entities: the organization that believes it is immune from criticism or fault.

Equally, I have spent many of my years in public relations practising so-called Integrity PR,[48] despite suspicion of the idea by an industry that took some time to accept that to believe in your client (or the cause you espouse) is essential if you are to be believed by the media you inform and lobby.

Interdependence is not unhealthy. It is simply a fact. Unless practitioners and journalists recognize this, and stop treating it like a dirty secret, the reputation of journalism will continue to be compromised and PR will gain more of the powers that journalists would least like it to have: increased control over client access and the use of limited leaking. Both should be big enough to make visible changes without having to rely on *Big Brother* to put us all on display. Now that would make a good story.

PR and the Press: Two Big Guns

Simon Jenkins

No two professions feel themselves so traduced as journalism and public relations. Both claim to be seekers after truth. Both complain that only a perverse and sinful world – composed of owners, managers, readers, clients and each other – denies them their goal. Only tell the truth, they cry, and nothing need go wrong.

One theme runs through these essays and that is that both journalism and public relations feel themselves to be handling a common product, objectivity. As a journalist, my inclination is to say that the similarity stops there. Journalism does indeed seek to describe the world as it is, not as someone might wish it to be. It is to be a witness to the world, and tell the truth, the whole truth and nothing but the truth. The profession of public relations is quite different.

Journalism must negotiate with public relations, as it must with many attendant professions. It deals with media owners, who produce and market its output. It deals with technicians who determine its speed of communication. It deals with lawyers for redress. It deals with those who need it to command the attention of the public. This embraces businessmen, politicians, lobbyists, artists, buyers and sellers, all guided by the craft of public relations.

In my experience journalism's relationship with all these professions is and should be cantankerous. As reporter, commentator and editor I have always found the best question for a journalist to ask is not, 'What is happening here?', since the answer will always be mediated by some interest is other. The question is, 'What is that interest trying to tell me, and why?' I have watched journalism from every angle and know that nothing is straightforward. News is a process of ceaseless exchange, governed by rules honoured more in the breach than the observance. When a big story is running the best metaphor is of news and public relations in constant artillery exchange, with ordnance hurled into the air in the hope that some of it hits a target. But every newspaper seeks to reflect the dictum that news is what someone does not want to see in print, all the rest is advertising (which can be bought). Revelation and conflict are thus instinctive to journalism. Public relations can never be real news. Yet as Shaw said in his satirical *Doctor's Dilemma*, all professions are conspiracies against the laity. To a world that must use the mass media to communicate its message – public relations in the widest sense – the conspiracy of journalism is impenetrably sceptical. The world views journalists as addicted to stereotype. They appear to fabricate news to fit the stereotype because that makes readers feel comfortable. Comfortable readers buy papers and pay salaries. Given this state of affairs, public relations understandably responds by often showing a similar lack of commitment to the truth in handling journalists. As if trapped by some original sin, both go to hell together in a handcart.

Hence the craving reflected in many of the essays from practitioners of public relations for the two activities to find common cause against some perceived common enemy. The enemy most cited is commercial pressure, the free market in mass communication. Here is where both professions live and have their being. Surely there could be some professional *entente cordiale*. Cannot the press lion lie down with the public relations lamb?

I think there are two wholly separate arguments at work here, one giving the answer no and the other, yes. Every

profession has its dignity and so do the two analysed here.
Journalism best defines itself by a commitment to accuracy as
evidenced in its response to its failures. The one charge no
journalist enjoys is that of factual inaccuracy, of having made
something up. It happens all the time, but it is a source not of
professional pride but of shame. The professional intention is
to give the best possible version of 'what happened', in the time
and space available. These constraints, as Charles Wintour
once wrote, are far greater challenges to professionalism
than the political or proprietorial bias beloved of Fleet Street's
critics.

I disagree with a number of contributors that bias and inaccuracy are more widespread today than ever before. There was
no golden age of journalistic or editorial impartiality. Both are
largely post-war inventions. Indeed, if there were ever a golden
age of responsible mass communication, it is today. Laws
affecting privacy and confidence and protocols on intrusion
and right of reply are beyond anything in place in the 1960s or
1970s – even if some might want them more extensively
applied. So too are such aids to accuracy as the worldwide web
and 'freedom of information'.

Gleeful enthusiasts for the internet see it as the final challenge to the journalists' conspiracy. It circumvents the newspaper back-bench and the editing suite. It puts information
directly into the public domain, unedited and unmediated and
free at the point of delivery. Purists protest that the editing
function is crucial to the professional ethics of journalism.
Without it web browsers cannot know whether what they see
has any bearing on the truth. But as Emily Bell points out in
this collection, just as the web aids the dissemination of falsity,
so it disseminates its correction. It replicates in public the
process that the mass media have customarily conducted in
private.

I do not see the internet as rendering journalism obsolete. It puts it on its mettle. It converts the editing process into a search engine and website designer, and places an additional premium on brand trust. The obsession of publications such as the *New York Times* and the *Guardian* with self-correction shows a growing sense that the institutional newspaper is nowadays about trust or nothing at all. This has to be good news. The internet thus promotes a skill which I believe should be taught in every school, as it was to the ancient Greeks, that of scepticism. Without scepticism the web is indeed a dangerous place.

To this extent journalism and public relations are wholly different pursuits. Much is made in these pages of the apparent similarity between selling a product and selling a newspaper. I disagree. To me public relations is first and last about marketing. True, that may apply also to the managers of a media outlet, but it is not the purpose of journalism, merely the raw material of what media organizations sell. With stark and well-known exceptions, news gathering and writing is not an activity subordinate to a commercial enterprise. It is not intended to contribute to profit. When it is, as in 'aditorial', it is rightly excoriated as unprofessional.

When I was researching a book in the 1980s on why people want to own newspapers, I noted that ownership seldom had anything to do with profit. Only a minority of titles in the previous quarter-century had made money and many had lost fortunes. It was not commercialism that kept them afloat but something quite different, an owner's pride in journalism or, at root, a lust for fame and access to fame. This was financed by cross-subsidy. That is why papers such as *The Times* and the *Guardian* do not wrestle each day to outsell the *Sun* and the *Daily Mirror*. The *Observer* was long a rich man's mascot. Whatever else British newspapers have been about, they have more often been spending money than making it.

Cynics might reply that, in this sense, journalists are merely lucky. They have sugar daddies to indulge their professional whim, their craving after truth. Like academics they can do their own thing with a measure of licensed tenure. Perhaps so. But this remains a different pursuit from that of public relations. While a reporter is supposedly enslaved to the truth, the whole truth and nothing but the truth, public relations must be enslaved to the client, the whole client and nothing but the client. It is a form of business activity no different in goal – and no less noble – than that of invention, design, manufacturing and advertising.

Hence my puzzlement that so many of the essays from the side of public relations seem to yearn after a parallelism with journalism. They wish to share its assumptions and even its professional bed. Public relations is surely a dignified economic endeavour in its own right. It seeks to tell the truth about its product or client but only insofar as it helps sales. It seeks not to tell outright lies or, if it must fabricate, at least to escape detection. Such masters of the art as Max Clifford and Alastair Campbell are essentially skilled at fudging, distorting, dissembling to a purpose. They are not in the business of reporting but of selling. The measure of success is profit or celebrity or some heady cocktail of the two.

So much for the professional differences. My second argument reverts to Shaw's doctors, confronted by the dilemma of art. All professions, when challenged by some higher truth, retreat into conspiracy. Surely instead they should have the courage to spread their wares openly before each other. Both journalism and public relations have a shared interest in the conduits of mass information in Britain. They have an interest in their plurality and fluidity. The first thing totalitarian states do is check such conduits, block them and censor them. The first thing democracies do is ensure they are kept open.

Thus while I believe journalism and public relations should be in natural conflict they should collectively guard the freedom of the press. They have a shared interest in short-term commercial imperatives not gaining the upper hand in the management of newspapers or broadcasting. They have an interest in editorial columns remaining unpolluted by advertising. They have an interest in news media retaining sufficient public esteem to call forth cross-subsidy, whether from capitalists in the case of serious newspapers or from taxpayers in the case of broadcasting. Above all they have an interest in numbers, in choice of outlets. The only thing more important than journalists being sceptical of public relations is that they should be sceptical of each other. That means a range of outlets to make that scepticism real.

This collection is by way of being a conversation. But it is a conversation to a purpose. It is between professionals with many conflicting interests but one that is shared, the maintenance of conversation as such. Long may it last.

'Consider Not the Beam, Focus on the Mote'

John Lloyd

I wrote a column recently, in the *FT Magazine*, about public relations. Its main point was that journalists' view of PRs – that of the dog to the lamppost – was largely absurd, because the standards of journalism in the UK were not always and everywhere higher than the standards of press relations.

I quoted two sources, both anonymous. One was a public relations consultant who believes, I wrote, that:

newspapers and news broadcasts are more often wrong than right on a simple factual level ... that most journalism that rises above the level of the reproduction of a press release (and he accepts that much journalism is the virtual reproduction of press releases or briefings) has an 'agenda' constructed by journalists, which generally consists of finding a wounding fact against the company or the executive who is the main subject of the article. And finally, that most public relations is far more accurate and honest than most journalism. It gets the facts right because it has to, otherwise journalists slaughter him, and other PR companies try to steal his work, and it makes clear what the agenda is because it's clear who the client is.

I had more hostility from fellow journalists on this than on anything else I have written on journalism. One colleague on the *FT* sent me all the emails he received for two days from PRs, to make the point that they were a slimy bunch of liars: at least, I assume that was the point – when I asked for a discussion with him, he refused (by email), perhaps because his indignation was too great to allow rational debate. The lesson I took from this was that it is a crucially important part of the journalistic self-image to despise PRs: and while the editor of this book has been one of a very few in the public relations field to confront this issue directly, no journalist I know of has done so. The default position is that 'spin' is what PRs (in common with politicians and others in public life) do: and what journalists spend their professional lives seeing through, correcting and denouncing.

I believe this is inadequate, and dangerous – above all for the profession of journalism. If we take away a wrong view of ourselves and our work, we won't be able to change it, when it needs changing. The reasons why it's wrong are:

• because much journalism is based on public relations: some of it *is* public relations. The great growth in newspapers/broadcast media in the past twenty years has been in areas where the PR content is high: there has been a large decrease in coverage of, for example, parliaments and foreign affairs, where the PR content is low.

• journalists and public relations people have ever closer unions, because newspapers and news channels are much more about consumption, personalities, and events of various kinds – including political events, which are now usually staged and which tend to merge increasingly into show business (think of the Live8/Make Poverty History projects).

• these ever closer unions have corrupted the media scene to a considerable degree. PRs have lavished and continue to lavish a great deal on journalists in pursuit of good copy – most of which is not declared by the journalist. This is one of journalism's biggest and dirtiest secrets: and while at least some news outlets in the US either don't take such hospitality and free gifts, or declare it when they do, very few British journalists working in this area do. As budgets are cut – especially on newspapers – it's likely that this will increase.

• PR people almost always have to declare themselves: they have to say, or it is anyway clear, that they are working for client X, and can thus be presumed to be putting the best possible spin on the client's behalf. The moral hazard for the PR is that s/he steps over the line from putting a good spin to distorting or suppressing information; the moral hazard for the journalist dealing with public relations people is that s/he spins a story about the client which takes little or no account of the genuine information provided by the PR.

There are two broad kinds of public relations – what one could call the public relations of consumption on the one hand, and on the other, the public relations of the public sphere. The first of these is well known to journalists who work on what has been the burgeoning area of the media of the past two decades, everything from leisure through cookery to travel, motoring, fashion, personal finance, health – and, to a degree, the arts. The second is public relations for, on the one hand, politicians and on the other, corporations – together with all kinds of other public actors, such as the monarchy, NGOs, trade unions, the churches, charities and voluntary associations. There is no clear dividing line between the two – and public relations people themselves often work across these different spheres in the course of their professional lives. But the two are best seen as distinct for the purposes of this argument, since they serve different purposes.

The public relations of consumption is that part of a market economy which introduces products, services and innovations to the market through the media, to complement (or occasionally instead of) paid advertising. Because, inevitably, it is seen by the corporations who do this kind of PR as strictly functional – that is, to sell more product – it is the most open to a certain kind of corruption and is, in fact, largely corrupt. By corrupt, I mean that the rewards given to journalists who cover this area are substantial, and usually not transparent: it is usually not clear to the reader that the journalist has enjoyed a substantial amount of hospitality, or has even been given gifts to keep, for his/her writing or photography. For the corporations and the public relations people, the temptation is obvious – give, in order to receive (good copy). For the journalists, the temptation is larger – to receive, with the obvious implication to give that plug, either as a matter of proper gratitude for the money spent upon the journalist, or as a prudent investment in receiving more of the same.

In his 1967 novel *Towards the End of the Morning*, Michael Frayn uses a 'facilities trip' to a new holiday development in the Gulf as the climax of a satire on what was still Fleet Street – the trip being described as an absurd mixture of pomposity, drunkenness and open greed, the absurdity and pomposity of the event then more obvious because, in the 1960s, consumption PR/journalism were still in their early days. Reg Mounce, a photographer, tells a colleague in the departure lounge his view of the trip:

'I'm doing it for a load of crap called Leisure and Pleasure *magazine,' said Mounce. 'They don't pay much but what the hell? It's a week off from the stinking office, with nothing to do but collect a few pix from the firm, slap some sort of crap together from the handout and get some serious drinking done.'*

Satire contains truth, but isn't fact: consumption journalism can be good, straight and hard-working. But the pressures on it are not getting less: and the approach to it by journalists must inevitably remain that exposed by Frayn – a search, more or less conscious, for the best 'freebie'. In a thesis written in March 2004 for his degree at the London College of Communications, the journalist Nick Leader describes the pressures on the *Independent*, a newspaper which had, from its founding in 1986, decided not to take freebies

'The policy in the end proved unworkable. "We had to

abandon it for pragmatic reasons," explains [Simon] Calder [the *Independent*'s Travel Editor]. "We went from four pages of travel a week to twelve. Consequently it became harder and harder to maintain the policy and fill the pages with very good writing. We looked at the figures and concluded that something had to give, and that was the 'no freebies' policy. Clearly I had mixed feelings about it at the time but I can see the logic of it. In newspapers you always need to be prepared to compromise ...'"

Many in the industry claim not to see what's wrong with taking freebies. If you commission quality writers, who aren't going to be pressured into writing something they don't believe in, what's the problem? The decision at the *Independent* to accept free trips resulted in the editor having more money to pay better writers, thus improving the quality of journalism and producing a more competitive travel section. As Melissa Shales (chairwoman of the British Guild of Travel Writers) puts it, 'Some people might think that when something free is given to you, objectivity might go out of the window, but it's a very fine balancing act, one that goes beyond whether the product is free or not.' The veteran travel writer Stephen Brook agrees: 'Ninety five per cent of stuff that appears in print is the result of a freebie, but that doesn't mean it's not objective.'

The description well describes the murkiness of consumption journalism. Many journalists who work within it can and do retain their balance and discrimination while accepting free trips and other facilities; others don't. (I see both where I work: the *FT*, like the *Independent*, does accept freebies.) The most vulnerable are the freelances, who – lacking a salary to buttress their independence – are more open to the implicit or explicit deals offered by PRs: that is, give us good copy or no more freebies. How – in a field where PRs are offering not just temporary luxury but the basis for a relatively privileged living – could it be otherwise?

More to the point, can it be otherwise? The imperatives of

consumption are not getting fewer: nor are the temptations. The only certain fact is that newspaper budgets are decreasing. That brings more pressure of the kind Calder describes, and more temptation. Public relations people would be rare human beings if they did not recognize this fact, and take advantage of it.

The response, which gives a basis to ethical journalism (as against leaving it up to journalists to be ethical) is regarded by most journalists and editors to whom I've spoken about this as impractical – but yet seems to be the only one possible. That is, to return to the *Independent*'s original stance, and ban freebies. The much less satisfactory fallback is to be transparent about their acceptance – but that transparency would, to be effective, have to detail the amount spent on the journalist by the company, in order to make clear to the reader/viewer what the relationship is. Would that be acceptable in the long term to the companies? We should at least try that: a very partial step, but it would give the consumption sphere a minimal self-respect. Journalists have to take the lead in this – because we have most to gain, and to lose, from a relationship which isn't clear. PRs already are at the first stage – they are transparent, because they must be.

The larger question is that of the public sphere. Larger, because the stakes are even higher than they are in the consumption sphere. Higher, since the notion of 'spin' – largely a presumed effect of public relations – has attracted considerable public attention, and is said to be a major determinant of the present, New Labour, government.

There's no question that New Labour used public relations techniques to the full. From the mid-1980s, when Peter Mandelson was appointed director of communications for the Labour Party and when Philip Gould became the pollster for the Party, Labour developed what became a formidable public relations presence. Tony Blair and other party leaders grasped that, in an era of constant news suffused with a much more aggressive and oppositional stance towards politicians than at any time in the post-war period, they must be constantly proactive. They also came to believe that the public relations function – that is, the necessity of informing the public of what they were doing clearly and repeatedly – had to be built into every stage of policy making. This was the definitive end of a political practice which put out a press release every so often to sum up what the leaders had decided. Instead, the task of informing the public via the media was assumed to be part of the art of politics itself.

The discovery of proactive presentation coincided with – though was not the same as – the remoulding of the party as a socially liberal rather than a socialist one. When Mandelson and Gould sought inspiration, they found it in the New Democracy of Bill Clinton: seeking a model, they found it in Clinton's victory over George Bush Snr in 1992.

Gould's testimony on this American influence – he was exposed to it most, and used it best – is revealing. He had gone to the US for five weeks to study the campaign: on 3 November 1992, he stood before the Old State House in Little Rock, Arkansas, waiting for Clinton to make his acceptance speech, having won the presidency; a BBC reporter, Martha Kearney, asked him: 'When is this going to happen for Labour? When will a Labour leader be making an acceptance speech?' He records himself as saying: 'When Labour has got rid of high taxes and trade union dominance. When we have changed as the Democrats have changed.' Some years afterwards, dispensing with false modesty, Gould wrote: 'These Little Rock days ... changed me, and I like to think they changed – in part through me – the subsequent course of progressive politics. Nothing would ever be the same again. Progressive parties would stop being victims and start to be aggressive; they would regain contact with the values and hopes of middle-class and working-class people; they would start developing campaigning techniques that meant that the Left started to win elections far more often than they would lose.'

Thus the presentation techniques came in on the wings of the third way – and the major task given to it was selling to sceptical media and public a party which was progressively ridding itself of the baggage of nearly a century. Both the presentation techniques and the third way ultimately suffered badly in media esteem in the process – even though both were a success on the policy level.

The nub of the issue is that identified by both politicians and business leaders, and given a powerful restatement by the Archbishop of Canterbury in a speech in Lambeth Palace at the end of June 2005. Rowan Williams said that:

There is a difference between exposing deceptions that sustain injustice and attacking confidentialities or privacies that in some sense protect the vulnerable. If we begin by assuming that the question to ask almost anyone – not just politicians – is the immortal 'Why is this bastard lying to me?', the effect is to treat every kind of reticence as malign, designed to deny other people some sort of power. Exposing what is for any reason concealed becomes an end in itself, because the underlying reason for all concealment is bound to be corrupt and mystificatory. The political culture of 'transparency' and the magic word 'accountability' reinforce an already sufficiently powerful trend. And there is the further problem of an unblinking determination to find buried (and probably discreditable) agendas in every public statement or decision ... but a moment's reflection ought to remind us that the templates at work here are inadequate. Various kinds of investigative process (including the actual processes of journalistic enquiry) require confidentiality and therefore concealment in order to guarantee fairness; certain things cannot be said while legal proceedings are in train; there is a convention about what can be said or shown about minors, especially the children of public figures. Even on the other end of the judicial system, when papers publish or threaten to publish the addresses of convicted paedophiles, most of us feel uneasy. It exposes individuals to mob law and does nothing at all to protect children. Medical and psychological records are confidential. Sensitive material around national security is confidential. Concealment isn't by definition unfair; it may be part of a system guaranteeing fairness. Which of us would happily contemplate our guilt or innocence being assessed by a casual majority poll or our medical records being public? And which of us relishes any actions or words of ours being subjected to exhaustive interpretation to reveal their true agenda? As even Freud said, sometimes a pipe is just a pipe ...'

This, the most exhaustive defence of confidentiality and privacy I've seen, is also a fine primer to my profession on how to approach public life: that is, with care. It prompts us to reflect that there are (at least) two time-lines at work here – one, that of the news media, which is as near to instant as possible; and the other, that of public policy and deliberation, which is often slow – sometimes, extremely slow. The media, either implicitly or explicitly, demands instant reaction and answers; the political, corporate and public spheres can often not give them, at least not completely, without betraying confidentiality, or running the risk of damaging the project under development. Public relations in this context is designed to fill that time gap: it can succeed in giving the news media some facts, atmosphere and aspirations, but it cannot do so completely. The news media and public deliberation live in separate universes.

This central fact is one which both public relations people and journalists should put at the centre of their work. Deliberation of all kinds – especially that which follows demo-

cratic routes – is slow. Media is fast. Can there be a public relations of the public sphere, which copes with, and educates the
news media in, that gap? Can the news media acknowledge it
while remaining vigilant against abuses in power. Ultimately,
can we both – PRs and journalists – develop a common practice which respects the necessary processes of decision-making
and which yet is able to investigate their corruptions? It is at
the heart of what we, in the two professions, could do together.

Trust

Deborah Mattinson

....

'I don't trust him. We're friends.'
Bertolt Brecht

....

Brecht, writing in the first half of the twentieth century, might have summed up attitudes to trust then but for the twenty-first century the situation has reversed. We now choose to trust those we know or feel we know – friends, family and wider social contacts.

Trust at its most basic level is about honesty – 'telling the truth' – and, about people keeping their word. It is about our reliance on the integrity and ability of a person or organization. In a wider context, in people's relationships with public services and business, trust is about confidence, satisfaction and accountability.

The conventional wisdom is that trust between authority and the public has been breaking down in many spheres of British life, a trend that is being felt by institutions everywhere. Yet, research shows that the nature of trust has not diminished but changed. People trust differently, transferring their loyalties from traditional business, governmental and institutional authorities to new alternative authorities. The shift has been towards trusting more personal contacts.

The decline in trust

Many key institutions and sectors of our society are suffering a depletion of trust with levels of suspicion and scepticism often more than double their 'trustworthy' ratings.

The findings of a new survey conducted with 'movers and shakers' from business, the City, politics, the media and the voluntary sector show current trustworthiness rankings for some of our key sectors.49 The church was the only organization with a positive net rating. Interestingly, of the organizations tested, government comes next and the media is at the bottom of the league, scoring only 9 per cent.

Table 1: Opinion leaders' trustworthiness ratings, July 2005

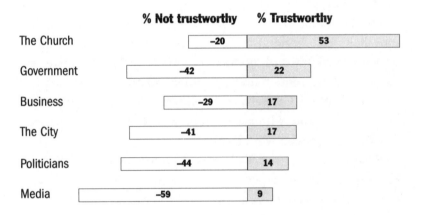

The 2005 general election turnout with only 61 per cent of the public choosing to exercise their democratic right indicates quite clearly the public's lack of faith and engagement in party politics. In 2001 the turnout figure was even worse at 59 per cent and confirms that these statistics were not blips but a worrying trend for politicians. Among our opinion leaders only 14 per cent thought politicians were trustworthy.

When the focus is turned on named politicians some individuals do better. Even so, few manage to gain the trust of over 50 per cent of opinion leaders. The exception is Gordon Brown, whose trust rating in July 2005 was 52 per cent; hardly changing from a similar survey we conducted in 2002.[50] The Chancellor was alone in maintaining his standing over this period with most other politicians suffering a decline in confidence. Charles Kennedy seems to have suffered from the poor performance of his party in the general election, sliding from a similar trustworthiness rating to Gordon Brown in 2002 to 38 per cent by 2005.

The Prime Minister, Tony Blair's own rating remains in decline. Just 35 per cent of opinion leaders thought he was trustworthy compared with 43 per cent in the 2002 survey, with qualitative research suggesting that the dip is a reaction to his handling of the war in Iraq.

Another twist to the analysis of confidence in political figures has been highlighted when the public is given a more detailed breakdown of 'politicians'. 'My local MP' is trusted by 44 per cent, far more than trust either Labour ministers (25 per cent) or leading Conservative politicians (20 per cent). This shows that people who are deemed remote tend to be trusted less than those who work locally.[51]

However, compared with other professionals, politicians' honesty comes into an even starker light. MORI research with the public shows doctors at the top of the league with a positive rating of 91 per cent of the survey. Other trusted groups include teachers and the police with scores of 85 per cent and 62 per cent respectively.

This weakening of confidence has been decades in the making: from the sleaze scandals of the Conservative Party's years in power to the dashed hopes for a 'whiter than white' Labour government in 1997, culminating in the breakdown of trust over the Iraq war and perceptions of slow public service improvements.

The use of spin, though a constant part of political and business communications for many centuries, is perceived to have intensified during the New Labour government. This has contributed to a belief that the truth is or can be manipulated to suit the teller and results in creating scepticism among the public about what they are hearing.

Further to this, Opinion Leader Research's findings suggest that the style of politics – its adversarial nature, witnessed by behaviour in the House of Commons – fails to engender confidence in politicians. And the lack of a significant opposition party compounds the problem.

Business and regulators

Things are little better in the business and financial world where mis-selling of endowment policies, pension fund mismanagement, corruption scandals and controversy over executive pay have all added to a prevailing mood of mistrust of and cynicism about organizational motives.

The automation of businesses and institutions, though part of society's technological advance, is also a device used by organizations to distance themselves from customers and prevent accountability. A common complaint is the inability to get hold of the person you want because of automation, the 'invisible' bank manager whom you have to talk to via a call centre. As society becomes more automated people become increasingly divorced from organizations that they used to know well. Anonymity is a source of mistrust.

The last two decades have seen a global increase in privatization. Companies that were once state-controlled monopolies have moved into private hands. As a consequence, regulation has become an important governmental tool in the policing of business but also in being transparent about the workings of that industry, being accountable and protecting the public's needs.

Government has also used regulators as a means of 'exporting' the problem of declining trust away from ministers to quasi-independent institutions.

There has been a significant growth in the number of regulators but despite good intentions often these bodies are not as effective or trusted as they could be. They are still too associated with 'official voices'.

Table 2 is a league table of regulatory bodies which indicates who is doing a good job in maintaining the confidence of the public. Heading the list is the Audit Commission, with most regulators scoring better than the government's trustworthiness score of 22 per cent (see table 1). At the bottom is the Qualifications and Curriculum Authority (QCA), which regulates public examinations and qualifications – it has suffered from perceived poor handling of a variety of examination crises. This was little more than the 9 per cent the media scored (see table 1).

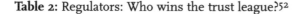

Table 2: Regulators: Who wins the trust league?[52]

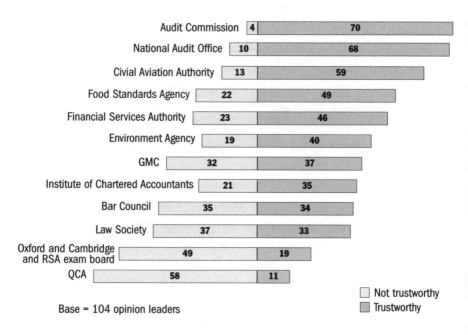

Despite the aims of regulatory bodies there is confusion about these organizations and particularly their independence – 97 per cent of opinion leaders felt that to 'be effective regulators the organization needs to be independent of government'. Many felt it was important for regulators to act on this independence – 87 per cent thought regulators 'must demonstrate that they have teeth; and have an obligation to promote their achievements'.

Opinion Leader Research believes that regulators need to be more effective at communicating what they do. They need to adopt a show-and-tell policy – to show the public who they are and to tell them what they do. Doing this provides opportunities to build a strong relationship with citizens. They need to demonstrate their independence and transform themselves into identifiable organizations.

The media

The relationship between the public and the media is complex and often contradictory. But we have found that trust in the media has been damaged on two fronts.

Firstly, its own reputation has suffered with 59 per cent of our opinion leaders not trusting the 'media'. A major concern is the media's lack of independence – 73 per cent thought society needed more independent media coverage. The public is also cautious and has a good understanding of the political allegiances that newspapers hold.

In the increasingly competitive media world the hunt for ratings or increased circulation has led to a culture of soundbites and tabloidization of 'serious' coverage of stories. Increased choice and competition mean outlets have to shout harder to gain attention. As a result there is an emphasis on simplicity over complexity and conflict over consensus. Challenging issues are frequently covered in an overly emotive and personalized way, such as the human rights issues in the London bombings of July 2005. In discussions with communication professionals 62 per cent blame the 'tabloidization' of the media for making it increasingly difficult to communicate intelligently with the public.53

There are, however, outlets of the media that are trusted – television programmes like *Richard and Judy* or *GMTV* are considered particularly highly because the public develop a relationship with the presenters through the frequency of the scheduling and the interactive elements of the programme which allow the public the opportunity to ask senior figures questions. This apparent intimacy enhances trustworthiness. Twenty-four-hour news and newsreaders are also regarded as credible as neither are seen as having the time or motive to 'spin' a story.54

Opinion Leader Research's work with the public for Sir Bob Phillis's review of government communications confirmed the public's mistrust of the media but it also illustrated its power. Our in-depth discussions with the public showed that despite their clear misgivings they went on to adopt those views and opinions that they read and heard as their own. And even among opinion leaders the contradiction exists, with 29 per cent trusting the media to provide them with facts more than any other group such as pressure groups, civil servants, companies, and politicians.

Shoot the messenger

The second problem for the media is that it is blamed for the general erosion of trust across society. Fourty-four per cent of opinion leaders believe that trust is a media-created problem because of the way news stories are presented and a huge 81 per cent believe that it is the media not politicians who influence public opinion.

Opinion Leader Research have found that the impact of frightening headlines, shocking personal stories and the 'spin' of politics often negates positive consumer experience of public services. The relative 'volume' of negative messages is so great that people believe their own 'good' experience is a 'fluke' and not representative – something we have termed the 'I've been lucky syndrome'. In a recent exercise looking at public attitudes to the NHS, researchers found that even though 87 per cent of people were satisfied with services provided by their GP and 92 per cent recorded high satisfaction ratings for inpatient treatment, only 62 per cent of the general public say they were satisfied with the running of the NHS overall.55

Trusting differently

This negative picture does not tell the whole story. There is clear evidence that we still trust but have transferred where we place that confidence. Instead of automatically trusting authoritative bodies, we challenge that trust. Eighty-five per cent of our opinion leaders agree that we don't trust less but we trust differently – we are more likely to trust people we have a direct relationship with than institutions who used to be trusted routinely.

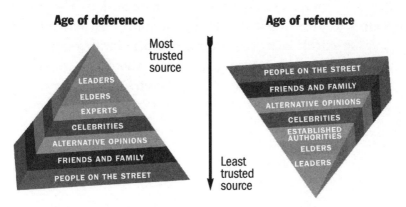

153

There has been a fundamental shift from an age of defer-ence, based on authority structures dating from the Industrial Revolution, when the public looked up to and trusted distant power, to an age of reference when the public is far less trust-ing of authority, preferring to seek out others with similar expe-riences to themselves or sources that have earned respect.

The debate that ensued around concerns about links between the MMR triple vaccination and autism is a good example of how the public deals with the mass of information available and who they trust. Interestingly Opinion Leader Research's findings also highlighted the different values opinion leaders place on the same sources.

Among opinion leaders there is a general disbelief about information presented by government authority. More than half select the medical profession's regulatory body, the General Medical Council (GMC), as their trusted source of accurate information with damningly few – only 16 per cent – choosing the then Minister for Health, Alan Milburn, to present the facts.

This was quite different from the public's choices. The gen-eral public is dismissive of both sources of 'authoritative' infor-mation, with Alan Milburn scoring a low 11 per cent and the GMC only 18 per cent, i.e. 38 percentage points lower than the degree of confidence expressed by opinion leaders. The public prefers to turn to popular TV programmes like *Richard and Judy* for reliable facts (34 per cent), compared with a very small number of opinion leaders (5 per cent) who do so, whereas a higher proportion of opinion leaders prefer to trust alternative medicine practitioners rather than TV programmes.

TRUST

Table 3: Who did the public and opinion leaders trust to give them accurate information about the MMR vaccination?[56]

	Opinion leaders	General public
The medical regulator	56%	18%
Health secretary	16%	11%
Popular TV programme	5%	34%
Alternative medicine	7%	10%

These findings were repeated in similar studies looking at the foot and mouth crisis, stem cell research and genetically modified organisms (GMOs). All found a mistrust of government authority and a migration of trust to those perceived as voices of independence. The public prefers information from people not sanctioned by authority.

Social influencers

Added to this there has been an increase in the socializing of society, and a rise in the memberships of clubs, gyms and voluntary organizations.[57] Through a network of friends and acquaintances the public are able to gather effective information which they trust.

Our research has identified that there are highly influential members of the public in all walks of life – you find them in the workplace, on the PTA and in the pub – who are trusted sources of influence. These are engaged, articulate and informed individuals who shape opinions within their peer

155

group. They have large networks of contacts and are very per-
suasive – we have called them 'social influencers'. Sixty-four
per cent of opinion leaders believe that the influence held by
traditional authority figures has waned; nowadays friends and
acquaintances are more likely to influence opinion.

Rebuilding trust: how can businesses and government turn around this mistrust?

Trust nowadays can no longer be assumed by those in authority; it has to be earned by every individual, commercial organization and public institution and a key factor in regaining that
trust is 'telling the truth at all times and being straightforward
about the limitation in that truth'.[58] Eighty-four per cent of a
panel of authoritative figures in the communications sector
believe that successful organizations are those that strive for
total transparency and openness.[59]

The increased volatility and aggression of the media and
public mean transparency is essential if companies and organizations are to build a relationship with the public in which
they are seen as trustworthy. Corporate social responsibility
(CSR) is believed to be an important method for organizations
to rebuild that trust and demonstrate transparency. A growing
number of companies believe that long-term business success
depends not only on a healthy balance sheet but also on social
and environmental performance, and that CSR directly affects
their economic performance. In a survey of companies[60] many
said a strong incentive for their involvement in CSR was the
desire to motivate employees and attract new recruits, as well
as to enhance their reputation.

The changing way in which trust operates in society means
that 'people we know' are the new influences. This creates a
need and real opportunity for organizations to find ways of
connecting with the individuals who are most influential.

Engaging 'social influencers' within an organization in a real conversation, actively listening, deliberating and responding will have a significant impact.

These hidden persuaders within each organization shape a company's culture, and are vital to its future success and prosperity. They may not be powerful in hierarchical terms, but they are the ones who lead opinion around the water cooler. The implication for companies is that their employees now play a major role in shaping reputation, both within and outside the organization. They are its most powerful ambassadors.

In the public sector, particularly, this can be taken a step further. By engaging an organization's users, and the community in which it operates, in debate and discussion about its services we believe trust can be regenerated and strengthened.

The more effectively communities are involved in shaping their services the more likely it is that better decisions will be made and quality delivered. Involving the public in the decision-making process, revealing how issues are dealt with and verdicts reached, can enhance confidence in that process as well as boost the legitimacy of the public sector organization.

The crucial three qualities for a trustworthy company chosen by our opinion leaders were: reliable products and services, transparency and being prepared to admit mistakes. This suggests that people want business to become much more human. They want business to behave like trusted friends.

Coca-Cola, the world's most recognized brand, has had to tackle the problem of being a remote icon of globalization and the suspicion this now engenders. In the past Coke had a 'think global, act global' strategy. This centrally driven marketing approach has been replaced in favour of a 'think local, act local' policy in an attempt to disguise its global status and attune itself to local markets. This illustrates a more general shift in branding which is increasingly about ideas, emotions and relationships. It is about building intimacy.

Table 4: The elements of a trustworthy company (showing as percentages the company values respected by opinion leaders)[61]

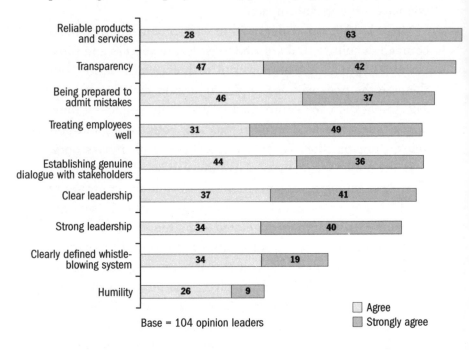

Base = 104 opinion leaders

☐ Agree
■ Strongly agree

In our findings on how political leaders could be more trusted, transparency and honesty were priorities. The public felt that honesty was such a key to effective leadership that 39 per cent were in favour of the introduction of lie detector tests in the selection of politicians.[62] One way of becoming more transparent is to publish milestones, report on these and consistently accomplish these aims. These allow the public to see the achievements while fostering a sense of trust. But top of the list for our opinion leaders was the ability of politicians to admit their mistakes openly rather than bury them.

Summary

Trust is vital to the success not only of government and business but of every profession, institution and even us all as individuals. We all need trust.

But the nature of trust and how people grant it has changed. Shakespeare famously said, 'Love all, trust a few', and that is certainly what we are seeing today; and those 'few' are no longer the institutions of authority that could previously assume they had that trust. Trust now has to be won. Credible and meaningful trust takes a long time to develop, but a short time to damage and destroy. Public trust is concentrated in people and organizations to whom the public directly relate and consider to have no hidden agenda.

Business, regulatory bodies and politicians need to find new ways to build effective relationships with the public and their staff. These organizations need to find relevant methods to influence public opinion; otherwise they may find that influence comes from elsewhere.

Where the Truth Lies, There Lie I

Baroness Julia Neuberger

Unlike facts, 'the truth' is somewhat value-driven. And that is an enormous problem when it comes to trying to work out how an argument is being played out, should be played out, and indeed will be played out in the media. Take any story – particularly about unpopular groups of people – and watch how different newspapers see it from different angles. 'Mad mullahs' are unpopular wherever you look, but while some of the quality press is struggling to come to terms with just who the so-called 'preachers of hate' are, and quite why some young Muslims are so affected and moved by their inflammatory words, others are arguing for their expulsion and for an order in society which demands that people behave according to 'British' values. Or simply get out.

Yet this needs to be teased out. First, it is unclear what the British values are that are being held up as an example of all that is good and fair. Are they the values of sexual morality so lax that many fathers do not know if their children are theirs (new evidence suggests one in twenty-five children are not their 'father's') – and ask for DNA tests? Of the one-night stands of drunken young people? Of the gay bars where a nightly pick-up is the norm? And straight bars which are much the same, but even more drunken? Or are they the sexual values of our parents and grandparents who thought that fidelity was important (whether or not they kept faithful) and whose fear of an unwanted, unmarried pregnancy was considerable? Are our values changed by scientific advance – the Pill, abortion? Or by changes in attitudes – the acceptance of having children outside marriage?

It is these sexual values that the so-called 'mad mullahs' decry – they see immorality, in their terms, all around them. Immodesty in dress. Girls being openly sexually active. Boys drinking and becoming lager louts and so-called 'yobs'. The laddish behaviour of young men and women. They see lack of respect for parents and grandparents, for older people. They see our treatment of elderly people as disgraceful, shameful, suggesting that, whatever we may say about being a caring society, we have no real idea what a caring society that looked after its old (where the women do the caring) would be like. Whose values? And are they wrong about how we treat our old people? And our unkindness? And are we right to take such a blithe attitude to marital and relationship breakdown, when children, who never ask for it, are so affected?

But are they right to treat their womenfolk so often as second-class citizens, to demand of them obedience and a life often behind closed doors, a private, often drudgery-dominated, domestic life? The values are clearly in conflict. While I would argue that we could learn from their attitudes to older people, they too could learn from us about the status, and lives, of women. But the debate does not lie there, although perhaps it should. One reason for real anger among some young Muslims is that they feel that there is no area in which their values, their upbringing, their lifestyle, are valued above the commonplace of everyone else or even equally. They want to hear us praise their family life, their familial loyalty, their respect for older people, their desire for modesty in dress and behaviour. And we do not. Instead, we flaunt our lifestyle and values – and why should we do anything else? – while they feel disempowered and sullenly angry.

But there is a values clash here. Add into this the view that we – in terms of the United States and the UK – attacked Iraq for no good reason, whatever we may think, and killed thousands of innocent Muslims and led to the slaughter of many more in the chaos that has ensued since the war, and you begin to get a picture of where values might be in conflict. The media tells part of the story, though the daily toll of civilian deaths in Iraq is rarely reported with any great noise. The politicians continue to defend what has been done in our name with the argument that life for ordinary Iraqis is better, that they have democracy, and that there will be peace in Iraq and the Middle East, despite evidence to the contrary. Looking at it from the perspective of an angry young Muslim man, one can see that the case is poorly put. Yet, in the wake of suicide bombings on London's tube and bus system, the media rarely tried to get inside the thinking of such men – with rare and honourable exceptions in *The Times, Independent* and *Guardian* – leading to name calling against mad mullahs, but no equivalent name calling against those who have invaded Iraq on false premises, for unclear gain.

So where does 'the truth' lie? With the media, however critical they might be of the Iraq war, who are essentially quite xenophobic and unsympathetic to the horror at our attitudes felt by many in our midst (not all Muslim)? If that is the case, how do ordinary people get a balanced view, understand the values conflicts here, and recognize that, whatever politicians and media may say, it is not possible to depict the world, or even our country, only in the image one would like it to have?

Young male Muslim anger (though a very small part of the Muslim communities' view of the world) is one good example of where the media cannot tell us 'the truth', for lack of a grasp of the concept of values conflicts and trade-offs. But there are plenty of other examples. Take one that concerns me more than most – mental illness in general and, in particular, people who have the great misfortune to have enduring serious and severe mental illness. Whenever there is a tragic killing (manslaughter) of an innocent bystander by someone with severe mental illness or personality disorder, the newspapers, particularly the red tops, trumpet aloud about how those people should all be locked up, about how staff were negligent in letting the person go free – or in accidentally losing track of them – and that public safety and protection must take precedence over the right to freedom of the people who are ill, and so on and so on. 'Murder in the park: mental patient seized', shrieked the *Evening Standard* on 3 September 2004, while its rather more sober leader that day stated firmly that 'this case suggests that the weight given to even a small risk that the patient will prove dangerous needs to be increased, and, with the Mental Health Bill now being considered, the procedures for approving a release rewritten to protect the public better.' Around the same time, Madeleine Bunting in the *Guardian*, taking a different view, from a very different philosophic standpoint, argued that 'the public association of mental ill-health with violence is re-inforced almost daily in the British media. One study found that two thirds of all references to mental health in the media included an association with violence; in the tabloids, 40 per cent of such references are liberally sprinkled with derogatory terms such as "nutter" or "loony".' She continued: 'In fact, for every murder by someone with a psychiatric disorder, 70 people are killed in car accidents. Men between 16 and 30 are more likely to commit a murder. Yet no one suggests that cars be banned or young men locked up, unlike the extraordinary "lock 'em up" response to those with mental disorders.'[63] Yet government wants to include measures to lock up those with so-called dangerous and severe personality disorder on a long-term basis, despite there being no certainty about who is dangerous, no ability to predict accurately who will become dangerous, and psychiatrists arguing that there is no suitable treatment. Whose truth rules here? Whose values? And is one section of the media playing to our fears of the attack by the mad axeman, while another – in this case the *Guardian* – is arguing that this does not make sense according to any logic, according to any examination of the facts? And, in this context, how can one have a serious debate about mental ill-health, and how it affects us all? How can Richard Layard's urgent plea for thinking seriously and differently about mental ill-health, in his recent book *Happiness*, be taken seriously, when the 'truth' is that we like to be frightened by threats of the mad axemen, and we accept derogatory terms of abuse about people who are mentally ill?

Or do we? For there is one dramatic instance of changing public values in this area, suggesting a greater degree of sympathy towards those with mental illness than the newspapers themselves had comprehended. The case of Frank Bruno is one worth looking at. The *Sun* began the day back in September 2003 with the headline 'Bonkers Bruno locked up', and finished the same day with 'Sad Bruno in mental home'. What was acceptable as 'truth' about Frank Bruno early in the morning – the middle of the night – about him being 'bonkers' had changed into a different truth, one of sadness at his plight, by later morning, because the public had reacted furiously to such a derogatory headline about someone they loved and respected.

But all that demonstrates is a public attitude shifting – in one case alone, though perhaps more generally – towards a more sympathetic view than the red-top newspapers. Usually, the red tops get the public mood right. This time, uncharacteristically, they did not. But they should not be blamed, other than for deep prejudice and an unwillingness to put both sides of an argument. What they reflect is often neither truth nor untruth, but simply our attitudes, our prejudices, our xenophobia, our unkindness.

Take prisoners, for instance, or indeed those who emerge from our prisons after sentences either long or short. In a society

that is increasingly inclined towards meting out ASBOs –
anti-social behaviour orders – to young and not so young trou-
blemakers, it is virtually impossible to get the press to take a
proper look at our young offenders and their lives. Yet, between
1990 and 2005, twenty-eight children in prison – those under
eighteen and in one case as young as fourteen, died, mostly at
their own hands, but in one case after being restrained. These
are children. They may be difficult children, troubled children,
and impossible children. But for them to lose their lives is an
outrage. The truth is that they should not be held in prison or
so-called secure training centres at all. Other western European
countries do not do it. But you can search for months to find a
mention of their tragic existences and tragic deaths, and you
can search even harder to find an explanation. Where does the
truth lie? Why did they die, each one and together? There has
not been a single public inquiry into any of these deaths. We
have not been told why, but presumably it is for two reasons –
first, that no one in a position of power or influence regards
these deaths as truly important. And, secondly, that no one
really wants to know the truth about what occurred. The truth?
The media stays clear of it here, for there are no votes, and not
much interest, in prisons. When it comes to the adult prison
population, with the appalling statistics showing the incidence
of mental illness among prisoners and the extent to which prisoners had been in care as children, again who cares? (72 per
cent of male prisoners and 70 per cent of female sentenced
prisoners suffer from two or more mental health conditions.)
So despite anger at crimes committed, the lives, the pathetic
lives and miserable existences of the prisoners and their families, is not part of the equation. The truth? Whose truth? And
when government prides itself on mandatory sentencing policies, and does not look at people's lives, who tells the truth, the
whole truth, and nothing but the truth if the anger and the sadness is not part of the evidence?

And that is the problem. Sometimes the popular press, surprisingly, tells the whole story, or at least attempts to, as the *Daily Mail* did in 2004 when it said: 'Too many who end up in jail are inadequate rather than inherently bad, people who are illiterate, mentally ill, or addicted to drink and drugs.'[64] But it is all too rare, as on the whole the press continues to shout for tougher sentences for child molesters, for burglars, for those who disturb the peace, and for drunken and disorderly behaviour. And yet we know prison does not work. They call for tighter sentences but the truth is that they are pointless sentences. They call for hatred, when tough love might work better, and they prey on fear rather than our courage, when an approach that encouraged us to look at things fearlessly, and analytically, might help us cope better.

And that is why, even when sometimes they tell us things as they are, the media cannot and does not tell us the truth. It tells us the story according to what it sees as our lights, our prejudices. And though it will sometimes be brave, it will rarely keep going for long enough to deal with the really unpopular, the mad, the bad, the inadequate, and evoke our sympathy, rather than our anger. That does not sell papers. But it might, quite literally, make the news.

Truth, Public Relations and the Media

Kate Nicholas

The truth, media and public relations are not three words that you are likely to see juxtaposed very often outside of the covers of this book. But despite their apparent antipathy each does have a relationship with the other, no matter how uneasy.

The extent and veracity of this relationship depend very much on the point from which you view this unholy trinity. From the media's perspective, the terms truth and public relations are unlikely to be emblazoned together across newspaper headlines anywhere in the near future. In fact in the minds of many journalists the two concepts are diametrically opposed and can never be reconciled. Which is somewhat ironic given that from the PR professionals' perspective, a perceived move towards greater transparency, or honesty, lies at the core of the increasing professionalism of the business.

But just as the PR industry has increased in importance off the back of a greater public desire for accountability, a wider public understanding of the PR handling behind the headlines has led to even greater cynicism about so-called 'spin'.

Yet despite all this journalists are if anything even more dependent on public relations professionals than ever before. So how did this relationship become so dysfunctional?

The working 'partnership' between journalists and public relations people has never been an easy one. For journalists who perpetuate a self-image as defenders and seekers of the truth, the admission that their investigations are in any way dependent on the goodwill of PR professionals eats away at the ego.

And this resentment has only increased in line with the rise in power of 'spin doctors' such as Alastair Campbell, the ultimate gatekeeper, who dispensed his and Tony Blair's favours to his favourites but effectively locked out lobby journalists who failed to toe the line; or of a communicator such as Pat Kingsley, the Hollywood celeb supremo who made it acceptable for PRs to insist on not only copy and photo approval but even pre-vetting of interview questions. In the corporate field, you only need to count the number of spokespeople and corporate communications directors now quoted in the national press, to assess just how powerful these individuals have become both within the organizations they represent and in terms of communicating with stakeholders.

This rise in power has, of course, has partially been driven by the increasing pressure that journalists find themselves under through a combination of the incessant 24/7 demand for news and content and proprietors trying to run ever tighter ships. At *PRWeek*'s 2005 'PR and the Media' conference, the editor of *GQ*, Dylan Jones, admitted that over half of the magazine's content was now PR driven, and the *Independent*'s editor-in-chief, Simon Kelner, said that the newspaper was becoming increasingly reliant on PRs for information, particularly in the government and NGO sector. At the lighter end of the spectrum, the number of 'case studies' and human interest stories – ranging from candidates to try new diets and cellulite creams to 'get away from it all' goat farmers in the South of France – featuring PRs or ex-PRs makes you wonder whether national newspaper features editors ever actually come into contact with anyone outside the media village these days.

The resulting backlash has been clear to see as the media bites the hand that feeds. To quote the *Independent*: 'Journalists are always among those most ready to sneer at PR.'[65] A survey undertaken for *PRWeek*'s 2005 'PR and the Media' conference by Echo Research shows that the term public relations is overwhelmingly associated with the concept of spin. And as a result of this automatic association between spin in the political field and broader PR, professionals were primarily portrayed in the media as manipulative and concealing or hiding truths. At the same time, many in the media are also suffering from a creeping post-Enron paranoia. Having failed to see this disaster in the making they are determined not to have the wool pulled over their eyes again by corrupt corporates, and some see obstructive Public Relations Officers (PROs) as the potential architects of their own downfall.

But is all this fair on public relations? Or have the media a distorted perspective of the activities of PR professionals and their relationship to the truth?

Most journalists certainly have an incomplete view of the work of PROs and corporate communicators. Their view is based almost entirely upon those PROs who are in regular contact with the media. But in reality media relations now only forms a part, albeit an important one, of PR activity. In this culture of celebrity, their views are also coloured, almost inevitably, by the activities of a few high-profile individuals such as Max Clifford, Sophie Wessex, Matthew Freud and of course Alastair Campbell.

The reality of everyday public relations is of course far more mundane and also more complex than the media portrayal suggests. A large number of professional communicators now have little interaction with the media, focusing instead on communicating directly with government ministers and special advisers, prescribers in the NHS and patient groups as well as the employees of the organizations they advise or represent.

But do PRs tell the truth? In a survey of 1,700 of them undertaken by *PRWeek* US in 2000, 25 per cent admitted that they had lied on the job.[66] This certainly sounds alarming, and there is no way that a cavalier treatment of the truth can be condoned. But what exactly constitutes a lie in PR terms, and just how serious are the ramifications of untruths?

In most cases what public relations people are most guilty of is either exaggeration or economy with the truth. In fact 39 per cent of respondents to *PRWeek*'s survey said that they had exaggerated the truth. This exaggeration manifests itself in many ways. In the most benign sense it may involve a young and inexperienced PRO becoming over-enthusiastic about the product that they are trying to 'sell in' to the media and making excessive claims for its merits. In the more malign, it may involve over-hyping an IPO (Initial Public Offering) to the extent that after the initial offering both client and shareholders feel the pain – still a relatively rare occurrence.

What is more common is the charge that public relations professionals are economical with the truth. To which the response could well be – well, they would be, wouldn't they? Surely that is what they are paid for, to present an edited version of reality to the outside world? That is the very purpose of public relations, to act as a filter between the media and an organization in order to encourage the most favourable interpretation of a set of circumstances or range of products, or of actions taken by that organization. Or in more serious cases to ensure that a story concerning information about an organization never actually sees the light of day, never makes it into the media and the public domain.

This of course has always been one of the problems with measuring and evaluating public relations activity. Judging return on investment on a proactive media campaign to promote a new product line is fairly straightforward but how do you measure the success of keeping a company or person accused of wrong-doing out of the headlines?

Such jobs in PR still exist of course. The midnight call from a frantic client desperate to prevent themselves being spread over the front page of the *Sun* the following day does take place. And it would be naïve to assume that deals aren't still done to prevent the truth about certain situations being aired.

But over the past few years, public relations has changed a great deal, and I suspect that if *PRWeek* were to ask the same question today, a far smaller proportion of the PR industry would have to admit to a passing relationship with the truth.

At the end of the day it is mainly a matter of confidence. From the time that public relations first emerged as a discipline at the beginning of the twentieth century until only a few years ago, it was primarily an adjunct of journalism, a fairly lucrative bolt hole for journalists who had passed their sell-by date in the mainstream media. And as such it was a fairly basic media-relations-related industry. The dynamic and the hierarchy of power were simple. The client or marketing director informed the lowly PRO that they had a fabulous story for the media. PR wrote press release which was mercilessly edited by illiterate marketing director until the news story had all but been eliminated, and the PRO then had the thankless task of stuffing envelopes full of said press release and ringing up media contacts to ask if they had received it. The PRO was purely a conduit for the company or organization's version of reality and rarely would they have the confidence or status required to challenge or question that truth.

Significantly, 44 per cent of the respondents to *PRWeek*'s 'ethics' survey also said that they felt uncertain of the ethics of the task they were asked to perform and 62 per cent said that they felt compromised in their work, either by being told a lie by their clients or by not having access to the full story.

But the industry is growing up and gaining in confidence all the time. These days a majority of consultants feel confident to turn away business from, for example, the tobacco industry, if they feel it does not fit their own values, and are far less forgiving about clients who are less than open with them.

At the same time, According to a *PRWeek* UK CEO survey, these days 63 per cent of chief executives take direct responsibility for liaison with their in-house departments and consultancies, with this number increasing in line with the size of the organization.[67] There are also a steadily increasing number of places at the boardroom table for corporate communications directors.

The reason for this sea change has been a gradual realization at board level of the immense value of that intangible asset – reputation. Quite when the shift began is not exactly clear but, as entrepreneurs like Anita Roddick so astutely recognized back in 1976, the consumer's relationship with brands has subtly changed. For years advertisers and marketers have sold product on the basis that when you buy a brand of hair shampoo, car, soup, you are doing more than making a purchase – you are buying into a lifestyle and the choice of that brand says something about your own values. During the heady years of greed in the 1980s, conspicuous consumption was in vogue, but as we moved into the more caring, sharing 1990s consumers wanted their choice of brand to say something more about their ethics and values rather than just confirm their earning power.

At the same time the media began to wake up to the fact that business was actually quite sexy. Business stories began to make their way on to the front pages of newspapers, broadcasters began to bring business news into mainstream news bulletins; this, together with the profusion of easily accessible information available about business on the internet, created a new breed of informed consumer. And this new informed consumer looked beyond the brand on the supermarket shelf, or the burger being served to them, to the values, and in particular the environmental and human rights track records, of the companies who brought them to the market.

Where the consumer goes, institutional investors and ultimately government will now follow and so the concept of corporate social responsibility was born. There are now £4bn of ethical funds under management in UK socially responsible indices (SRIs); the UK government's Energy Minister has a corporate social responsibility brief and encouraged by the government at least half of the FTSE 250 now produce glossy annual reports on their sustainability and human-rights records.

And where once organizations were able to deal with each myriad range of these 'stakeholders' as a separate audience, delivering discrete messages, this is no longer a realistic option. An organization's employees can also be its consumers as well as shareholders, and they obtain their information from a bewildering variety of media and sources ranging from news channels to unofficial blogs. As a result organizations have to take into account all their stakeholders when deciding their official position on an issue or situation.

All of which has rapidly elevated the status and role of the public relations professional. Companies have come to recognize that years of trying to second-guess the media make them experts in reading the climate of public opinion – internally and externally. They have become the guardians of the company's most valuable asset – its reputation – an asset which they now realize needs nurturing and which can be devalued in a matter of minutes with resulting loss of sales, share price and staff loyalty.

These days the best PROs and corporate communicators are highly valued advisers who have a direct impact on company policy. And the message that they have brought to the boardroom table? Ironically that the truth is usually the best policy.

What PROs have realized is that the greatest threat to an organization lies in the gap between perception and reality. While once that gap might have passed unnoticed, now consumer activists armed with internet access and 24/7 news channels with space to fill are almost sure to spot the discrepancy. Add to this the paranoia generated by corporate scandals such as Enron and Worldcom and transparency has become the name of the game.

Given a good old-fashioned corporate crisis, public relations people and lawyers are likely to be battling it out over the boardroom table with PROs arguing for the kind of transparency and 'people before profits' approach that would make a legal brief blanch.

And the range of issues that need to be managed and potential crises that face corporates are ever expanding. In addition to the increasing pressure from government for transparency, financial services firms are coming under scrutiny for apparently irresponsible lending to vulnerable communities, FMCG (Fast Moving Consumer Goods) manufacturers are being criticized for fuelling the tide of obesity and only the brave or very powerful (or friends of George Bush) would now be seen to be openly defying the climate change lobby.

In this atmosphere honesty and trust have become a potential differentiator in the market. Hence Nike's decision in 2005 to go the extra mile and publish an extensive 'warts and all' account of is supplier chain, highlighting its weaknesses as well as the advances it has made since criticism of its labour practices in Asia in the 1990s; and the decision by leading pharmaceutical firms such as GSK and Merck to publish all their clinical trials, including results which could have a negative interpretation.

So where will it all end? And what does this new era of transparency mean for the public relations industry? If you take the concept of adherence to truth to its logical conclusion, and all organizations become completely transparent, then perhaps there will be no need for public relations professionals and the industry will have rationalized itself out of existence. But the reality is that honesty will always have to be weighed up against the value of proprietary information. It still takes skill to communicate price-sensitive information in a highly regulated and complex global marketplace and there will always be CEOs who are pathologically afraid of the media and require coaxing from behind their desks to provide the sound-bites necessary in the 24/7 media environment.

The ironic reality is that, as media and stakeholders become ever more exacting in their demands, it is PR professionals who are likely to be the ones who are going to have to face up to CEOs and boards in order to advise them on how their organizations and their policies are perceived; in other words, to tell them the truth. Perhaps, if the truth be told, this is an industry more spinned against than spinning.

Servants of the Truth

Peter Oborne

These last few years have seen a climacteric period for relations between government and the press. Historically the press is on the attack, government driven back on the defensive. Recently the government, along with its allies, has set the pace. It has set out to claim that the media in general, and the written press in particular, is intent on distortion, falsehood, trivialization and even the ultimate destruction of the British democratic process. The central assertion is that the British press is a narrow, sectional interest group, without legitimacy of its own.

New Labour want to change the terms of trade between government and the media. Ministers say that they are aiming at a 'new settlement' with the press. This is a longstanding New Labour ambition. In the eighties, when still Neil Kinnock's director of communications, Peter Mandelson spelt it out with engaging candour: 'Of course we want to use the media, but the media will be our tools, our servants; we are no longer content to let them be our persecutors.' In some respects New Labour has already come surprisingly close to reaching Mandelson's objective.

The most important part of this battle is the over-arching war of ideas. Government ministers and their numerous press sympathizers have set out to establish, in the words of Cabinet minister Charles Clarke, that much criticism of the government 'is pious and hypocritical, sometimes entirely manufactured, coming from parts of the media which themselves have done their best to bring democratic politics into disrepute.' This message has been supported by other government ministers. David Blunkett before his (first) resignation claimed that the media was 'almost on the verge of insanity'. Similar attacks have been launched by numerous others, including Jack Straw, John Reid, Peter Mandelson and Alastair Campbell, the former government director of communications.

At the same time government apologists or partisans in the press – Michael White of the *Guardian*, Roy Greenslade in the *Daily Telegraph*, David Aaronovitch and Alice Miles in *The Times* to name a few – have rallied behind the government argument. A series of longer articles have appeared in the periodical press giving support to Charles Clarke's general proposition. In the *Political Quarterly* Steven Barnet, professor of communications at the University of Westminster, made the extremely debatable assertion that 'evidence is growing' that political journalism manifests an 'increasingly hostile tenor' as we enter the twenty-first century.

The journalist John Lloyd has made the same claim in a series of influential books and articles. He blames 'the media' for the Cabinet resignations of Stephen Byers and Peter Mandelson (twice), and takes newspapers to task for putting Derry Irvine and Robin Cook through 'media hell'. Lloyd's contention is that 'they were pursued not for large derelictions of duty, or crimes, or corruption – but essentially for being human. They were pursued by men and women who would deeply resent the same kind of "standards" being applied in this way to them.' A related argument was made by the philosopher Onora O'Neill in her Reith Lectures in 2002. She argued that the press have played a malign role in destroying the trust which societies and institutions need to survive.

It is fair to say that the government and its allies have managed to establish a near consensus, stretching through academia into high journalism, that reporting as practised in Britain is destructive and must be changed. It is surprising that not one editor has attempted to launch a sustained defence of the integrity of our trade. This essay will be devoted to answering the attack on the press made by government ministers and their allies.

The first point to be made is an easy one, though no less legitimate for that. It concerns the motivation of these critics of the media. Take Alastair Campbell's claim that the press is fomenting 'cynicism about politics, about politicians, about people who work in public life'. How Campbell had the audacity to make this criticism – and carry on making it – defies belief. As a writing journalist he wallowed in a culture of media arrogance that still makes the reader boggle, and has no parallel of any kind among political reporters today. In one column he boasted that he had dismissed a friendly advance from John Major, the elected Prime Minister, with the phrase: 'Oh, sod off, Prime Minister, I'm trying to do my expenses.' It was Campbell who propagated the story that John Major tucked his shirt inside his underpants, thus turning him into a figure of ridicule. On another occasion he referred to 'this piece of lettuce that passes for Prime Minister'. He was more scathing still about members of the royal family – Princess Diana was denounced as 'vacuous, shallow, silly and egomaniacal' while her brother, Lord Spencer, was described as a 'hypocritical upper-class little pillock'.

But this hypocrisy is not the main problem. These ministerial expressions of outrage against a venal press would be convincing if New Labour had not been so ready to import its own culture of mendacity and deception into government. Governments deserve trust if they tell the truth. But New Labour's use of deception, its manipulation of statistics and the secretive smear campaigns aimed at prominent figures – Mowlam, David Clark, Filkin, Livingstone, Keith Halliwell and many others have been victims – denies it any right to be trusted. Reporters dealing with this government have a professional obligation to be cynical and to regard with deep suspicion a government which repeatedly demands one set of standards from the press, but itself practises another sharply lower set of standards.

Indeed, pro-government critics of the British media have conveniently failed to note that the largest deceptions have very rarely come when newspapers take issue with government accounts of the truth. They have ignored the fact that the most egregious misreporting has always occurred when newspaper reporters have believed what ministers and government spokesmen have told them. The list of victims who have been suckered in by government disinformation is too numerous and embarrassing to dwell on for long. Again and again journalists take on trust false claims from ministers and government spokesmen, publish them, only for the information provided to turn out to be false. There are all kinds of examples of this, many of which are set out in my book *The Rise of Political Lying*, which was published in 2005.

The most famous of these episodes concerns the *Sun* and the *Evening Standard*, which disastrously gave front-page prominence to the false claims that Saddam Hussein was ready to release his celebrated 'weapons of mass destruction' within forty-five minutes. Ministers knew these claims to be wrong even at the time, but did not lift a finger to correct the bilge being pumped out by the government information machine. Indeed, the then government director of communications, Alastair Campbell, later informed Lord Hutton that this completely misleading press coverage had 'gone very well, all around the world'.

So it would be extremely foolish to accept too readily the numerous protestations from New Labour and its allies that it is horrified by the mendacity of the media. What it really dislikes is media truth-telling. The *Scotsman*'s Joy Copley once complained to Alastair Campbell that his briefing on a Tony Blair speech had caused her to mislead readers. Campbell showed no concern or alarm that he had caused a falsehood to appear in the newspapers, merely contempt. During the Kosovo war, Downing Street went to extreme lengths to undermine the credibility of the seasoned BBC foreign correspondent John Simpson, who was reporting from the Serb capital Belgrade. In private briefings it accused him of 'falling short of the standards of a leading journalist' and 'swallowing Serb propaganda'. The real objection to Simpson was not that he was reporting lies, but inconvenient truths. Likewise during the Afghan war the full weight of the Downing Street machine was turned on another BBC correspondent, Rageh Omaar, one of a handful of journalists reporting from inside Kabul. Once again, Downing Street alleged that Omaar was being 'duped' by the Taliban, but the real reason for the anger at his brave and measured reporting was that he could not be readily controlled by Number 10. It is unhappily the case that the British government is extremely happy to see lies being published in the newspapers, so long as those lies are helpful.

As with the attacks on the BBC, there are grounds for caution before accepting at face value the New Labour explanation that it despises the *Daily Mail* because the newspaper systematically lies and distorts the facts. When Downing Street issued powerful assurances that there was not an ounce of truth in the story that the conman Peter Foster had given financial advice to Cherie Blair, its account was credulously accepted by most newspapers. But it was the *Daily Mail* who then published the emails that proved he had done precisely that. When the Home Secretary, David Blunkett, promised that there had been no impropriety over the visa obtained by the nanny to his lover Kimberly Fortier, it was the *Daily Mail* who showed that he had indeed intervened to 'fast-track' the visa. The refusal of the

Daily Mail and its sister paper the *Mail on Sunday* to collaborate lazily with the lies and equivocations from the Downing Street machine is, as much as anything else, the reason why the papers have earned the undying hatred of Tony Blair and his inner circle.

But it should not necessarily be assumed that just because ministers' motives are wretched and their objectives sinister, that their arguments are automatically wrong. And even if the attacks by ministers are so obviously self-serving that they can be entirely disregarded, it is still necessary to counter the eloquent critics within our own ranks like John Lloyd of the *New Statesman* or Polly Toynbee of the *Guardian*, as well as powerful outsiders like the philosopher Baroness O'Neill in the Reith Lectures of 2002.

O'Neill maintains that the power of the media in the twenty-first century is a danger to society because it destroys the trust that must exist if institutions are to work. She would rather that the media did not expose medical negligence, because in that way the reputation of the medical profession is diminished. She would prefer newspapers to let politicians get away with corruption rather than undermine the authority of government. And so forth. O'Neill believes that truth is less important than the 'trust' with which institutions are regarded. At the heart of her argument lies an overwhelming arrogance: that voters and the users of public services are not fit to know the truth and must be content to rely on the judgement of an elite who know better than they do what is good for them. Her instinct for suppression is shared by some pro-government journalists. One interesting manifestation of this state of mind was when the columnist Polly Toynbee, in the wake of the (first) resignation of David Blunkett, wrote that nothing that Blunkett had done 'was really a sacking offence in itself'. She then went on:

> *But through Britain's lack of privacy laws and grossly prurient press, aided by unfettered chequebook journalism buying up nannies to spill beans, we know far more than we ought to. Once it's known, we can't unknow it. Like it or not it undermines a home secretary's dignity. It shouldn't – which is why the press should be reined in – but inevitably it does.*

Toynbee assumed that the press coverage, not David Blunkett's use of power to pursue private ends, forced the Home Secretary to quit. She was therefore making the striking argument that the Home Secretary's abuse of office, and the falsehoods which he used to cover it up, should be tolerated. For her the greater villain is the British press, the agent which brings the abuse and falsehood to light and causes us to 'know far more than we ought to'. This is the kind of argument favoured by ruling classes everywhere.

Any journalist with integrity can only find the Toynbee/O'Neill case repugnant. The job of a reporter is to root out the truth. That must be a primary motivation, and is the ultimate vindication. He or she does so in the light of a profound conviction that shining a light in places those in power would rather remained hidden makes the world a better place. He or she must reject with great force the obscurantist O'Neill analysis that societies can only be maintained through falsehood.

It is all too easy to understand why government ministers have found the O'Neill thesis so beguiling. But the readiness of so many newspaper reporters to be attracted to this doctrine is baffling. John Lloyd quotes her with approval and articulates many of her assumptions. He expresses sympathy with the Cabinet ministers Peter Mandelson and Stephen Byers, rather than the journalists who wrote about them and played a proper role in their eventual resignations. He frequently portrays Peter Mandelson as a victim of the media, ignoring the fact that it was a parliamentarian, the Liberal Democrat MP Norman

Baker, who asked the questions which led to his (second) downfall. To judge by their writings, Lloyd or O'Neill would presumably have preferred the fact that Byers was an individual who repeatedly found it very difficult to tell the truth and who made a shambles of the British public transport system to have gone unreported. Both of them, and O'Neill explicitly so, seem to be aiming at a world divided according to Plato's notion, between a handful of enlightened 'guardians' – government ministers, officials, 'experts' and others in establishment positions – and an ignorant populace sustained by useful myths.

This is a sinister doctrine. Historically it has been linked to totalitarianism. It fails to take account of the connections between a free press and a properly functioning democracy. This demented belief that it has suddenly become illegitimate for the press to criticize politicians or reveal their lies, corruption and incompetence has now become embedded in the new establishment. And that is a disturbing state of affairs. Reporters should never be servants of anything, or of anyone. They should simply be servants of the truth. Revealing the corruption and incompetence of Cabinet ministers is part of our role in a properly functioning democracy. It is most emphatically not an abuse of power.

PR in Developing Countries

Anya Schiffrin

I spent ten years overseas, mostly writing about business. During that time I worked in Spain, England, Turkey, Amsterdam and Vietnam. In every country I dealt with PR people, often speaking to them several times a day. Reporting on business and economics is a technical matter and PRs became my trusted allies in many cases – guiding me through balance sheets and complex profit and loss statements, giving me background when I was new to a country and didn't know the history of what I was covering, setting up interviews, offering me scoops and helping me locate sources when I didn't know who to call. Their press releases were the bread and butter of my coverage; each day began with reading what came through on the fax (this was before the internet) and writing spot stories based on the latest corporate announcement. As I travelled around the world, it was interesting to see the differences in the PR people I dealt with. In the Netherlands they tended to be older men who had been in the job for years. In the US, during the internet boom in the late nineties, the PRs were hungry youngsters who called our magazine dozens of times a day without bothering to study our book to see if we would even be interested in what they had to pitch. But it was working in the developing world – where there was hardly any PR at all – that made me most concerned about the relationship between journalists and those in public relations.

After spending ten years overseas, I came back to the US and studied finance and economics, learning many things I should have known while I was a working journalist. Inspired, I decided to get involved in teaching reporters around the world how to cover economics and business. Today I organise journalism training programmes for a small think tank, the Initiative for Policy Dialogue, based at Columbia University. We run seminars for journalists around the world, host an educational website (www.journalismtraining.net) and produce a series of textbooks on covering economics. I do this work because it is needed: journalists all over the world are now covering something they never wrote about in depth before – globalization and how it has affected their readers. Usually, this means economics, so business journalists are now writing about privatizations, trade, energy contracts, corporate social responsibility and macroeconomic policies.

It turns out that these stories are no longer local ones. The global and the local are intertwined and today reporters everywhere cover global issues. Even what looks like a local issue is a global one. This has placed a huge burden on reporters all over the world. It is not enough to know about your local company any more. You also need to know about global trends in the sector in which your local company operates. You can't write about labour in Jakarta or Hanoi without knowing about the Nike boycotts in the US and Europe. Writing effectively about a local privatization or banking crisis means having to know about what has happened in other countries. This is necessary as it helps journalists understand what will work in their country and what won't work so they can explain it to the public and help set the policy agenda.

Unfortunately, reporters around the world are covering these often complex topics with very little background information, either about the experiences of other countries or the alternative interpretations that have been given to them. In many less-developed countries (and some developed ones) journalists are generally (with some notable exceptions) ill-prepared to write about the complex economic issues facing their country; and they have limited information about what has happened elsewhere. In these areas there are a lack of sources equiped with the international experience and technical training to provide information to journalists. I think it's fair to say that PR has failed them and we are trying to fill the gap.

In Ecuador we met reporters who needed to know about privatizations because Ecuador was thinking of privatizing electricity and they had never covered a privatization before. A few months later we went to Bulgaria and found that reporters there were also supposed to be covering electricity privatization. They didn't know much about the subject and they had no idea that it had been discussed in Ecuador. In Turkey, a country beset by financial crises, reporters asked about the debt crises in Argentina and Brazil.

Inevitably, this lack of knowledge hurts coverage. Business and economics reporters are especially vulnerable because the subjects they write about are so technical and require so much knowledge. Naturally, reporters will turn to the nearest available sources and, regrettably, they sometimes report what they learn uncritically, not realizing the biased perspectives. When a journalist is on deadline and writing about an unfamiliar topic, it is all too easy to take the nearest press release and repeat it verbatim. The problem is that those who devote resources to public relations usually have a motive for doing so. They typically want to convince others to support the positions that they advocate. But too often reporters take press releases as 'facts' rather than as 'advocacy'.

The international economic institutions, for instance, have well-honed and well-funded public relations departments. Officials at these organizations may be the only ones around who have worked in a number of countries and who have experience in economic policy. If they are urging a country to privatize its water supply, for example, they naturally will explain why this will allow more investment, and therefore greater access to clean water. They will typically not mention the enormous opposition to water privatization in other countries, and if the issue gets raised in a press conference, they will either quickly dismiss such opposition or explain why it was misguided. They are unlikely to emphasize the problems that have occurred elsewhere – the increase in prices, making clean water unavailable to some who previously had access; the one-sided renegotiations – if the foreign concessionaire bids in a way that leads to low profits, he insists on new terms, often with pressure brought to bear by the foreign government; but if the foreign concessionaire has high profits, pressure from the government to renegotiate is strongly resisted. If there are discussions of an electric power agreement, the emphasis will be on the increased availability of electricity, not on the price or on the large risks which the government may assume.

Other readily available sources of information often reinforce these biases. The water company obtaining the concession or the international firm signing the electric power agreement often have well functioning and well financed public relations departments that attempt to shape public opinion. When I was asked by Caspian Revenue Watch (part of the Open Society Institute) to help reporters in Azerbaijan cover the effects that the country's vast oil wealth has on economic development, I found the only group doing training on oil reporting was BP. Clearly British Petroleum has a lot to offer journalists and can explain things like production-sharing agreements and how oil revenues flow into the government budget. But equally clearly, BP has a certain bias in favour of oil companies and so should not be the only organization training young reporters.

In some cases, NGOs may attempt to provide counter-information. But they are typically nowhere near as well-financed, and sometimes, in their zeal, accuracy is lost. If the views of the

NGOs are presented, reporters are seldom in a position to do more than simply report; they can provide little assistance in understanding the sources of such marked differences in opinion.

The only thing worse than bad PR is no PR. When journalists are not informed is that they revert to their natural biases and assume that their government or national companies are in the right in any business disagreement. In Vietnam, I noticed the local press naturally took the side of the Vietnamese government or business whenever there was a dispute with a foreign entity. In part this was because the media was heavily controlled by the ruling Communist Party, but it was also because the journalists tended to believe the government line. In most developing countries, reporters tend to be suspicious of foreign companies and advisers, and often with good reason.

In developed countries' press, bias is also evident. US reporters often write patronizingly about the European economy and the need for reform and restructuring of the labour market. They take the view that developing countries are lucky to get foreign investment. When Enron was trying to build the Dabhol power plant in the Indian state of Maharashtra, US reporters didn't question why power prices for the plant were so high or why the government should have to bear the risk in the deal. As a result, they did not see the real story: that protests against the plant would grow and that the deal would fall apart. When it comes to covering economic development topics, reporters again trust people from their own government. So the foreign reporters based in developing countries will write about the need for economic reforms such as privatizations, the restructuring of the banking system, the loosening of labour laws and the importance of fiscal austerity. They will often assume the World Bank and International Monetary Fund are in the right when it comes time to negotiate with the government of a developing country. Journalists from the developing country will often assume the IMF and World Bank are giving bad advice. Neither side looks at examples from other countries to see whether the policies being proposed have worked in other places.

PR people working for government or international financial institutions such as the ADB and World Bank need to do far more to educate journalists. But this must be separated from their roles as spin doctors and disseminators of information. It is well known that governments 'leak' good news stories to reporters who are likely to provide the favourable spin they want. Those who must rely on others for their primary sources of information need to be aware of the distortions that result. These 'connected' reporters know that their continued access to 'breaking' news requires that their stories be favourable to those providing the inside information, or at least as favourable as the facts allow. There is a symbiotic relationship between these reporters and the government officials who provide them with the inside information. This should not affect the education of journalists but should be a separate activity.

Less easy to control is the symbiotic relationship between the press and sources of information in the private sector as well as the public. Reporters covering markets are especially vulnerable, not only because it is the markets that provide the information which reporters require, but also because it is the experts and market traders who train the reporters, as they are the ones who know the materials. Their agendas and biases are naturally instilled into the reporter.

At the other end of the spectrum is the culture of media scepticism about the information being provided. This creates its own bias: a media which is highly sceptical, perhaps overly so, and that may see conflicts of interests or incentives to provide distorted information when none exist. Doing so often plays up to readers, who frequently want to question 'authority', to believe in the pervasiveness of corruption. Good reporting needs to be aware of these biases in the media, the incentives it has to overplay certain types of stories, as it is aware of the biases in those providing information to it.

Related to the problem of scepticism is the type of reporting that has a hectoring and moralistic tone. This undermines the dispassionate, analytic tone which should be the hallmark of good reporting.

The 'moralistic' tone is especially prevalent when discussing corruption and cronyism. Reporters see one of their responsibilities as uncovering wrongdoing, and it is natural that accordingly they take aim at corruption and cronyism. Yes, corruption is common in developing countries, and research at the World Bank and elsewhere has shown that such corruption can have a strong adverse effect on a developing country's growth prospects. But corruption is often blamed for all a country's ills. As a facile explanation, one which readers can easily understand, it diverts attention from the harder issues.

Worse, the moralistic tone does little to contribute to an understanding of the underlying forces behind corruption, the multiplicity of forms in which it can be displayed, and to the design of policies and programmes to root it out. For instance, for every bribe, there is a briber and a bribee. It is often companies from the richer countries who pay the big bribes. BP's attempt to reduce corruption, by publishing what it paid to the Angolan government, was unmatched by other oil producers. The governments of the advanced industrial countries have it within their power to force such transparency – simply by not allowing any payments that are not so disclosed to be tax-deductible. It may be that bribes were paid when power contracts in India and Indonesia were signed. But the US government actively intervened on behalf of US companies as well. In at least one case, there were well-documented instances of cronyism and campaign contributions.[68]

When readers perceive that there is a double standard, this moralistic tone may undermine the credibility of the media. During the East Asian crisis, much of the media talked about the need for Asian countries to adopt American accounting practices and American-style corporate governance. The Enron, Arthur Andersen, and Wall Street scandals made it clear that American accounting practices and corporate governance were not all that they seemed. The problems should have been apparent –the Financial Accounting Standards Board had complained about the treatment of executive options years before. But most of the media failed to note this – until the scandals broke out. The moralistic approach led the media to 'scold' the developing countries, rather than to enquire more deeply into what good corporate governance or good accounting entailed. Had they done that, they would have recognized the failings in America.

Particularly problematic is moralistic reporting that is used to advance hidden agendas – often those of the people who 'control' the main sources of information. Such messages are often expressed with a standard set of clichés. Reporters talk about 'market discipline', or the importance of 'reform', and lay out a set of reform measures by which the success of the government is to be measured. They often cover debates about government 'commitment' to reform, and those who oppose government measures, it is suggested, are either corrupt and beholden to special interest groups or just playing at politics. But reporters frequently do not ask the hard questions: To what extent are these 'reform measures' simply symbolic? How big a difference will they actually make? Most importantly, to what extent are the reform measures themselves consonant with ideology or special interests? How would such reform measures fare in, say, the United States?

Reporters often talk about how, if the reform measures fail, markets will be 'disappointed' and 'punish' the country through higher interest rates. The problem is that there is often a self-fulfilling nature to such reporting: if everyone believes that the failure of the measures to be enacted will lead to higher interest rates, this will happen – regardless of the economic significance of those measures. They often do not give a full hearing to the legitimate arguments against the 'reforms'.

The importance of the media[69]

I want to conclude with a few words on the central importance of the media – of good reporting – for developing countries. One of the ways in which developed countries are different from developing countries is in their 'information density': in developed countries there are a large number of channels through which information flows between government and the citizens, between markets and consumers, between individuals in one part of the country and those in another. With so many channels underdeveloped or blocked in developing countries, it is all the more important that those channels which do work should work well; that they disseminate information which is accurate and unbiased. The absence of think tanks puts additional burdens on reporters to interpret the information. Thus, reporters need to get the information that will help them become more informed *and* think critically about this information. PR has a responsibility to help provide this information.

There are by now a large number of studies that show the critical importance of the media in both corporate and public governance. Sen's work shows, for instance, that countries with a free press are less likely to have famines; other work shows that a free press helps to limit corruption and ensure individual rights are not abused. The press played a central role in exposing corporate scandals in the United States, and in the continuing pressure being exerted for reform. Interestingly, there is some evidence that a foreign press may be particularly effective, not suffering from what we referred to earlier as 'national bias', and being less beholden to powers within the country that would resist such exposure. The *Financial Times*, for instance, was particularly active in exposing the problems in the New York Stock Exchange; even though the *Wall Street Journal* first noted the excessive salary of the Board's CEO, it did little to push the story.

Development is a process of transformation,[70] and such transformation is best effected through the creation of a national dialogue on the need for change and through achieving a consensus on what changes are required. It is largely through the media that such a national dialogue occurs. The media helps frame the issues and provides the information which forms the basis of such a dialogue. How the media characterizes a reform may doom even a good reform to a premature death, or may allow a 'bad' reform to continue to be debated. As participants in the debate increasingly realize the power of the press to help shape it, pressures will inevitably be brought to bear; reporters will be increasingly confronted with information and arguments from those wishing to shape the debate in particular ways. Well-informed and unbiased PR can help journalists improve their coverage. This, in turn, will assist decision makers and policy makers to come up with better economic policies – something we will all benefit from.

Nano-Truths and the Story

Jean Seaton

What scale of truth do we live our own lives by? After all, a life of stark verity would lead one to be intolerably discourteous to other people and it would be pretty miserable if everyone one met was scrupulously honest to one. Meanwhile, as off-the-cuff judgements often prove later to be quite wrong, so polite dissembling, up to a point, may also produce greater realism over time. As an individual, too bleak an appetite for truth without hope (even though hope in turn can be a terrible burden) would also be hard to bear. Then what scale of media-policed truths do we conduct public life by? Surely government cannot be conducted properly, despite the current obsession with 'transparency', without confidences and discretion? Exploring options frankly helps test them. News is one of the ways we discuss in public what a 'truth' is. It is also one of the places where we agree in public, together, what matters to us.

Is the news therefore the truth shop? Recently it has often squirrelled away into the inner life of stories, without shedding any light on what matters. The fierce rivalry by which journalists and news organizations metabolize the swirling storms of official information, expert evidence and human fallibility into stories which engage us is supposed to guarantee us a measure of reality in how we grasp events. The media's competitive struggle for commercial survival – it is also assumed – is ultimately dependent on their legitimacy. They are certainly accorded political and commercial privileges because of the role they play in informing the public, but the idea is also that, in the end, the public trusts (and consequently buys) the media which experience has shown is trying to tell some kinds of truth that the public needs (as well as a lot of stuff it does not need but enjoys, some of which like a raucous exploitation of scandal also plays a role in keeping institutions and political players on their toes).

What we value from news, and can scarcely survive politically without, is not simply information, but an editorial intelligence, an informed assessment of circumstances and events that guarantees the value of information. This requires judgement. News also puts competing stories into a ranked order (called news values) and combines assessment with a shrewd salesmanship that commands and directs our fickle attention to what matters. News both evaluates evidence and then makes a fuss to sell it to us. However, the underlying assumption for two hundred years has been that commercial survival and political utility are bonded chemically together, to produce a vital realism. De Tocqueville observed that 'People in a democracy are frightened of losing their way in visionary speculation. They mistrust systems; they adhere closely to facts and study facts with their own senses.'[71] But are these assumptions valid any more?

The business of news production has certainly altered. We have few mechanisms for discussing how the media is changing and what the consequences might be. Indeed, while the news is an old form, and newspapers date back to the seventeenth century, what the public got then was information often merely reproduced from other sources combined with partisan propaganda. Reporting and reporters – in the sense of an independent exploration of events – are the inventions of the European and American nineteenth-century middle-class public and its institutions. Reporting emerged at a historically specific moment. It is always evolving and is never untouched by the world around it. It does not necessarily transfer easily to other cultures at other moments.

Similarly, contemporary news, at least in the form we currently finance, construct and politically rely on it, was created – and has evolved – accidentally. As the American sociologist Robert Park observed in 1925 in the *The Natural History of the Newspaper*, 'The newspaper, like the city, is not a wholly rational product. No one sought to make it just what it is. In spite of all the efforts of individual men and generations of men to control it and make it something after their own heart, it has continued to grow and to change in its own incalculable ways.'[72] Just because trustworthy information is necessary for a democracy, and just because wild rumour may be exciting but is no secure basis for getting sensible government, there is nothing inherent in the structures of news as an industrial product that guarantees these key values will survive.

The commodity that keeps all of this important democratic stuff flowing, at least in mature democracies, is the manufacture and trading of audiences' attention, usually to advertisers. The only exception to this is public service news, which also depends on audience attention but which 'sells' it for its own legitimacy and for the public good. Public service news, like the BBC, is sustained by a political will, but its market situation is as fiercely competitive as any commercial producer. However, not only are there now many more reliable and cheaper ways of harvesting audiences' attention than news (celebrity stories, online chum reunions, games, mobile-phone downloads), but our long-term dependence on the traditional form of the news subsidized by advertising means that we are unfamiliar with the real cost of the news, and seem not prepared to pay for the more expensive model online. We have become accustomed to getting our news on the cheap, subsidized by advertising. Now, news as it has been traditionally produced and financed, especially in newspapers but in much broadcasting as well, is in commercial decline, and may be, like the dinosaurs, about to hit an evolutionary catastrophe. It is the news vehicles that traditionally have provided the democratic glue, that depend most on adjudicating evidence and least on shouting, that are most threatened by the swift delivery of information on the net. Of course, new kinds of reporting are emerging, from participants ever closer to the heart of dramatic events, to concerned communities and partisan groups, but for the time-poor modern citizen reliable adjudication of events may be increasingly elusive: the market as it works at the moment, at least, may not deliver such values.

Moreover, the assumption that news vehicles survive because audiences find them reliable may need some modification. Which media, reliable about what, for what purposes? The bitter struggle for survival has driven news reliability down some odd paths. On the one hand, news stories often seem concerned with fragments of experience that are tiny and detached from the context that explains them. On the other hand, they also often seem to fashion these particles into narratives of good and bad, success and failure, that pre-exist in relation to the facts and are stubbornly resistant to any amendment by reality. Particularly in hunt mode, the media often combine a sweeping, unstated presumption of guilt with obsessive minutiae of evidence, so that the public gets perplexed and lost. Moreover, there are few rewards for cautious evaluation, even though when things matter (like when there are bombings) these are then what the public values.

On a minor level, anyone who has ever been even adjacent to a story knows that once a potential piece of news is in the hands of some kinds of journalism the last thing any of the practitioners wants to hear is what has actually taken place, or what it means: they do want a quote, they may pursue a 'fact', they do want colour for the story they intend to construct, but they are not actually interested in the 'real' story. Moreover, news is destructive. It is not so much that news has always been in attack mode, which can be one of its most valuable public functions; it is rather that there are now few penalties for attacking incorrectly. As the media has had to fight harder to get attention so the self-righteousness has increased. As with the playground bully, news insecurity stimulates news aggressiveness. Moreover, although the media often feeds on celebrity reputation and fame (which it has created), all across *public* life it feeds on experience, accomplishment, achievement and responsibility. When the proverbial Hack-ette phones one at home on a Sunday night you know what she wants to ensure is that someone gets wounded, never whether the story makes sense or is just. Leaving aside those cases when the media hunt to kill (a not inconsiderable subset, and one with distinct historical roots; 'getting' politicians as a badge of journalistic success stems from Watergate), even less-heated stories are often based on preconception, habit, news values and cliché. In particular journalists also frequently want the story everybody else is getting, the sturdy bonds of the journalists' pack life reinforce their collective understanding of an event.

The important issue is not in any simple sense 'truth and accuracy'. Many journalists are scrupulous about sourcing their reports, and rightly defend their professionalism in doing so. However, the relentless and forensic exploration of detailed evidence can expose a genocidal crime or the embarrassing private sexual behaviour of a public figure. It can paint a conspiratorial picture of the intentions of a government policy, perhaps because that is more interesting, more 'story-like' than the mundane truth – that there was no plot. On occasions, it can give apparently sober circumstantial reality to an entirely fabricated and misleading story. The issue is not so much reliability but rather about the definition of what should, and what should not, rate as news. Increasingly, in most of the broadsheets as in the tabloids, it is the neatly packaged human interest story or the noisy attack against easy targets that wins the day. Meanwhile broadcast news, having won one news battle – re-engineering the role of the press in breaking stories – still seems to accept the press definition of what counts as a story. It may help explain why audiences are sometimes bewilderingly indifferent to important issues and perplexingly obsessed with trivial matters.

Indeed, there have so far been three responses to the new media revolution. Firstly newspapers have become increasingly opinion-led. If you cannot deal in information any more perhaps you can deal in views. These views have also broken away from the older political regimentation of party politics. But television news has become more opinionated in a narrow sense too – now celebrity reporters ventriloquize politicians.

The second response has been that of broadcasting: faced with acres of channels because of the new technology it has been to produce permanent 'twenty-four-hour' news, but it is a sadly repetitive, empty format.

The third response has been to pursue stories into their micro-hearts, aided and abetted by the odd contemporary conventions of invasive rights; stories are often propped up by an incremental detail. This is not the 'investigative' journalism of the past which went away and dug and sifted reality, it is different. It is often based on the assumption that any discretion is a lie.

One overarching problem is that audiences have become more elusive for news producers to capture and sell, they are more fragmented, more difficult to engage, more busy with other things, less secure in their habits, more comfortable, perhaps hungrier for more highly charged fun than before. Everywhere, from politics to classical music, from selling books to art galleries, from city centre shops to broadcasting, there is an anxiety about audiences. It is those who have produced content for a market who are most insecure: there is a real sense of tectonic plates being about to shift across many sectors. Driven by technology, and changes in how they live, audiences want personalized communication, their own down-loaded entertainments (portable); they want to compose their own video-clips, express their own views and take and distrib-ute their own pictures. Much of this, of course, the public knows how to do because it has learnt from the media. A BBC news website will get 10,000 messages on an average lunchtime. They will only be read, in the main, by increasingly sophisticated software, but the urge to perform rather than observe has to be accommodated in the news. News may become more pleasurably gossipy and rumour-driven, yet if things really matter rumours are the last thing we need.

Another odd aspect of contemporary experience is the extraordinary availability of the heritage; technology means that every past performance is now accessible. Who needs a new live version of a symphony or its CD when they have thou-sands to choose from or a new comedy when there is all of the past available? The modern and the real are under extraordi-nary pressures.

Another related and urgent problem for modern journalism is distinguishing itself from the noisy crowding that surrounds it. It is not just that other media compete for the audience's attention, with more glamorous, more thrilling, more gratify-ingly complete events or that there are many other things to do, though these may be important. It is not just that the media depends on other structures, like education, and indeed poli-tics, to provide audiences with the skills and understanding to bring to stories, or even that the times change – some epochs (for example, the inwardness of the immediate post-Cold War) are not good for foreign news, and although we pay the price of our ignorance later that's just as it is. But the real problem is how to distinguish the reality of news events from the pseudo-news which often surrounds it: it looks like news, it has the right pictures and makes the right sounds, but it is not based on facts or evidence. Even more critical for news is the competition with many other records of real events available which have none of the scruples of news about reality, or taste. Only the careful news organizations that attempt to sift and categorize honestly really feel these pressures. So many news organizations feel challenged in many areas. They are sometimes a depressed, anxious lot, journalists.

The response has been, so far, largely to attempt to stir the familiar embers of audience interest. The idea has been to shout louder about the things that have traditionally comfortably enraged audiences and to set agendas with an eye on circulations. This has had consequences. Some news coverage, driven by these forces, threatens the very heart of sensible government: the politics of appearances now saturates the whole policy-making process. Do we really want policy driven by fear of headlines? Take two examples: numbers and people. Serious, expert, knowledgeable mandarins really do sit around in the Home Office worrying, wrangling, chewing over how to handle statistics. So they ought: how else can we understand the pattern of crime? But what worries them is not whether the numbers are true or could be counted more meaningfully, but how to media-manage the numerals. Let us take that dear favourite of the *Mail* and the tabloids (and to be frank, my mother) and our old teaser 'violent crime'. The current definition of violent crime includes 'common assault', which as it turns out is not all that it seems. Common assault makes up 37 per cent of 'violent crime', yet involves absolutely no physical contact; though it does include the local yob being lippy on the street. I am as keen on courtesy on the streets as the next one (more so probably – we once had a brick through our window when I intervened in a fight between a gang of boys outside). But such a definition is a nonsense. Yet does the Home Office worry about that? Well, yes and no. Interminable meetings have been concerned with weighing the costs of changing the way in which the numbers are counted, not as it influences policy, but rather as it will play in the media with whom, of course, it is impossible for the Home Office to have a rational discussion.

This irrational state of affairs is not just the media's fault; in our target-driven culture when computers counting things are the measure of success and failure, missing your target is very important (as it has real consequences in terms of money and careers). Nevertheless, it is a weird kind of free media-driven Eastern-Europeanization of the world. This is an example of media nit-picking, scrutiny damaging policy and more importantly driving greater unrealistic public fear and inefficient government.

But then take another rather contrary example, in which the happy hope of non-media scrutiny plays a formative part: regulators. Now there is nothing sexy or publicly thrilling about regulators. Their impact on our lives rarely makes it beyond the business news pages, and when it does (as perhaps a little in the Hatfield rail crash story) they are rarely seen as the problem. The personal lives of regulators may or may not be blameless, but, for example, 'Water regulator's nanny scandal' would probably not shift many copies of a paper. No wonder politicians like regulators. They can download responsibility in the name of independence and at least not get blamed.

There have been, of course, serious regulatory failures which have played havoc with financial services (and a generation's pensions), water, the railways. Yet, while anything that a minister, for example Tessa Jowell, does is likely to be held up for some kind of scrutiny, much that a regulator, like Ofcom, does will potter about in the business pages or the media supplements. Regulators really affect the public's everyday life but are never subject to serious exploration. Yet the rise and rise of the regulatory state, rather like the rise and rise of the NGO state, is at least in part a response to media pressure on politics. Get it out of government, get it neutral and get it some quiet media specialism – despite acres of woodland being felled for the massive mission statement documents they produce, no one will notice.

The media creates a pseudo-environment which is all most people can know of large areas of public life – the public in contemporary complex communities have many sources of information but are paradoxically more dependent on media-mediated reality to make sense of them. The quality of news gathering and dissemination may not matter that much when what it is concerned with is the jolly cut and thrust of humiliating minor publicity-vehicles, but sustaining our capacity to survey the world does matter. There is a traditional, rather pious plea for more 'serious', 'responsible' media. When actually the issue may be to attract audience attention to what matters by any innovative means you can. Calibrating stories for importance is not trivial, selling is vital.

The headline news is that we need some new models for what news does, pretty fast. Such models need to use the new noisy, outspoken desire to have your say, and somehow still sustain editorial thinking power. Moderating views, listening to the communicating public, must also be part of news. Indeed, synergies between kinds of media work even more effectively than in the past, and this multi-media mobilization needs to combine public as well as commercial purposes. The good news is that the British public still discriminates rather well, in the common-sense way it often has, between trustworthy news organizations and the rest, at least when things matter. So, all we have to do is invent some new ways of making sure the reflection they sometimes turn to evolves. The newspaper may have been an accident, but what succeeds it may need some conscious thought – if the public is not going to be lost in a storm of micro-facts.

A Place Called Hope:
On Inauthentic PR

Alice Sherwood

1 May 2003

Covered live on television, and published front-page around the world, a Navy S-3B Viking with President Bush in the co-pilot's seat executes an exhilarating picture-perfect landing aboard the USS *Abraham Lincoln*, after making two fly-bys of the carrier. The President disembarks, *Top Gun* style, wearing a green flight suit and holding a white helmet.

The carefully staged PR photo-op is, in part, to underline his role as America's Commander-in-Chief. But in order for President Bush to perform his dramatic stunt – the navy submarine-hunting and refuelling jet was brought to a screeching halt by cables across the *Lincoln*'s deck – the aircraft carrier, which had been only a few miles from home, had to turn around and head back out into the Pacific. In front of a banner declaring 'Mission Accomplished' Bush announces that 'major combat operations in Iraq have ended' and that 'in the battle of Iraq, the US and our allies have prevailed'.

Despite evocative pictures of a uniformed President surrounded by returning combatants, journalists are quick to highlight the gap between the image of Bush as wartime leader and the less than glorious reality of his military past. Many newspapers give lists of the week's casualties in Iraq, questioning what, if anything, has been accomplished or ended.

PR gets a bad press. Journalists regularly and unaccountably feel free to bite the hand that feeds them. The public is jaded by daily spin. And the industry itself is, as Americans say, a little bit 'conflicted'. Part proud, part embarrassed by its fairground past, PR now yearns for respectability. The rise of corporate social responsibility (CSR) is just one graphic example of this yearning and positioning. But can it, or anything else, deliver the reputation for integrity the industry so fervently hopes for?

PR's bad press is more than a neat contradiction in terms. It is a failure of the communicators to communicate. But it's also structural. The inauthenticity paradox at the heart of much of PR is that in order to work it has to pretend to be something it's not. The pressure on corporate PR is to fake its purpose; in marketing or product PR, to fake its source.

At the root of the paradox is a philosophical question: are you describing or prescribing? Are you telling me how things *are*? Or how they *ought* to be? To fudge the question, PR camouflages itself: promotion masquerades as editorial, product placement as set design and 'socially responsible' PR disguises self-interest as philanthropy. 'Look,' it says, 'good causes can maximize shareholder value too!'

It's not the message or the medium that makes for phoniness, rather the gap between what you say and what you are underneath. The joy of PR is that it can use any means, channel, format or idea that it can lay its hands on in order to communicate a message. A glamorous party can promote an unglamorous cause, carefully worded communiqués can simplify complex financial reality, point of sale motivates, nods and whispers over lunch get a result – a 'guerrilla' PR company can even promote a magazine by projecting a naked woman on to the Houses of Parliament.

Take three – on the face of it similar – messages. All use place as the fulcrum: all are by political leaders.

Bill Clinton's campaign film, *A Place Called Hope*, used his inspirational-sounding birthplace to reposition the candidate as small-town fellow made good, rather than 'Slick Willie' the liberal Ivy Leaguer. Clinton reprised the theme at the 1996 Democratic National Convention to thunderous applause: 'I told you about a place I was born – and I told you that I still believed in a place called Hope.'

'Officially a Roman emperor is said to be born in Rome, but it was in Italica that I was born; it was upon that dry but fertile country that I later superposed so many regions of the world,' writes the Emperor Hadrian in Marguerite Yourcenar's fictionalized *Memoirs of Hadrian*. Hadrian was born in Spain of provincial Roman stock and became Emperor in 117.

'I was a teenage stowaway'

In 1996, Tony Blair told a story on the *Des O'Connor Show* of how as a fourteen-year-old he tried to smuggle himself aboard a flight from Newcastle to the Bahamas. Blair's father, Leo, rubbished the tale: it later emerged that there were no such flights from that airport.

Clinton's message of hope underpinned a successsful, feel-good campaign advert – a successful one as it turned out. Hadrian's fib was an acceptable bit of presentational lily-gilding for the benefit of his Imperial stakeholders. Oddly more serious is Blair's comic attempt to self-mythologize, revealing his craving to be constantly in the spotlight and his addiction to using almost every event as a PR opportunity.

But no wonder. It's estimated you're on the receiving end of 300 promotional messages a day – that's two million by the time you're twenty-one. No surprise that companies, governments and individuals clamour to make themselves heard above the clutter and din. Yet PR arouses ambivalent feelings, particularly among its audience, even though it's a proven and cost-effective way of breaking though the noise. Is it just that we suspect people in the industry of getting a lot of glamour, freebies, good pay and insider info for producing something – well, rather insubstantial?

Advertising, PR's brash elder sister, is straightforward. You know where you are with her. Advertising is the paid promotion of specific goods or services, sometimes companies and even ideas, by an identified sponsor. Note the clarity in the definition. The promotion is paid for and the paying sponsor is identified as part of the promotion. The audience is never in any doubt as to who is talking to them. Secondly, it's clear what the products, services, people or ideas being promoted are. Most importantly, it's clear what the paying sponsor wants you to do about them. They want you to buy them (or buy their shares) or, in the case of election advertising, vote their candidate in.

Straightforwardly prescriptive, advertising says something is desirable or recommended and then attempts to prescribe certain actions for you. The rules of engagement between advertiser and audience are well understood. I, the sponsor, am paying for this advert in order to persuade, cajole, seduce, shock or amuse you into buying this particular product or service, give money to this cause, or vote this candidate in. You, the advertising consumer, can choose to take it – or choose to leave it.

By contrast PR is both more subtle and more sly. Textbook definitions of PR classify it as descriptive, about dissemination, presentation and communication. It is defined as 'the means and industry of influencing public opinion towards an organization, a company, political party or person and its products or services'. It aims to change your awareness, attitudes, understanding, opinions, belief in and goodwill towards the organization/entity and its products and services, but is distinct from advertising as the communication is not about promoting specific products or services. Corporate PR, in summary, is there to influence your opinion but not explicitly to propose any action.

But action – action that leads to profit – is what business exists to do. Try to elevate corporate philanthropy to the status of profits and the company accounts will prove you wrong. That visual hierarchy that puts action on top of description, 'above the line' advertising higher than 'below the line' PR, is clear if you look at a company's profit and loss statement.

Imagine the profit and loss (P&L) as a ladder, sales right at the top rung. Immediately below sales are the costs you can control to increase those sales. These include the advertising budget and count as 'above the line' costs. As you descend the ladder, you move 'below the line' into admin expenses. These costs are further removed from the all-important making and selling but are things you have to pay for in order to run your company. Things like head office costs and overheads that protect your company: insurance, corporate PR, expedient philanthropy and social initiatives. Right at the bottom is a netherworld of expenses that contribute nothing to your profits but that you have to pay out regardless: taxes, interest and dividends. The further from the top line a cost is, the less it has to do with the cutting edge of day-to-day operations. And the less it's perceived as essential. The P&L is a linguistic ladder. The prescriptive – what ought to be done – is at the top, whereas the merely descriptive 'it is/it would be nice if ...' is further down.

Informative-descriptive PR is an honourable and valuable trade. However, presentational corporate PR and brand identity, producing glossy well-designed accounts, neutral-as-you-can-make-them factsheets for constituents, or ensuring that the CEO keeps her foot out of her mouth when she answers analysts' questions, is not the issue here. Nor is purely reactive 'crisis' PR. Problems start to creep in when companies create communications that look like description but are in fact value-laden statements containing implicit calls to action. If you promote corporate brands as lifestyles, use social or political movements to add in 'brand meaning', run greenwash campaigns that are more about share price than ecology, devise CSR initiatives so you can be more profitably irresponsible elsewhere, you cross the line from description to prescription, whether you realize it or not. The risk to your reputation is the gap between what you say and what you are: 'brand boomerang' is what happens when the public spots the gap.

The more the image you project is a construct, the greater the risk that the public will perceive you as phoney. Shell, British American Tobacco and Coca-Cola have all been criticized for CSR programmes that are more cosmetic than systemic, paying what a 2004 Christian Aid report referred to as "lip service". And Stowaway Tony, the self-proclaimed Little Britain-lover and Franz Ferdinand-aficionado, has picked up a credibility problem through his addiction to PR.

The Nike brand boomerang of the 1990s showed the danger of moving too far and too fast from the descriptive to the prescriptive. The footwear provider began to associate itself with sporting values and empowerment of the underdog – mostly black, sometimes female – with its 'Just Do It' brand message. Sporting ideals, black empowerment and female emancipation are serious causes that people devote their lives to. So Nike's communications inevitably carried a lot more moral, emotional and prescriptive baggage than a simple description of footwear ever could. When anti-corporate activists exposed Nike's sweatshop manufacturing and the distinctly unempowered underdogs who toil in them, reality hit image head on. In the ensuing fracas, Nike attempted a retreat into the descriptive with 'We're not political activists, we're footwear manufacturers.' But the swoosh, however temporarily, was tarnished.

So, resist the temptation to plaster over a communications crisis by devising instant social accountability or other codes of conduct for your company. This can rebound. 'Greenwash' became part of everyday speech because people didn't believe the added layer of spin. Public immunity to PR messages is on the increase: counter-messagers, subvertisement sites like 'Adbusters', ethical shareholders and shoppers, logo-cops and culture jammers continue to proliferate.

PR does not exist to increase the sum of the public good. Nor is it there to find out the truth any more than barristers are. Both are performing the role of advocate for whoever is paying them, be it a business, an individual or an organisation. Businesses exist to increase sales, profits and shareholder value. Government organizations want to show they're doing a good job, in order to get your vote next time. Charities need donations and volunteers. If PR delivers those things by using the language and tools of description in such a way as to make it understood as a prescription, there is a fundamental tension between the declared purpose and the actual purpose. Dissembling and manipulation are built in from the start.

What's true for corporate communications is equally true of product PR. But here the paradox is that PR works best when it conceals its source. PR can't promote a product, identify the sponsor and urge people to buy it – that would be advertising. So PR has to find another way to get its message across and the contradiction is that its message is most effective when the source is most disguised.

Take this report on the press coverage of a recent event:

> 29 articles in national newspapers including The Times, the Sun, Daily Star, the Independent and Daily Mail. National broadcasters including BBC TV, Radio 1, 2 and 4, ITV and Five covered the event as did... magazines. Web coverage featured on... Guardian Unlimited and bbc.co.uk... all mentions... were positive.

Major political speech? Natural disaster? Sporting triumph? Much-loved public figure gets married? None of the above. It was a launch of a new hotel format for Butlins at its Bogner Regis resort, as featured in the Measurement and Evaluation section of a PR trade magazine. This particular assessment didn't quantify how much the column inches would have cost as paid advertising, but they often do.

However world-weary or knowing we may think ourselves, it is still quite shocking to read a report which says: this is how many times your story was placed, by a paid company, into the editorial and feature spaces of the media.

Editorial space is more valuable than paid space precisely because it is still presumed to be impartial. The industry rule of thumb is that editorial is worth *three times* paid space. Disguising your source is definitely worth it from a PR point of view. But each time the public apprehends that the real source is not the apparent one, it becomes a little more disenchanted and a little more cynical.

The public don't read the trade press, but they're not naïve either. They're wise to – envious of – journalists' freebies. Canny magazine readers will spot the correlation between inches of editorial and pages of advertising. They are sophisticated decoders, intuitive Logical Positivists who know that the 'boo-hurrah' use of 'must' as in 'this season's *must*-have lipstick' does not carry the same force as the 'must' in 'you *must* get out of the way of that speeding juggernaut'. *Private Eye* regularly highlights literary log-rolling, cross-media plugs and product placement, all examples of PR whose source is concealed. Is it any surprise that the public are increasingly disillusioned?

Disenchantment is a bigger problem for the media channels than for the industry. A loss of credibility takes a long time to repair for a serious newspaper or television channel. PR, however, will always find new channels and new routes to market as soon as old ones become tainted or lose their effectiveness. PR is using online review websites to replace feature sections that are seen as too close to advertorial, viral marketing instead of print, and has infiltrated the once fiercely independent message boards and blogs.

There will always be creative ways around a problem. But the greater the rewards of a newly-minted reputation for integrity, the higher the price of failure if the public perceive the bubble as bursting. Perhaps there is no solution to the paradox of an industry that has to deceive to succeed. If there is, I suspect it will come from greater transparency of means and objectives, allied to a greater clarity about sources, channels and context. More figleaf PR and you simply raise the stakes: the more you try to disguise, the greater the backlash when you are found out.

The risk is that PR believes it can take George Burns's famous advice to actors: 'The secret (of acting) is sincerity. If you can fake that, you've got it made.' But it can't. If there is a fundamental inauthenticity at the heart of PR, you won't cure it by pretending to be authentic. The public knows that acting is make-believe: they suspend disbelief in order to be entertained, moved or enlightened. But for PR to go down that route would be simply riding higher, to fall further.

Crises and Their Discontents

Andrew St George

....

This is the course in advanced physics. That means the instructor finds the subject confusing. If he didn't, the course would be called elementary physics.

Luis Alvarez, Nobel Laureate, 1968

....

I'd like to share some of my confusions with you. The matter of crisis management is for the most part straightforward in the application but complicated in the fashioning. In fact, the application has not changed since Nelson set out the model in the Gibraltar Memorandum:[73] establish an intent, formulate a strategy, commit your resources, draw up a contingency plan, and inspire where necessary. While the application may not have changed much the circumstances and environment have.[74] In fact, the circumstances of the media environment are such that change is the only constant, the only sure thing that can be relied on.

Let me set out three areas where some useful thinking might be done. First, why is it that a crisis is such an important event for the principal (company, organization, individual, government, institution)? Second, what does this tell us about the relations between the principal and the representatives of the media? Third, what conclusions might usefully be drawn from this?

1. Why is a crisis important?

Before momentous events occur in a city or province, there are signs that foretell them or men that predict them.

Niccolò Machiavelli, 1532

Machiavelli can still teach us much, not just by being abstract and cynical enough to match the qualities of the twenty-first century, but in recognizing that there are rules in the game. Rule one in crisis communications is that we live life forwards but we have to try to understand it backwards.[75] Rule two is that a crisis puts us on a wave between the two, between event and explanation. This is why it is often so taxing for the participants, so interesting for the advisers, so enticing for commentators. A mature, chaotic crisis can produce unexpected results: events unfold rapidly while understanding is made to follow. Rule three is that, given enough good fortune in a crisis, the events and the interpretation of them can be related with some degree of success. Rational deduction can follow from known causes. But not always.

Crises of all kinds tend to underline two things: first, they reinforce our prejudice that there are real explanations for why things happen; and second, they tend to pander to our sense that life must be less random than it in fact is. There must be an explanation, we say, someone must be responsible. From the outside, a crisis often appears as if it will admit of this kind of causal thinking. Media commentators want to know the *who*, *what*, *why*, *where*, *when* and *how* of any story. But the agents within the crisis are often unable to line up cause and effect: this is because they find themselves in the midst of experiencing the chaos that a crisis brings. It is as if one group – the media – is living in a world of cause and effect, a universe run by Descartes where proof is possible;[76] and the other group – the principals or actors in the crisis – are in a world of half-truths, a world according to Wittgenstein, where proof is impossible. The job of good crisis counsel is to mediate between the two. This describes the work that I do.

There is another complication. Journalists tend to be selected and trained because they excel at analysis and description rather than examination and hypothesis. They also excel at eloquent and apt opinion, the best maintaining high standards of accuracy and acuity delivered under great pressure. They are rarely researchers, statisticians, academics or professionals in the areas they cover. So understanding what is really going on in a crisis, and writing about their own – often very high – level of understanding are two different things. Why don't journalists realize that they know much less than they think? For that matter, why don't the so-called experts whom journalists rely on learn from their past failings or inaccuracies? In theory, as an expert you could be wrong every time if you believed strongly enough each time that you would get it right next time. In fact, the very notion of expertise is coming under proper scrutiny, with a renewed sense of trust in the smartness of the many rather than the individual.77

Crises invariably condense the uncertainties of everyday life. They frequently demonstrate that knowledge and information are shared unequally. For example, the burden of proof often rests on the principal: it has to demonstrate time and again that it did the right things; yet all the media has to do is to produce one exception to the principal's diligent approach, and the principal loses face. The US and British armies in Iraq have to deal with this precise problem. Countless instances of good behaviour mean nothing; one instance of bad behaviour means everything. The philosophical version (from David Hume in the eighteenth century via John Stuart Mill in the nineteenth) is clear, too. No matter how many white swans you count, you can never prove that all swans are white; but if you see only one black swan, you can prove that all swans are not white.78 This is an example of what statistical theorists call asymmetric information: it happens all the time in the relationship between the principal and the journalist during a crisis. The principal wants the median of behaviour, the journalist wants the statistical exception. Of course, what looks like an exception may well turn out to be the norm: an instance of defalcation in a company may really be the way things are done there (and that is proper, bad news for shareholders).

So, asymmetric information is one of the rules of the interaction. There is another important one. It is best explained by thinking about the chaotic implications of entropy. While, for an ordered company, there is one place for everything in its strategy, as in a well-ordered kitchen there is an infinite number of ways in which each individual thing can be out of place – like the mess that ensues after a hasty breakfast or a large party. There is only one way a factory or installation or policy can be perfectly ordered, but a myriad of ways in which it cannot be. This means that there is a tendency for information to become even more asymmetric. The principal counts white swans, the media looks for black ones.

2. What does a crisis mean for principals and journalists?

Always deny what you don't want to be known, and always affirm what you want to be believed. For, though there be much – even conclusive – evidence to the contrary, a fervent affirmation or denial will often create at least some doubt in the mind of your listener.

Francesco Guicciardini, Ambassador, 1527 79

Crises are ideal news. They have velocity, direction, plot and finite life. For these reasons they also make excellent entertainment. The 2005 hurricane season in the US was a case in point: Katrina, Rita, Wilma were dramas played out in real time; the stakes were high, involving destruction and death. Hurricanes also feature – in addition to myriad appearances of everyman – those crisis actors whom journalists love so much to cover: police, emergency services, medical and legal professionals. Why? Because all three deal with outcomes that are final: an arrest, a rescue, a life-or-death result in theatre, a conviction in court. All three produce story and plot.

Crises have a pattern, like hurricanes: sometimes forewarning, always immersion and aftermath. In this, they operate not only like movies but like everyday news. Each news item appears on a news website (and that of thousands of interested investors, commentators, advisers) in order not of importance but of time: latest, thirty minutes, sixty minutes, two hours. If a piece of news is older than twenty-four hours, it falls off the site. And the site is updated, like many news sources now, every fifteen minutes. Around the world, at countless editing desks, screens, editorial meetings, the same time standard is applied. How many of these stories are true? Accurate? Researched?

Over the last five years we have all become more connected, better informed, quicker to receive and to transmit information. In Marshall McLuhan's global village the biggest problem is that fact and fiction now travel at the same speed; here, distance is dead and time is compressed. News now travels faster and further to more people. If something dire happens in your business, more people now know about it sooner than before, at the speed of light, and probably before you do. The medium – celerity in all its forms – is the message.

This has produced a heated-up environment where speed is regarded as a value.[80] In the meantime, pared-down news organizations are busy running to keep still, reusing (they call it repurposing) news material easily accessed digitally. TV news is replicable and can be rebroadcast around the world at different times, with different sound-tracks, and with subtly different weight and bias. We have entered an era of what some call 'drive-by' journalism, where stories are casually and quickly put together. News coverage is becoming more expensive, so it makes sense to reuse where possible.[81] News itself does not make money. Reused, recycled, 'repurposed' news makes money. News is no longer a service but a product. For example, NBC used to be one organization. It is now NBC, CNBC, MSNBC.com, NBC Superchannel Europe, NBC Asia, NBC Latin America. Yet NBC has not increased the number of journalists to match its increased output. It has created the news repurposer, whose function is to cut, edit, augment, reshape and rebroadcast news pieces wherever there is a gap in the news output round the world. Business programmes in particular have flourished, because business is rich in information.

News is becoming another form of entertainment. The ownership of the TV news industry bears this out: CBS is now owned by what used to be Westinghouse; NBC is owned by General Electric; ABC is owned by Disney; Fox is owned by News Corporation. Depending on their cultures, news organizations are driven by ratings or profit or both. And depending on how their success is measured, usually by audience share or by advertising revenue, their news tends towards the form of entertainment rather than fact. In the UK, for example, political news is tending towards prurient docu-drama; this is raw gossip pasted over with the patina of sobriety. John Lloyd of the *Financial Times* is particularly astute in thinking about developments in this area.[82] There is class at work here, too. The acceptable upper-middle-class version of a tabloid is the faux-documentary charting the downfall of some political figure. Such a figure may or may not merit the attention, but style rather than the form is important here. All lives are given the tragedy treatment, not particularly original, but served up by smart editors who both elevate and reduce all to the level of

Chaucer: *a dittie of prosperitie that endeth in wretchednesse* with breaks for ads.

To understand the pressures on journalists, their professional and economic environment, is to understand the fundamental needs in operation during a crisis. For the principal, a crisis can take many forms: a fall in share price, a terrorist attack, a product failure, an unreliable mistress, an environmental disaster, an unforeseen political move, a rogue website, a challenge from a pressure group. Each defines its own rules and each needs a range of tactics and techniques if you are to survive and even prosper. For the media, a crisis takes only one form: the story.

Crisis communications evolved through the 1990s in order to meet those needs. I learned from a great guru called John Scanlon. We worked mostly in litigation in the US, in product liability and class action, in fraud and financial shock. We advised clients to start a dialogue and take control of it, speak with one voice, and choose their media outlets. We limited access. I told clients: 'Tell the truth now.' We would hope to manage the news cycle of morning radio, daytime print journalists and night-time TV. With dedicated phone lines, press releases and news interviews, the crisis would resolve itself or move on to a place where it could be more easily managed. All our clients had to do was know themselves, be honest and consistent, and trust the facts, however bad they may have looked. Time was on their side. Not now.

In the digital world time is not on your side, because events unfold at the speed of light. Now there is no news cycle, but rolling, churning 24/7/365 information. In this context the internet has made us all into publishers and spokesmen. It is gossip and conjecture and analysis and truth and hearsay and rumour and fact all blended together. It offers a different view of the world, and as a result alters our view. Because of this, traditional crisis management falls short. There is still a place for rushed meetings, airport summits and limousine trysts, last-minute faxes, press releases and media statements. They may achieve much, but these are poor tools because they cannot speak immediately to enough of the people you need to speak to.

Think of the number of constituencies you have in your internal and external organizations: staff, clients, partners, suppliers, sub-contractors, investors and shareholders, regulatory authorities, stakeholders, trade and media and so on. These are many and disparate publics, and each one needs a subtly different version of the same message from you. How do you reach them all?

Forget the technology for a minute. How do you convey qualities? How do you show concern? How do you sit down with the 5 million people who may have some interest in your difficulties? How can you be yourself with so many different people? You can only answer these questions in a crisis if you understand that the Net is not a place where you broadcast but a market forum in which you talk. Markets are forms of gossip, conversation, rumour and exchange. And since all information now travels digitally and can be replicated, or distorted, in an instant, markets based on that information tend to change rapidly. You must be able to change with them. You must also be able to provide reassurance and information in the right form, matched to the audiences to whom you are talking: figures for the bankers, common sense for the public, plans for the staff and so on. You must be human at the speed of light; you must talk in many voices; you must show your publics that what they see makes you more and not less like them. People react to concrete and visible things; our brains are made, as Stephen Pinker says, for fitness not truth. So a crisis must be made available, somehow representative.

You can no longer do nothing and no longer do everything. You need to think of yourself as a part of a conversation that determines your future. That conversation, about your product or your environmental policy or your share price, is happening faster than you can imagine. It is bigger and wider than the present crisis. However you choose to see your own part in it, your reputation, status, brand, market share, profit will be affected by how you do. A crisis is simply the point at which your underlying values are tested against realities beyond your control.

3. Some conclusions

Truly powerful republics and princes do not buy friendships with money but with ability and reputation.

Niccolò Machiavelli, 1532

The internet was created in the 1960s by the US Defense Department to enable the military to communicate internally during times of crisis. In 1964 Marshall McLuhan predicted that the information technologies would turn us into a global village. All forms of media were an extension of the human sense. McLuhan was right about many things but he did not predict the digital age because he probably did not know what the US military was doing with technology. We are still in the village, but digitization has made it a much more dangerous place. Dangerous because information can travel anywhere at any time and to anyone. It can do this because all digital information is expressed as configurations of 1s and 0s, or bits of information. These are the smallest element of the DNA of information. They know no boundaries, they have no loyalties, they recognize no nationalities. They can translate from voice to print to picture to sound.

There are two salient features of the digital age. First, digital data contain information about information: everything can be tracked, referenced, stored and found. Second, digital communications technologies allow many-to-many communication: message boards, chatrooms, emails, intranets, extranets, podcasts, web-logs. While publishing or broadcasting sends one message to many people, the internet is capable of carrying many messages to and from many people. Journalists should feel uneasy. They used to be at a point where access and information narrowed, a fast-flowing conduit between their subjects and their readers. Now many rivers of information flow between people.

Just as internet technology has removed the middle-man, so the journalist is in danger of extinction, or is at least in need of an evolutionary boost. Worldwide, the internet has linked consumers *directly* with producers, buyers with sellers, cappuccino-drinkers on Fifth Avenue with coffee farmers in Colombia; auto-workers in Germany with parts workers in the Philippines and distributors in Africa. While journalists still have exclusive sources, they do not necessarily have all the information they need to report properly (because they lack time and because there is so much more information to be had). Moreover, they face competition from the very people they are writing about because in the digital age we can all become our own broadcaster, write our own blog, set up our own website, issue our own news. *Everyone their own Boswell*, as Geoffrey Bowker says.[83] And, most seriously, even excellent journalists face challenges to their credibility. The philosophical version of their problem, to paraphrase Wittgenstein, runs like this: unless you have confidence in the ruler's reliability, if you use a ruler to measure a table you may also be using the table to measure the ruler.[84]

OK, some might wearily object, of course technology always brings political and commercial change. The printing press changed the political map of Europe in the seventeenth century; the railways changed the commercial standing of countries in the nineteenth; the fax machine and cable TV changed our perceptions of nationhood and warfare in eastern Europe. We make more phone calls on one day in 2004 than in all of 1984. So what? Well, in the digital age, business is different. Information moves faster, globally, unchecked. Stock markets and financial services were the first to go digital: money, information, risk are exchanged around the world in seconds, each and every second of every day.

The future depends upon a company's ability to render its products and services in a digital form. Status, standing, reputation, worth: all will be represented in digital form. The nation states of the digital age are its corporations, their ambassadors are its brands; and, like their precursors in the seventeenth century, they must be ahead of technology in order to survive. A company's results and global reputation may be in the hands of a news repurposer who has no knowledge, no interest and no stake in traditional news values.

With the exponential growth of news, the information atmosphere is becoming polluted, and there is more potential for errors of fact and substance than ever before: more noise, less signal. A news report – accurate or inaccurate – can now be filed, edited, shortened or lengthened by archive material and broadcast in any language worldwide. There is no right to reply. Ironically, the more global the event, the more parochial and limited the news agencies look and the more they struggle to fill their schedules. Cable, satellite and network TV in the USA currently provide between 2,700 and 3,000 programmes per day. The global TV philosophy of 'anything, anytime, anywhere' has already created a vacuum in TV, and the economics of TV production mean that documentaries, infotainment, rebranded and repurposed news, audience chat-shows and sector-specific news will dominate for the simple reason that these are cheap to produce. News organizations now use digital technology to plunder and recycle film archives, publishers' backlists, vaults of information in libraries or in newsgathering companies. We make information the way we used to make automobiles.

At the same time as opening up new sources of news content, the news media is mounting a technological assault on the consumer through the four routes into the home or office: cable (copper and fibre optic); phonelines; airwaves (satellite, radio, phone and network broadcast); and mailbox. It is an inevitable result of digital technology that the cable TV industry has entered relationships with IBM, Apple, DEC, HP and Microsoft. But how might all this be controlled, delivered, known about and charged for? Remember, the internet is unique in that it catalogues itself, and contains information about information.

And here is the key to the future: search. The last time in history we came face to face with something that met our capacity for wonder and knowledge was when we attempted to catalogue the great library at Alexandria. Now, we have Google. All media are now forms of search: a news website, a TV show giving links, a bookstore even; all are portals on to some other place. This used to be the role of the media. Not now, because we live in a search culture. The searched-for information on companies, organizations and individuals is now within the grasp of the searchers, ordinary people like you and me. A crisis is only the last place it feels like the old world, because it is the last place the relationships between principal and media are clear. But it is changing.

A Long Way from Watergate

Simon Walker

The weakening of professionalism among journalists and strengthening of competence within corporate communications is combining with financial regulation and the absence of any meaningful press regulatory regime to create a paradox: corporate PR is actually becoming more honest than retail journalism.

When I left Oxford thirty years ago, if any careers adviser had suggested working in public relations, my contemporaries and I would have rejected the idea with contempt. Fortunately no job counsellor attempted such lèse-majesté. We all went off cheerfully to be lawyers, bankers, civil servants, politicians or – as in my case – journalists.

Times change. The brightest children of my university friends now regularly ask for advice on how to get into corporate communications. Last year an unscientific but plausible survey of Oxbridge leavers put 'spin doctor' at the top of job aspirations.

The key to such a turnaround is power. We have Alastair Campbell to thank for much of this. The Prime Minister's press secretary was certainly perceived to have more clout than any politician, except his immediate boss, and power matters. The Hutton Inquiry made that painfully clear, with the once senior Cabinet position of Secretary of State for Defence reduced to a cipher whose main role was to fob off tiresome MPs. And obituaries for Mo Mowlam noted matter-of-factly that the former Northern Ireland Secretary had been reduced to pouring tea for President Clinton while the PM ran peace negotiations with his immediate advisers.

With that as a template for power, why would a politically active graduate, anxious to achieve change, slither slowly and patiently up the greasy pole as an MP when he could wield real influence rapidly as a press aide or special adviser?

The trade of journalism, especially business journalism, is suffering from a different version of the same assault. PR agencies and big companies regularly pluck out rising talent, leaving a yawning gap between business editors and inexperienced recruits. Even the *Financial Times* – where a senior common room atmosphere used to compensate for inadequate pay – is far from immune.

When I first moved into corporate PR, a former reporter who'd taken the same route warned me ruefully that my social status would plummet. As a journalist, he claimed, when you go to a cocktail party people typically look at you as the most important person in the room; when you become a corporate flak, you immediately become the least important.

Not any more. What's changed?

One reason is that today's newspaper journalism no longer beckons to idealistic graduates as the champion of truth and integrity. A news agency, like Reuters, does still champion its historic values. But the combination of celebrity reporting, set-ups, made-up quotes and pitiless paparazzi has prompted a general distaste for the media.

There are reasons for the increasingly tabloid approach of the British media. The press scene is intensely competitive, without the strong regional bases of US newspapers or the genteel and clubby continuity of the serious continental dailies. There are fewer reporters, less time and more space. This is dog-eat-dog. Economic pressures mean the demands on British journalists are far greater than they used to be. There is no money to pay for the degree of specialization seen in serious US newspapers, still less legions of fact-checkers.

Secondly, and crucially, companies have changed. They have come to appreciate that straightforward communication is one of their most valuable assets. Big companies to whom public profile matters (and that's most of them) have brought the PR function to the top table. And clever people are going into corporate communications departments.

Heads of communications departments routinely report to the chief executive, which amplifies effectiveness. Rather than Byzantine internal structures, corporate PR plans are rapidly assessed and, if endorsed, quickly implemented.

When British Airways executives met an hour after an Air France Concorde crashed over Paris, the image issues around its own Concorde operation were second only to actual safety concerns. Should BA suspend its Concorde service? What public impression would that create? How could the company reconcile continuing its Concorde flights with TV news and front-page photographs of the world's most advanced aircraft bursting into flames, causing 250 deaths? 'Perception is reality' the textbooks tell us, and it was public perception that drove corporate strategy and the company's management of that crisis.

Buckingham Palace's planning for the Queen's Golden Jubilee gave huge weight to the community's likely response to the event. Therefore, the question 'How will this be reported by the media?' was key to every aspect of the celebration. The royal household was understandably concerned about the precedent of the government-sponsored millennium celebrations two years earlier, when the public had reacted to being told 'You will enjoy this' by saying 'No, we bloody well won't.' The Jubilee promotional strategy was deliberately low-key and heavily regionalized, away from the cynicism of the London press corps. Information was made available with unprecedented openness: but it was given to the *Falmouth Packet* just as readily as to the *Sun* or the *Guardian*.

The Palace privately welcomed *The Times'* lead story six months out, headlined 'Apathy threatens Queen's Jubilee'. The resulting low expectations among the chattering classes helped make the delivery of a competently managed public celebration look positively spectacular.

Look what happens when strategy isn't set with robust proactive communications at its core. The principles of accountability now apply just as much to obscure investment groups and dull accountancy practices as to retailers and more visible public companies.

Shell, Sainsbury, Prudential and Jarvis are all case studies in poor communication with City, media and public opinion. I used to quote Amvescap, formerly the world's second-largest fund manager, as an example of a FTSE company that might not 'need' active corporate public relations – until Eliot Spitzer forced it to pay $450 million to settle charges of 'late trading' and 'market timing'. Arthur Andersen (particularly outside the US) collapsed not because of the Enron-related misdemeanours of a few senior figures, but because of its substantially inadequate reactive response to bad publicity.

Of course, PR is not a silver bullet that can magic away ethical or managerial failure, despite the fact that that is what some businesses would like and what many anti-business activists suggest. The image of public relations may historically have been associated with sleaziness, but its practice today is squeaky-clean in most reputable agencies and corporations.

The experience of the corporate PR practitioner is brutal. 'If it can come out, it will come out', especially if it's bad news, and crises are best salvaged through the recognition that factual honesty is the underpinning of all good corporate communication. If you have a pile of dung in your front hall, you must take the biggest shovel available and get it outside as rapidly as possible. It minimizes the damage, and gets over what is inevitable.

Whenever I have departed from this principle, I know I have made a mistake. My most public disaster at Buckingham Palace was attempting to stitch together a deal with the tabloid press which would limit their revelations of a taped conversation with the Countess of Wessex. With copies of the transcript in circulation, and rampant rumours based on half-heard saloon bar conversations, the 'deal' was doomed from day one. The drip-drip of new rumour and occasional revelation over a fortnight gave the story continued reporting legs which enabled it to run well beyond Alastair Campbell's stipulation that no story lasts more than nine days.

Of course, what we should have done was say 'publish and be damned'. The immediate firestorm would have been gruelling. But it would have closed the story down, and that is why putting out all the facts early is the best PR remedy.

A good example is from politics. Four years ago the Conservative MP (my friend and university contemporary) Julian Brazier killed a motorcyclist. It was an appalling tragedy, and one that could have happened to anyone. On holiday in Italy, he turned one morning on to the wrong side of the road and ran straight into a young man on a motorbike. He was devastated, but how did he respond? By going to the Italian police immediately. Then by calling a morning press conference in London, admitting fault and acknowledging that he would plead guilty in court and expressing his primary concern for the victim of a terrible accident. The incident made immediate headlines but properly faded from public consciousness: he had not been drunk or malevolent. Julian received a suspended sentence and (rightly) remains a respected constituency Member of Parliament. No 'spinning' was necessary or desirable.

Making difficult news public is the most basic PR function. When Reuters – a genuine pillar of integrity – unveiled an investment strategy involving a near 30 per cent reduction in consensus earnings estimates for the next year, it was obvious that the share price would take a hit. That's the basic way a normal market determines the value of a company. What was important in PR and IR terms was to reassure the market of the credibility of the company's belief that reduced short-term earnings would eventually be offset by medium-term growth.

When Sky had announced similar plans but provided little rationale on future earnings, its share price fell by 20 per cent. The Reuters share price fell around 8 per cent – well within internal expectations.

A principal concern of Reuters was to avoid media reporting that would oversimplify and so distort accurate understanding of our plans. For example, modest expansion plans into India and China are less technical and easier for a journalist (or reader) to understand than the development of risk management platforms. They are also sexier and tied into well-trodden globalization themes. I understand why a business reporter will devote ten paragraphs to buying into Indian TV stations for every line on algorithmic trading. As a journalist, I might – rather lazily – have covered it that way myself. But it would have been wrong for us to take the easy way out, and give a false impression of where the real money is.

Alfred Einstein told us everything should be made as simple as possible, but no simpler. The age of *Celebrity Big Brother* is inevitably the age of oversimplification.

Shortly after Jeff Randall became the BBC's business editor, he covered Philip Green's 'bid' (which never in fact became a bid) for Marks & Spencer. He was scheduled live on one of the BBC's explanatory interviews at 6 o'clock, and had prepared himself against every (largely technical) question – until the newsreader started the interview by asking: 'Jeff, what does this mean for shoppers?'

Randall was completely flummoxed. A Green takeover of M&S was important for the City, for the retail sector, for government and regulators. But for shoppers any consequence was remote and theoretical. Basing the story on the impact on Mrs Housewife was a wrong-headed simplification of the issue.

Of course television must be relevant to its viewers, but the feverish determination to prove direct connection sometimes distorts the truth. ITV has a different response: it simply does not cover business news. In an economic democracy that cannot be the right answer.

Some news/information cries out for simplification. I hate the fact that forward-looking Reuters strategy announcements have to be accompanied by fifty pages of legally mandated, utterly impenetrable IFRS statistics. The Enron whistle-blower, Sherron Watkins, said: 'The overriding principle of accounting is that if you explain the "accounting treatment" to a man in the street, would you influence his investing decisions?' I think the IFRS data would make his eyes glaze over. Little wonder journalists show no interest in wading through the statistical thickets.

The changes in professionalism in both businesses, and the external constraints on corporate communications (and absence of constraints on the press), have had an unpredictable effect. In the topsy-turvy world of today's journalism the *News of the World* won the 2004 Press Award for a kiss-and-tell story about football celebrity David Beckham, which it obtained by paying the Beckhams' nanny a very large sum of money. In less-democratic countries this sort of activity might be seen as a bribe. We've come a long way from Watergate.

With honourable exceptions, the lack of consequences within journalism often means corporate spokespeople end up being more reliable – perhaps even more honest – than those who report on them.

C. P. Scott, the iconic editor of the *Manchester Guardian*, held that 'opinion is free but facts are sacred'. The great American writer Walter Lippmann qualified this by saying: 'The facts have become so inordinately complicated that they are by no means self-evident ... fact-finding is inevitably an interpretation and there is no single and sacred version of the facts. The best reporters have not merely to note down what has happened. They have to explain how it happened.'

Up to a point, Lord Copper. Serious broadsheets now use opinion-led, interpretive reporting as a substitute for journalism of record. Every newspaper has a parliamentary sketchwriter but none of them feels obliged to report what MPs actually say in the House of Commons. And business journalists use that flexibility to pursue their own (or their newspaper's) hobby horses at the expense of covering news. No wonder bloggers, who have even less accountability in reporting fact, are drawing ever larger audiences.

We have all witnessed the relish and sanctimony with which so-called business reporters have covered 'corporate fat-cat' stories ever since a thirty-five-year veteran of British Gas named Cedric Brown was driven from his CEO job by a press posse which lapped up a well-planned publicity stunt to unseat him over his relatively modest salary.

The same tactic of mock indignation is used in reporting MPs' salaries. To the average newspaper reader earning £400 a week, a salary of £59,000 a year is substantial. Middle-brow columnists (who reliably earn much more than £59,000) will always be able to tut-tut any pay hike, without allowing practical considerations to intervene. Like sending a journalist into an airport or Buckingham Palace with a toy gun, it is the sort of story that can be guaranteed to provide a couple of pages twice a year.

The former *FT* editor Richard Lambert has written of how 'an intelligent examination of business starts to become a crucial component of democratic choice'. The key word is 'intelligent'. Much business coverage these days owes more to *Celebrity Big Brother* than to the tradition of hard grind City reporting.

The *Guardian*'s business pages have devoted more attention to the Reuters CEO's terms and conditions than to the investment programme he has implemented, which has quadrupled the company's share price. Of course, it's much easier to understand than corporate strategy. Some readers will be stirred up without needing to know background details, so the reporter's story generates more column inches without more light. Such lazy pseudo-journalism crowds out proper analysis. It is a temptation to be resisted.

Some CEOs are indeed overpaid. A case in point was Tyco's Denis Kozlowski. No doubt his purchase of a $6,000 umbrella stand or the party where a mock-up Manniken Pis peed vodka into guests' glasses added a splash of colour to otherwise dull reporting. But the primary focus should have been the analysis of corporate disintegration which cost thousands of pensioners their savings and earned Kozlowski his eight to twenty-five year prison sentence.

Fraud, fat-cattery and executive compensation issues will always stir the British press but journalists would do well to focus equally on issues of business incompetence as well as on occasional instances of venality. Where government declines to investigate corporate failings, it has been a traditional role of the fourth estate to expose them. Sadly, such painstaking investigations now go routinely into the 'too hard (or too expensive) basket'.

In early 2004 (post-Enron, post-Worldcom) the US shareholder activist Robert Monks asked a group of British fund managers, with some degree of irony, 'what had they learned from the Marconi hearings?'

Of course, there had been no hearings into Marconi, or Railtrack or many other companies which cost British pensioners billions. But Railtrack's scandals were officially generated and hardly likely to induce government-sponsored inquiries from a secretary of state who acknowledged lying to

Parliament in explaining them. As for Marconi, the *Financial Times*' John Plender noted almost in passing the 'dismal omission' of any inquiry into 'the most impressive feat of value destruction in British corporate history'.

Much of the media is infinitely distractable. When I worked for British Airways (as opposed to when I worked at Buckingham Palace!), senior management was almost sanguine about sex scandals, whatever we may have said at the time. Four pages of topless Tina, sometime stewardess, would entertain readers without having a negative effect on either the share price or, we suspected, ticket sales.

I believe in capitalism. I also believe in freedom of speech – not just for those articulating fashionable causes, but for companies outlining corporate strategy or justifying unfashionable but clearly democratically desired production plans.

Corporate PR has to be more accurate than journalism. The rules are old ones. Behave honourably. Tell the truth. Be realistic. Don't do deals with bandits. Relationships matter so act for the long term. Of course you can deceive any reporter once. But he or she will never believe you again.

Good journalism really matters, and will be revivified if it becomes more accountable. But I enthuse when the children of my friends look to become spin doctors. They won't make as much money as bankers and lawyers, but they have the potential to enjoy much more varied careers with a role that is critical to their communities. I loved being a reporter, but I followed Lord Northcliffe's advice by 'leaving journalism in time'. May they have such luck.

The New Media and Trust

Derek Wyatt MP

....

There is no religion higher than truth.
Mahatma Gandhi

....

I watched the 1992 general election results on television. The key seat if Labour was to win was Basildon. If we won it, Neil Kinnock would be Prime Minister. We lost it. At that moment I turned to my wife and said, 'I'm going to stand in the next election.' She replied, 'You'll feel a lot better in the morning.' In 1992 I was one of the rare viewers who had chosen to watch the results on Sky News. This was part of a new multi-channel satellite subscription service from the Murdoch empire. Sky News was a twenty-four-hour always-on news channel. It wasn't the first such channel – a billboard company in Atlanta had been metamorphosed by its owner, Ted Turner, into a twenty-four-hour news service called Cable News Network (CNN to you and me). But in the fierce channel environment of 1992 there were only two providers of news – BBC and ITN. They couldn't have been more different. The Beeb was stuffy and arrogant; ITN was serious but lively. The Beeb tried to position itself as the old *Times* while ITN owed more to the late *Express* and the reinvigorated *Mail*. I doubt if either of them took Sky News very seriously in 1992. After all, Sky had sold fewer than 200,000 subscriptions that year.

Sky and CNN were products of the 1990s, when the stock markets of the world moved gradually to a 24/7 environment, making it easier for capitalism to flow unheeded. At about the same time, Tim Berners-Lee was putting the finishing touches to his worldwide web pilots at the CERN laboratory. In the spirit of the early computer clubs in the Bay Area of San Francisco which spawned Steve Wozniak and Steve Jobs, he released his suggestions free of charge into cyberspace, and the internet for Joe Public was born.

These developments were a pretty rich cocktail. They were compounded by a third, twenty-four-hour news channel. We could now watch communities being bombed in Iraq or Afghanistan or the Balkans while at the same time we could be bombarded with emails from those citizens being bombed to tell us how much they loathed what we were doing. For most of the twentieth century, receiving news was a passive activity. People had no choice over its content, nor, with broadcaast news, over the time at which it was available to them. But in the 1990s, news became a two-way street. Today, 3G mobile digital cameras make it possible for us to see, through podcasts and websites, iNews (individual news) as opposed to oNews (our news). Trust has moved on.

Indeed, as media became a 24/7 activity, so too did trust. Whatever the UK does, we can see an alternative view. Until Al Jazeera, the only news about the Middle East conflict between Palestine and Israel used to come from Israeli cameras backed up by Western sources; that is no longer the case. Al Jazeera itself has shown terrorist scenes that some Muslim countries have found hard to stomach. It has also seen its offices bombed – some claim deliberately – by US forces. The proliferation and instant availability of alternative views on any event have had profound implications for conventional media and for all governments and political institutions. None of them can guarantee to persuade people to accept their interpretation of events – or even to accept that reported events actually happened. In short they cannot guarantee trust.

I was able to witness early case studies of the loss of trust and authority by government during the 1980s and 1990s when I worked in the media as a freelance journalist at the *Observer* and *The Times*, in publishing with Allen and Unwin, William Heinemann, Octopus and Virgin, in the independent television sector and with the big boys and girls at Flextech and Sky. At William Heinemann I was a board director when we published a rather dull and innocuous book called *Spycatcher*, and I was at the meetings with our chairman, Paul Hamlyn, when he was offered first a knighthood and then a peerage if he'd pull the book. This was my first brush with Mrs Thatcher, who was then in her East Ham phase, just one stop short of Barking. Paul refused to budge and because she feared the worst he was then asked to name his price. He asked if his wife could be made a duchess. We published. Without Mrs Thatcher it had a 3,000 print run. With Mrs Thatcher it sold 3 million.

The *Spycatcher* case in Sydney, for which we were brilliantly advised in the UK by David Hooper and in Australia by Malcolm Turnbull, was my first realization that Thatcher had more than fulfilled Lord Acton's homily that power corrupts – absolute power corrupts absolutely.

She was at the zenith of the control over her Cabinet just before the 1987 elections. As she fell, the machine that she had created went into freefall – Harrods, with Neil Hamilton as the Widow Twankey, became the new Christmas pantomime; Tory MPs accepted cash for questions; the late lamented Robin Cook brilliantly skewered the Tories over the Scott Report on Arms to Iraq. By this time I had ignored my wife's wisdom on election night 1992. I had gone in search of a seat and duly won the nomination to Sittingbourne and Sheppy in north Kent. It was a safe Tory seat with a 16,000 plus majority. I thought I would learn the ropes in 1997 and then find a winnable seat in the election after that. Instead the cumulative collapse of authority in John Major's government pole-vaulted me into parliament with a majority of 3,501. No one could have been more surprised. It proved that the public had completely lost faith in John Major.

There were so many new MPs in 1997, and so many unexpected ones, that unless you were already in the Blair– Brown–Prescott axis you remained outside both the government and the party at large. It gave a new meaning to the phrase 'brass ceiling'.

If the Prime Minister was accused of walking on water in those heady days of 1997, we 'ordinaries' floated like butterflies as we started our grubby life holding the executive to account. One of these 'accounts' was David Clark's outstanding Freedom of Information Bill. By the time it won the Queen's approval it had been mauled by the Home Office and else-where and been reduced to a thin gruel. It was such a disap-pointment. It was as if the government was still in opposition; still in denial. *Trust was the casualty.*

Meanwhile, as New Labour struggled to impose its agenda on the British People, new media for receiving news and views continued to proliferate and serve more and more people across the world, breeding ever greater challenges to authority. Against this background, two events in America changed first the European, and then the Muslim, view of itself, the reper-cussions of which are still being felt and which to my mind have seriously destabilized 'trust' and brought out the lack of independence and integrity in the old media.

If you believe President Bush, America stands for liberty, freedom and democracy. That cuts little ice in Europe, the Middle East and China. A trust chasm has developed between America's Republican political elite, its own people and the rest of the world. The reasons are twofold. The first is the fact that Vice President Al Gore won the general election in 2000 but had the decision overruled by the US Supreme Court whose judges are political appointees. Naturally, the Republican appointees outvoted their Democratic counterparts; the second was 9/11.

After 9/11, our global response in the West has been pretty feeble. The four organizations that pretend to be world bodies – UNO, the World Bank, the IMF and the World Trade Organization – are there to represent the major powers and are controlled as such. They are not global and three of them reside in America. Thus, for me, the nature of media and trust and new media and trust has to be globalized. Before we can reach a new understanding of the relationship, the old Second World War bodies have to go or they all have to be refashioned to better represent the world, not the Western perspective of it.

The current rules of engagement reinforce America's hegemony. They remind me of Palmerston's nineteenth-century 'gunboat diplomacy'. Gunboats can win obedience but not trust.

Fourteen years since I watched the 1992 election, and after eight years of life as an obscure backbench MP, I look at a vibrant new media scene, matched by a stagnant political scene, dominated by apathy and mistrust. From its small beginnings, Sky News regularly wins the annual Baftas for news coverage and now over eight million homes have it as one of the 400 or so channels on offer. But Sky News has rivals too. Bloomberg, Fox, BBC 24, ITV News, Euronews (and Al Jazeera) have all subsequently rolled out twenty-four-hour news channels. And these channels came into their own especially at the time of the mortar attack on Downing Street (CNN), Princess Diana's death (Sky), 9/11 (Sky and CNN), the Iraqi war (Sky, BBC and ITN), the tsunami (CNN and Sky), the tube bombings (Sky and ITV) and, more recently, the hurricanes in America (blanket coverage). And when there's good news like England winning the Rugby World Cup or the Ashes, the news channels have given us the best coverage. This accessibility has had a serious impact on how the BBC produces news, on BBC1 and BBC2, and on ITV (ITN having been rebranded). Nonetheless, in terms of a trust marque, all the news on UK television (except Fox) is regularly worthy of high fives even if their production values vary.

This accolade could not be awarded to many of our national newspapers; they have been caught by the twin pincers of twenty-four-hour news channels and of the internet and digital photography. Into this mix has come a brand of magazines on a continuum – beginning with *Hello!* and ending with *Nuts*.

The only way newspapers can compete is by becoming more intrusive, creating more 'exclusives', buying rights to more 'exposé' books, linking more into the 'personality' of a new genre of twenty-four-hour entertainment programmes which began with *Blind Date* and moved on to *Big Brother*, *I'm a Celebrity*, *Wife Swap* et al, copying more of Sky's coverage of sport, especially soccer, and moving into lifestyle guides. This development has been exacerbated since 1992 with the demise and distrust of John Major's government and after 1997 because Tony Blair and his Cabinet ruled with impunity. The trust vacuum that this has created has been filled by the Tory papers (the *Telegraph* and the *Mail*) as well as by the *Indy* and the *Guardian*. The *Mail* has become, to all intents and purposes, the Leader of the Opposition; it could well be retitled 'The Fox News–Sky TV' compact. Year on year, but for tiny swings here and there, every national newspaper's circulation is falling and the move of the broadsheets to compact or Berliner size may have been their last throw of the dice. How they respond to Gordon Brown as Prime Minister and David Cameron as Leader of the Opposition will be fascinating.

Perhaps, because I have seen how my own diddly life story as a low-lying MP has been misreported since 1997, I no longer trust what I read in the newspapers, especially on Sundays, when editors strain the meaning of the term 'exclusive'. By the following week, these exclusives have long been forgotten. On the other hand, maybe because I do not have to think as hard, I find myself watching news on television. It's not just the way the stories are reported; it's because I trust Jon Snow (Channel 4) and that trust ensures my viewing loyalty.

Into this mix has come the term globalization, a phenomenon which was greatly advanced in 1991 when CNN covered the first Iraq war. This was a pivotal time for the media and trust. To be able to film the war, CNN had to agree to be embedded with the American generals. This stretched the nature of independent news provision but it brought war directly to our comfortable living rooms in the West and spurred News International to reinvest in Sky News and eventually other news services on the emerging Fox and Star platforms. It was the same in 2003, when in the second Iraq war all correspondents were once again embedded.

My guess is that the second Iraq war will bring back a Tory government faster than anyone could have anticipated. Labour's third-term victory was hardly that; it was to a large extent a vote against the Prime Minister and the way in which the information we were all given took us to war. Over fifty Labour MPs have majorities of under a thousand with three of us in double figures (mine, since you ask, is seventy-nine).

The most unsettling aspect of media and trust has been the way in which the second Iraq war was called. Trust was the only issue. Going to war is the hardest decision any politician has to take. And in trying to decide how to vote, I went to a Noam Chomsky lecture and another by Hans Blix. I read as much as I could (aside from Michael Moore's epistles) and noted the hundred or so marches across America that went largely unreported there. I know that because I joined the tail end of one in San Francisco where 100,000 turned out, but it was hardly mentioned in the media. In the end it seemed to me that we had promised a second resolution at the UNO and that there were no weapons of mass destruction. As a result, I twice voted against my own government's decision on going to war.

The Prime Minister genuinely took a different view and he had all the information to hand. He was persuaded by the evidence, I was not. But, life is never as black and white as that. Robin Cook, whose death will be mourned for years, said:

> The reality is that Britain is being asked to embark on a war without agreement in any of the international bodies of which we are a leading partner – not NATO, not the European Union and, now, not the Security Council.
>
> To end up in such diplomatic weakness is a serious reverse.
>
> Only a year ago, we and the United States were part of a coalition against terrorism that was wider and more diverse than I would ever have imagined possible. History will be astonished at the diplomatic miscalculations that led so quickly to the disintegration of that powerful coalition.

Whatever view one takes about the merits of the Iraq war there is no question that events since have dramatically accelerated mistrust of Western governments, by their own people and across the world. New media can claim much or the responsibility for this, particularily Al-Jazeera, because they led mainstream media in presenting a counter-narrative to that offered by Western governments. In the end, this counter-narrative proved more accurate and attracted more trust than the "official" version: Saddam was not an urgent military threat, the occupation of Iraq was incompetent, brutal and detested, the insurgency was spreading, not shrinking. All these once dissident views have crossed into the mainstream of public and even official opinion and unsurprisingly people have turned against the leaders who took them into Iraq on premises which have since proved to be false, and who refuse to acknowledge this.

We talk the talk about globalization. Global companies such

as BP, Gap, Levi's, Sony, Coca-Cola and Nike spend time think-ing about the worth of their brand and by association which other brands they admire and with whom they would like to be associated. Political parties (except the international socialist movement) do not; nor do their governments. Yet in this trust game, one bad trust call, such as Iraq, poisons for a time your own well too. I'm not sure politicians have understood the impact of the globalization of twenty-four-hour news channels and that 'trust' has also gone global. Voters have.

And introducing a new element of a brand, as in 'New Labour' as opposed to 'Labour', has been fraught with difficul-ty. More and more people distrust 'New Labour' and as a con-sequence the original brand, 'Labour', becomes damaged too.

In the end it is the 'disconnect' that worries me most. I no longer feel that Parliament is the only place to change the world. You can change the world just as much, if not more, out-side the febrile world of politics. The Labour government betwJeen May 1997 and May 2005 had a massive majority in the House of Commons; it frittered it away. Its spin of the daily news, good and bad, took its toll both on the Prime Minister's inner circle and in the media. This disconnect was then fed through to the population at large (as if they hadn't spotted it already).

Opposition MPs cannot do much except turn up and vote against anything and everything the government throws at them; they can sometimes find a life in a select committee but membership of these is decided by the Whips and few of the twenty or so committees actually have much effect on govern-ment. Backbench MPs are just fodder for the Whips office. It is a great credit to so many of them that they have voted against their own government but the net result has been that the gov-ernment has usually had its way because of its large majority. This will not be the case in this Parliament as our majority has been reduced, such that fifty or so Labour MPs voting against the government could result in its losing a vote, as happened on ninety days (Terror Act). Health and Education beckon.

In the nine years I have been an MP, I have learned that there are two sides to the notion of 'truth'. One is *perceived truth* and one is the *actual truth*. Many people hold the perceived truth that the MMR vaccine causes autism: quite untrue. Even more people hold the perceived truth that genetically modified food is intrinsically dangerous to mankind: not true, or certainly not justified. These beliefs are now deep-seated, and their proponents do not believe anyone who tells them the contrary, not experts or scientists and certainly not their governments. The reasons why these differences between perceived and actual truth occur is largely due to the way that we, as politicians, put messages into the public domain and then the way in which the media reinterpret these messages to the punter.

If the politicians have not lined up the 'right' decision for an issue with the 'right political' decision (the left and the right hand) then they can experience a torrid time – as has happened with the Licensing Act, the Casino element in the Gambling Act, the Primary Care Trust boundary changes et al.

David Cameron's appeal is that he has been a breath of fresh air for an outdated and disconnected Tory Party: that was Blair's appeal back in 1994. Can the Labour government be reinvigorated by Gordon Brown's 'trustworthiness'? The polls suggest it can. It therefore follows that the longer the delay in the handover period, the greater the damage to the trusted brand. The one certain thing is that whenever Brown inherits – or perhaps Cameron after him – he will find more and more electors using the media to access the news they choose and not necessarily the news he wants them to receive.

Notes

1 Institute of Public Relations paper, 1970. Cited in Jacquie L'Etang, *Public Relations in Britain: A History of Professional Practice in the 20th Century*, Lawrence Erlbaum, 2004.

2 Andrew Marr, *My Trade: A Short History of British Journalism*, Macmillan, 2004.

3 Private correspondence, Niccolò Machiavelli, 1499, quoted in Phil Harris, Andrew Lock, Patricia Rees (eds.), *Machiavelli, Marketing and Management*, Routledge, 2000.

4 A Public Relations Consultants' Association report in 1998 estimated that up to 80 per cent of financial news and 40–50 per cent of general news is directly influenced by PR. As reported by *The Times*, 10 April 1998.

5 *The Anatomy of Britain*, Hodder & Stoughton, 1962.

6 The title of a classic text on public relations by Scott M. Cutlip, *The Unseen Power: Public Relations, a History*, Lawrence Erlbaum, 1994.

7 Philip L. Graham, publisher of the *Washington Post*, in an address to his staff, recalled on his death, 3 August 1963.

8 *Sunday Times*, May 2003.

9 Professor Steven Barnet's inaugural lecture, University of Westminster, 27 November 2002.

10 Roy Greenslade, *Press Gang: How Newspapers Make Profits from Propaganda*, Macmillan, 2003.

11 Neill committee, 2002.

12 Andrew Marr, *My Trade: A Short History of British Journalism*, Pan, 2005.

13 John Stauber and Sheldon Rampton, *Toxic Sludge is Good for You: Lies, Damn Lies and the Public Relations Industry*, Constable and Robinson, 2004.

14 BBC4's *The Thick of It*, 20 October 2005, written by Armando Iannucci.

NOTES

NOTES

15 Maureen O'Dowd, *New York Times*, 22 October 2005

16 Marshall McLuhan, *Understanding Media: The Extensions of Man*, Routledge, 1995 (first published 1964).

17 Robert Jackall & Janice M. Hirota, *Image Makers: Advertising, Public Relations and the Ethos of Advocacy*, University of Chicago Press, 2000.

18 Malcolm Gladwell, *The Tipping Point: How Little Things Can Make a Big Difference*, Little, Brown, 2000.

19 Lance Price, *The Spin Doctor's Diary*, Hodder & Stoughton, 2005.

20 Quoted in the documentary *Why We Fight*, directed by Eugene Jarecki, 2005.

21 Author's interview with Hassan Ibrahim, 2004.

22 Carne Ross, 'War Stories', *FT Magazine*, 1 February 2005.

23 In November 2001, 69 per cent of those polled said the press 'stood up for America', and only 17 per cent found it too critical. 60 per cent said the press did a good job of protecting democracy. Now 67 per cent believe coverage is too critical, and only 47 per cent think it protects democracy (Pew Research Center for the People and the Press, quoted in *International Herald Tribune*, 27 June 2005. No public outcry (and few expressions of admiration) followed the decision of the *New York Times* reporter Judith Miller to go to prison rather than reveal her source in an investigation of a national security leak within the administration, in relation to which she hadn't even written a story.

24 Walter Lippmann, *Public Opinion*, Free Press, 1965 (first published 1922).

25 Print journalists, in Britain at least, tend to believe themselves immune to economic laws; they tend to despise television, believing it to consist of showbiz and self-importance. A cause of the press's dislike of New Labour was the latter's connections with posh TV folk like John Birt and Greg Dyke. Peter Mandelson was once employed by Birt, and his pretensions to govern with the assistance of television were widely resented. On the other hand, journalists found equal reason to dislike Alastair Campbell, who had started his career as a tabloid journalist.

26 Marshall McLuhan, *Understanding Media: The Extensions of Man*, Routledge, 1995 (first published 1964).

27 John Dunn, *Setting the People Free: The Story of Democracy*, Atlantic, 2005.

28 Edward S. Herman and Noam Chomsky, *Manufacturing Consent*, Vintage, 1994.

29 Author's interview.

30 George Orwell, 'As I please', *Tribune*, 7 April 1944, in *The Selected Essays*, Everyman, 2002.

31 R. Pearson, 'Business ethics as communication ethics: public relations practice and the idea of dialogue', in C. H. Botan and V. Hazelton (eds), *Public Relations Theory*, Lawrence Erlbaum, 1989.

32 R. L. Heath, 'Shifting foundations: public relations as relationship building', in *Handbook of Public Relations*, R. L. Heath (ed.), Sage, 2001.

33 M. Josephson, 'Teaching ethical decision making and principled reasoning', *Business Ethics*, Annual edition 1993, Daskin Publishing Group, 1995.

34 P. Parsons, *Ethics in Public Relations*, Kogan Page, 2004.

35 R. B. Potter, 'The Origins and Applications of "Potter Boxes"', paper presented to the 'State of the World Forum', San Francisco, 1999.

36 R. R. Sims, 'The challenge of ethical behaviour in organizations', *Journal of Business Ethics*, 1992.

37 *Sunday Mirror* editorial, 8 January 2006.

38 Margaret Atwood, *The Handmaid's Tale*, McClelland and Stewart, 1985.

39 Echo Research for Editorial Intelligence, November 2005.

40 Quoted in Andy Hobsbawm, '10 Years On: The Internet a Decade after Mosaic', AGENCY.COM, 2003.

41 Hobsbawm, '10 Years On'.

42 David Michie, *The Invisible Persuaders: How Britain's Spin Doctors Manipulate the Media*, Bantam Press, 1998.

43 *Sunday Times* News Review, 8 January 2006.

44 www.wikipedia.org

45 UCAS Lists 2006.

46 Edward L. Bernays, *Crystallizing Public Opinion*, Liveright, 1961.

47 Standard industry definition of Public Relations.

48 First coined by my PR firm, Hobsbawm Macaulay Communications, founded in 1993.

49 Opinion Leader Research interviewed 100 'influencers' drawn from politics, the media, the city, business, NGOs, think tanks and

academia between 25–29 July 2005.

50 Opinion Leader Research conducted telephone interviews with 104 opinion leaders in September 2002.

51 YouGov polls with the general public, February & March 2003.

52 Opinion Leader Research conducted telephone interviews with 104 opinion leaders in September 2002.

53 Opinion Leader Research survey with 100 senior and mid-level figures from the communications and marketing sector, May 2004.

54 Opinion Leader Research carried out a quantitative study with the general public for Sir Bob Phillis' review of Government Communications in 2003.

55 Public perceptions and patient experience of the NHS, 2005.

56 Opinion Leader Research studies, conducted October 2002. Base of 104 opinion leaders, 1001 members of the general public.

57 The Office of National Statistics Social Trends Report, 2003.

58 94% of opinion leaders agreed with this statement in a survey conducted October 2002.

59 Opinion Leader Research conducted a quantitative survey with 100 senior and mid-level figures from the communications sector in March 2004.

60 KPMG survey of the 250 top companies in the Fortune 500 and 100 biggest companies in 16 countries, June 2005.

61 Opinion Leader Research conducted telephone interviews with 104 opinion leaders in September 2002.

62 Opinion Leader Research commissioned a telephone poll of 1001 members of the general public, October 2002.

63 Madeleine Bunting, 'The Last Taboo', *Guardian*, 5 July 2004.

64 Quoted in the press pack for 'Rethinking Crime and Punishment', an initiative of the Esme Fairbairn Trust, 2004.

65 *Independent*, 24 April 2004.

66 'PR Week Ethics Survey', *PR Week* US, 1 May 2000.

67 'PR Week/Countrywide Porter Novelli CEO Survey', *PR Week* UK, 8 September 2000.

68 In both instances, the US ambassador took an active position in pushing the American firm's interests; in at least one instance, the ambassador was rewarded with a seat on the board, after he left public service. See J. E. Stiglitz, *The Roaring Nineties: Why We're Paying the Price for the Greediest Decade in History*, Penguin, 2004.

69 For a broader discussion of the issues raised here, see

Roumeen Islam, *The Right to Tell: The Role of Mass Media in Economic Development*, The US World Bank, 2003.

70 J. E. Stiglitz, 'Development as Transformation', in J. E. Stiglitz and Ha-Joon Chang (eds), *Joseph Stiglitz and the World Bank: The Rebel Within*, Anthem Press, 2002.

71 A. de Tocqueville, *Democracy in America*, vol. 2, ed. P. Bradley, Vintage, 1995.

72 Robert Park, *The Natural History of the Newspaper*, 1925.

73 Off the city of Cadiz, 9 October 1805.

74 I have used this approach in highly public internet investment cases in the US, in large civil actions in the US, and in government scandal in Poland.

75 I am grateful to Charles Handy for this insight.

76 I appreciate, also, the sceptical qualities of Descartes in this regard.

77 See James Surowieki, *The Wisdom of Crowds*, Doubleday, 2004.

78 The best modern discussion of this is in N. N. Taleb, 'Chapter 7', in *Fooled by Randomness: The Hidden Role of Chance in Life and in the Markets*, Texere, 2004. This excellent book is a source of thinking on asymmetry and on the problems of reasoning by induction.

79 Guicciardini is interesting for being the exact opposite of Machiavelli in his belief that men are essentially good. The two face each other from opposite piazzas in Florence.

80 See Malcolm Gladwell, *Blink: The Power of Thinking without Thinking*, New York, Little, Brown, 2005.

81 That said, TV news is still relatively cheap to produce (around $500,000 an hour, while *Seinfeld* or *Friends* used to cost $1.5 million an hour).

82 See *FT Weekend*, 22 October 2005.

83 Department of Communication, University of California, San Diego.

84 See also Taleb, *Fooled by Randomness*, introduction to part III.

List of Contributors

Emily Bell has worked for the *Observer* and the *Guardian* for the past 15 years, setting up mediaguardian.co.uk in 2000 and becoming editor-in-chief of *Guardian Unlimited* in 2001. *Guardian Unlimited* has won multiple awards, including the prestigious Webby in 2005 for Best Newspaper on the World Wide Web. Bell writes a regular column for the *Guardian* about media policy issues and for *Broadcast* magazine.

Sarah Benton has been a journalist and a lecturer in journalism.

Mark Borkowski is a publicist and founder of Borkowski PR, a central London PR agency. Clients and brands which have benefited from the Borkowski treatment include Action Man, Gordon's Gin, the Bolshoi Ballet, Vodafone, Selfridges, Sir Cliff Richard and Mikhail Gorbachev. He is also a writer and contributes to a wide variety of TV and radio programmes.

Colin Byrne is CEO of Weber Shandwick, the UK's largest PR consultancy network. His PR career has included work with the Automobile Association, the National Union of Students, the Inner London Education Authority, the Labour Party, the Prince's Trust, the National Farmers' Union and ten years as a PR and public affairs consultant.

Michael Cockerell is an award-winning political documentary maker and reporter. He is author of *Sources Close to the Prime Minister* and *Live from Number Ten – The Inside Story of Prime Ministers and Television*.

Leonard Doyle is foreign editor of the *Independent*.

Kim Fletcher has worked on Fleet Street since 1981, in journalism and in management. He has been deputy editor of the *Sunday Telegraph*, editor of the *Independent on Sunday* and editorial director of Telegraph Group Ltd. He is now a business consultant. Fletcher is chairman of the National Council for the Training of Journalists, writes a fortnightly column for the *Guardian* and is author of *The Journalist's Handbook*.

Nick Fraser is editor of Storyville, BBC TV's acclaimed series of world documentaries. He is the author of four non-fiction books, including *The Voice of Modern Hatred*, a study of race hate and anti-Europeanism. He has written for many British publications, and he is a contributing editor to *Harper's Magazine*, New York. *The Importance of Being Eton*, which he describes as 'a study of privilege and the workings of English elite society' is published in 2007 by Short Books.

Janine di Giovanni is a writer for *The Times* and *Vanity Fair*. She has reported on war and conflict for nearly fifteen years, and is also the author of four books including *The Place at the End of the World: Stories from the Frontline*. She has won two Amnesty International Awards, Granada TV's Foreign Correspondent of the Year and the National Magazine Award in America. She has been the feature of two documentaries on women war reporters.

Anne Gregory is the UK's only full-time professor of Public Relations and director of the Centre for Public Relations Studies at Leeds Metropolitan University. She has a background in consultancy and in-house public relations and was President of the Chartered Institute of Public Relations in 2004. She works extensively with public and private sector clients as well as researching contemporary issues in public relations.

Julian Henry worked as a music journalist prior to working in public relations. After ten years with Lynne Franks he started his own company, Henry's House, one of the most highly regarded communications agencies in the UK. He is also a director of the ICA and writes for the *Guardian* on marketing and media.

Julia Hobsbawm is a pioneer of 'integrity PR' and Britain's first professor of Public Relations at the London College of Communication. She founded and now runs Editorial Intelligence, the first networking organization for people in PR and journalism, which monitors and analyses the worlds of comment and opinion. She is a trustee of the Prince of Wales' charity In Kind Direct, and is a Vice President of the Hay Festival for Literature and of the Facial Surgery Research Foundation.

Simon Jenkins is a journalist, author and broadcaster. He writes a column twice weekly for the *Guardian* and weekly for the *Sunday Times*, as well as broadcasting for the BBC, and is former editor of *The Times* and the *London Evening Standard*. His career began on *Country Life* magazine and continued on *The Times Educational Supplement*, the *Economist* (political editor) and the *Sunday Times* (books editor). His books include works on London architecture, the press and politics and, more recently, *England's Thousand Best Churches* (1999) and *England's Thousand Best Houses* (2003).

John Lloyd is the contributing editor of the *Financial Times*, where he has also been Labour editor, Industrial editor, East Europe editor and Moscow bureau chief. He is the founder and editor of the *Financial Times Magazine*. He has also worked as the editor of *Time Out* and the *New Statesman*, as well as being a reporter and producer on LWT and *Weekend World*. Lloyd is on the board for *Prospect* magazine and the Moscow School of Political Studies and is the author of *Loss without Limit: The British Miners' Strike* (1985), *Rebirth of a Nation; an Anatomy of Russia* (1998); and *What the Media are Doing to Our Politics* (2004).

Deborah Mattinson, joint CEO of Opinion Leader Research, is one of Britain's leading practitioners of issue-based research and consultation. She has unparalleled expertise in accessing and understanding public opinion, in stakeholder dialogue and in citizen engagement. She writes and broadcasts widely on public opinion. She is a Commissioner of the Equal Opportunities Commission and a Trustee of the Green Alliance.

Baroness Julia Neuberger was educated at Newnham College, Cambridge, and Leo Baeck College, London. She became a rabbi in 1977 and then a fellow of the King's Fund Institute and later the Harvard Medical School. She has been a member of the General Medical Council, the Medical Research Council, the Committee on Standards in Public Life, the Board of Visitors of Memorial Church and a trustee of the Runnymede Trust. She holds honorary doctorates from thirteen universities, is an honorary fellow of Mansfield College, Oxford, the Royal College of Physicians and the Royal College of General Practitioners and was Chancellor of the University of Ulster from 1994–2000. She is currently a trustee of the Imperial War Museum and the British Council, as well as of the Booker Prize Foundation. She is also the author of several books including *The Moral State We're In* (2005). She was created a Life Peer in June 2004.

Kate Nicholas is associate publisher and former editor-in-chief of *PRWeek*, the leading weekly title for the public relations industry. Nicholas worked in PR in London and Sydney before embarking on a career as a freelance business journalist, writing for titles such as *Business Age* and *Marketing*. She joined *PRWeek* as features editor in 1996 and became editor in 1998, relaunching the magazine in 2004. She also regularly speaks at, and chairs, international conferences and is a high profile media commentator on PR, reputation management and CSR. She writes a weekly column for *PRWeek* and has written on issues relating to reputation, PR and CSR for titles such as the *Independent, Observer* and *Business Life.*

Peter Oborne is political editor of the *Spectator.* His most recent book, *The Rise of Political Lying*, was published by Simon and Schuster in 2005.

Anya Schiffrin is co-editor of *Covering Globalization: A Handbook for Reporters* and co-director of the media programme at Columbia University's School of International and Public Affairs. For more information, please see www.journalismtraining.net.

Jean Seaton is professor of media history at the University of Westminster. Her most recent book is *Carnage and the Media: The Making and Breaking of Violent News*, published by Penguin in 2005. She is writing the official history of the BBC in the 1980s which is funded by a grant from the Arts and Humanities Research Council.

Alice Sherwood is a writer and producer. Following degrees in Philosophy and Chemistry at Bristol University, she worked for Anderson consulting before taking an MBA at INSEAD. After a period in venture capital, she became a televison producer and then a multimedia producer, most recently for the BBC and London Gifted and Talented.

Andrew St George advises individuals in commerce, government, the media and the military. He has written twelve books on a range of subjects from linguistics and social history to business issues and leadership. He was educated at Cambridge, Harvard and Oxford, and advises three UK business schools.

Simon Walker is director of communications for Reuters. Prior to that he was communications secretary at Buckingham Palace and director of corporate affairs for British Airways.

Derek Wyatt MP was first elected to the House of Commons for the new constituency of Sittingbourne and Sheppey in north Kent in May 1997 and was re-elected in June 2001 and again in May 2005. Before being elected as an MP he was director of the Computer Channel at BSkyB and travelled extensively throughout America to research the internet and to assess its impact. On arriving at Westminster he formed the All Party Internet Group of which he is the chairman.

Index

INDEX